MEDITATIONS ON GANDHI

Gandhian Studies for Peace and Research Series

1. Gandhian Model of Development and World Peace – *R. P. Misra*
2. Conflict Resolution Through Non-violence : Role of the Univ. Vol. 1 : Science and Ethics – *K. D. Gangrade* and *R. P. Misra*
3. Conflict Resolution Through Non-violence : Role of the Univ. Vol. 2 : Development without Destruction – *K. D. Gangrade* and *R. P. Misra*
4. The Social Philosophy of Mahatma Gandhi – *K. S. Bharathi*
5. Gandhian Humanism – *Mohit Chakraborty*
6. Gandhian Holestic Economics – *Shashi Prabha Sharma*
7. Gandhian Spiritualism : A Quest for the Essence of Excellence – *Mohit Chakraborty*
8. Gandhian Perspective on Population and Development – *A. K. Sharma*
9. Thoughts of Gandhi and Vinoba : A Comparative Study – *K. S. Bharathi*
10. Economic Philosophy of Mahatma Gandhi – *Shanti Swarup Gupta*
11. The Political Thoughts of Mahatma Gandhi – *K. S. Bharathi*
12. Gandhi and 21st Century – *Janardan Pandey*
13. Gandhian Philosophy of the Spinning Wheel – *Mohit Chakraborty*
14. Gandhian Satyagraha : An Analytical and Critical Approach – *Ajay Shanker Rai*
15. Gandhi and His Religion – *P. A. Raju*
16. Mahatma Gandhi : Vichar Vithika (Hindi) – *S. P. Agarwal*
17. Poverty of Gandhian Philosophy – *Himansu Roy*
18. Right to Equality in the Indian Constitution – *S. N. Saraswati*
19. Meditations on Gandhi : A Ravindra Varma Festschrift – *M. P. Mathai, M. S. John* and *Siby K. Joseph*

About the Editors

M. P. Mathai is Reader in Gandhian Studies attached to the School of Gandhian Thought and Development Studies, Mahatma Gandhi University, Kottayam, Kerala. He is one of the founder members of the National Alliance of Peoples' Movements and is a Visiting Professor at the Institute of Gandhian Studies, Wardha, Maharashtra. He has recently published a book on Mahatma Gandhi's World View. His areas of interest include ecology, social and environment movements in India and Gandhian philosophy.

M.S. John is Reader in Political Science and Peace Studies at the School of Gandhian Thought and Development Studies, Mahatma Gandhi University, Kottayam, Kerala. His areas of interest include Panchayati Raj and Participatory Planning, Peace Theory and Conflict Resolution, and Gender Issues in Development Planning and Sexual Health Interventions. He has co-authored a recent book in Malayalam on the Sen Committee on Panchayat reforms in Kerala and has also published in national and international journals.

Siby K. Joseph is a Faculty Member of the Institute of Gandhian Studies, Wardha. He has researched on the unemployment problems in Kerala, the functioning of Gram Sabhas in Tamil Nadu and aspects of good governance in Kerala.

Gandhian Studies and Peace Research Series – 19

MEDITATIONS ON GANDHI

A Ravindra Varma Festschrift

Edited by
M. P. Mathai
M. S. John
Siby K. Joseph

CONCEPT PUBLISHING COMPANY, NEW DELHI-110059

ISBN-81-7022-961-8

First Published 2002

Published and Printed by
Ashok Kumar Mittal
Concept Publishing Company
A/15-16, Commercial Block, Mohan Garden
NEW DELHI-110059 (India)

Phones : 5648039, 5649024
Fax : 091-11-5648053
E-mail : **publishing@conceptpub.com**

CONTENTS

Introduction by *M.P. Mathai, M.S. John* and *Siby K. Joseph* ix

PART I : IMPRESSIONS

- Ravi 3
  – *N. Krishnaswamy*
- Natural Leader 10
  – *Manoranjan Dutta*
- A Jewel in the Gandhian Crown 17
  – *Brij Mohan*
- A Very Happy Association 20
  – *A.K. Damodaran*
- The Young Ravindra Verma 24
  – *A.P. Mahadevan*
- A Dedicated Gandhian 27
  – *K. Janardhanan Pillai*
- A Human Dynamo 29
  – *K. John Mamman*
- Recalling our Days in WAY 32
  – *Piet Dijkstra*
- An Inspiring Personality 34
  – *S.K. Bandopadhaya*
- A Politician with a Difference 38
  – *Sadiq Ali*
- My Teacher 40
  – *Sanjay Matey*
- A Unique Personality 41
  – *Neema Vaishnav*

PART II - ESSAYS

1. Social and Environmental Violence : A Buddhist Perspective 45
– *Sulak Sivaraksa*

2. Gandhi's Lessons for the Twenty-first Century 63
– *Gene Sharp*

3. Honouring Gandhi and Gandhians 76
– *Peter van den Dungen*

4. Gandhi and Tolstoy 96
– *Anthony J. Parel*

5. Spiritual Living, Gandhian Economics and Well-being 113
– *Romesh Diwan* and *Shakti Bethea*

6. Gandhi on Modernity : A Revisionist Paradigm 151
– *K. Raghavendra Rao*

7. Is a Gandhian World Social Order Desirable and Possible? 162
– *T.K.N. Unnithan*

8. Breaking the Shackles : Gandhi's Views on Women 179
– *Usha Thakkar*

9. Development Paradigm Transition : From the Second to the Third Millennium 189
– *Amalendu Guha*

10. Religion and Nation-State : The Untenable Linkage 200
– *T.K. Oommen*

11. Education and Living : The Sustainability Connection 210
– *K. John Mammen*

The Contributors 220
Index 224

Introduction

It is only befitting that a festschrift is brought out as a tribute to Ravindra Varma on the occasion of his seventy-fifth birth anniversary. It will be a matter of joy for all those who have associated with him or are familiar with his life and work. The idea of a volume of this kind was mooted by some of his colleagues, friends and students who met during an International Workshop on Non-violence, organized in New Delhi in October 1999. The volume places on record Ravindra Varma's multi-dimensional services to the nation and contributions to the study, propagation and understanding of Gandhian studies. Before proceeding to discuss the contents of the volume, a brief account of the life and work of Ravindra Varma is in order.

Ravindra Varma's public life spans almost six full decades. Having imbibed the spirit of the Indian national movement and inspired by Mahatma Gandhi's ideas, he devoted his life fully to the service of his motherland, with total devotion and commitment.

Born in a royal family at Mavelikkara, Kerala, on April 18,1925, Ravindra Varma was educated at The Maharaja's College of Arts, Trivandrum and later at the Madras Christian College, Tambaram, Madras. The clarion call of Mahatma Gandhi during the Quit India Movement to 'do or die' was so irresistible that the young Ravindra Varma left his college studies and took the plunge. He was arrested and imprisoned For Ravindra Varma it was commitment for life and there was no looking back afterwards.

He was called upon to organise the All India Students' Congress. In fact, Indian students' politics during the struggle for independence was moulded under his dynamic leadership.

He was President of the All India Students' Congress for three years (1946-49). It was in recognition of his dynamism and organising ability that he was elected to the Executive Committee of the International Students' Service – World University Service (1945-46). He was also elected Leader of the Indian delegation to the International Students' Conference at Prague (1946) and of the Indian delegation to the International Students' Service Conference, Aurora, New York (1949).

Ravindra Varma played a central role in organizing the Indian Youth Congress as well. He was national Secretary of the Indian Youth Congress (1949-51) and President , All India Youth Congress (1957). He was elected Leader of the delegation of Indian Youth Cong ess to China in 1958. He also served as Secretary of the Indian Committee of the World Assembly of Youth (WAY) for two terms. He was elected International President of WAY in 1958 in which capacity he served the cause of youth for over four years till 1962. As President of the WAY he travelled extensively in Asia, Europe, Africa, Latin America as well as North America and contributed substantially in bringing the youths of different parts of the world together. Ravindra Varma succeeded in imparting to the members of the WAY the ideals of freedom, justice and peace, and a sense of colonialism, which contravened these ideals.

Ravindra Varma served as a member of the All India Congress Committee (AICC) from 1958-77 and was the General Secretary of the AICC (O) during 1971-74. He entered electoral politics in 1962 and was elected to the third Lok Sabha (1962-67) from Kerala. He was also member of the sixth (1977-79) and seventh Lok Sabha (1979-84). During these terms as Member of Parliament he was member of various important consultative Committees for Ministries of External Affairs, Defence and Finance, besides being member of Privileges Committee and Rules Committee. In addition, he was member of Government of India's delegations to UN Conference on Trade and Development, Geneva 1964; Afro-Asian Governments' Conference, Algiers, 1965; Government of

India's Observer Delegation to the African Heads of States' Conference, Accra, 1964; and Government of India's Delegation to the ECAFE Conference, New Delhi, 1967. He was leader of the Parliamentary Delegation to People's Republic of North Korea and represented the Government of India in the 61st, 62nd and 63rd Sessions of the International Labour Conferences. He had the honour of presiding over the 63rd Session of ILO in Geneva in 1979.

Ravindra Varma played a leading role in the Lok Sangharsh Movement during the emergency (1975-77) and directed the underground movement against the emergency by travelling all over India (in disguise, of course) and organising underground cells of resistance. He was arrested in Bombay in February 1976 and was detained in Thana jail until his release on February 24, 1977. He served as Union Cabinet Minister for Labour and Parliamentary Affairs from March 1977 to August 1979.

Ravindra Varma's association with the Gandhian Constructive Movement dates back to the days of the Mahatma himself. He was associated with the All India Spinners' Association and All India Village Industries' Association. Countless are the Gandhian study camps he has been organising all over the country ever since he joined the national movement, targeting particularly the students and the youth. He has delivered innumerable lectures on Gandhian themes all over the world (holding his audience spell-bound). He is the author of a number of tracts and books on various aspects of Gandhi's philosophy and method, as also on current socio-economic and political questions. Ravindra Varma was mainly instrumental in founding the Gandhi Vichar Parishad (Institute of Gandhian Studies), Wardha. He has been serving as the Chairman of the Gandhi Peace Foundation, New Delhi, for many years. He is also the Chairman of the Second National Commission on Labour, Government of India.

This festschrift is organized into two parts. The first part contains impressions and personal recollections of some of those – who include persons belonging to different generations and various persuasions – who have the privilege of knowing Ravindra Varma personally and intimately. There is no need to paraphrase these impressions and recollections lest the emotions accompanying these accounts should be lost. These accounts throw a flood of light on the nature of involvement of Ravindra Varma in the national movement. The second part of this book contains articles on Gandhian studies by scholars of international repute. The articles cover a broad range of Gandhian themes. This includes some aspects of Gandhian thought, environment, development, world order and nationalism.

In the first article entitled "Social and Environmental Violence: A Buddhist Perspective", Sulak Sivaraksa criticizes neo-liberal capitalism which prizes accumulation of profits over human well-being and environmental sustainability. He says that the main beneficiaries of the present economic reality are the transnational corporations, big investors and their allies. He contests the reasoning that the profit generated by the system will trickle down to benefit the mass of humanity. While admitting that capitalism does generate some benefits, Sivaraksa argues that they are unintended by products of the system. The values created by capitalism under the guise of free competition and efficiency will usher in a "grotesque society of violent, selfish, anti-social environmental plunderers", according to him. He counterpoises Buddhist values as alternatives to those of neo-liberal capitalism. Buddhism approaches a human being holistically unlike capitalism which looks only at the economic (possessive) dimension. Cultivation of values like loving kindness towards oneself and others, compassion, joy at the happiness of others, equanimity, sharing, pleasant speech , working for one another's benefit and equality constitute essential elements of Buddhist practice. He also targets his attack on consumerism that "nourishes the unlimited greed of soulless trans-national corporations" and undermines the sense of community. Consumerism is self-defeating in as much as "the insatiable desire for goods ultimately leads to despair or boredom". Buddhism looks upon prosperity as the result of collective enterprise with an emphasis on spirituality rather than the outcome of egoistic pursuit of individuals. Sivaraksa speaks about the merits of the Buddhist *Saṅgha* model of social organization that existed in the Vajjian republic in ancient India. The *Sangha* model is quite similar to Gandhi's village republic, according to him. Living in such small communities in harmony with nature where individual and societal interests are not in tension offers the only way out of the present neo-liberal capitalist order characterized by greed, hatred and delusion. He says that one unintended result of globalisation is the emergence of transnational alliances of people against global capitalism. In this century, the clash between cultures and capital is more likely than between civilizations, argues Sivaraks.

Gene Sharp has spent his entire life researching and teaching the theory and practice of non-violence, especially of the strategic kind. Small wonder that it is the strategic dimension of Gandhian non-violence and its implications for reshaping politics that enamours Sharp most. Sharp starts his piece with a criticism of commentators who question the universal applicability of Gandhian non-violence by attributing Gandhi's success in India to factors such as the gentle nature of British rule, his personal charisma as a Mahatma and the passing historical circumstances of that time. He says that those who excessively revere Gandhi without studying him with detachment actually are doing a great disservice to him. Sharp sees Gandhi's thought and work to be of great relevance throughout the twenty-first century. Gandhi operated on two levels, personal and societal, independently without allowing either to dominate the other. Not satisfied with personal non-violence, he felt obligated to apply it in society and politics. Gandhi recognized the importance of constructive work as an essential ingredient of struggle against oppression. Development and application of non-violent struggle, which remains Gandhi's major contribution, was not his own invention, as he himself acknowledged. Sharp argues that Gandhi "presented non-violent struggle as an expedient" in the societal context. He sees Gandhi as a person who brought "strategic sophistication to the technique" of non-violence. Sharp then proceeds to summarise Gandhi's lessons for us in the present century and ends with a number of questions on how non-violent action can be adapted and applied in a wide range of conflicts. He also says that if non-violent action is planned properly, the chances of success can be enhanced and the casualties of conflict can be reduced.

Peter van den Dungen laments the non-award of the Nobel Prize for peace to Gandhi who deserved it more than anyone in the last century and traces the events surrounding the effort to recommend Mahatma Gandhi for the Prize. He adds that this failing has not in any way affected Gandhi's standing, who, as a symbol of peace, is "without peer and is likely to remain so." That several Nobel laureates have acknowledged their indebtedness to Gandhi is perhaps a greater recognition, according to him. Peter van den Dungen feels that the work of peace and non-violence needs to be encouraged and publicized. Instituting prizes, awards and honours is one of the means of achieving this goal. He details the various awards instituted in India and abroad in honour of Gandhi. The Alternative Nobel Prize or the Right Livelihood Award instituted in Sweden can be regarded as a Gandhian award. The author says that more significant than the awards, that accompany peace work, are the rewards in the form of opportunities for personal growth that such work entails. Even though Gandhi was only runner-up in *Time* magazine's 'Person of the Century' contest, the words of Albert Einstein, who won it, about Gandhi are quoted by the author approvingly: "Generations to come will scarcely believe that such a one as this ever in flesh and blood walked upon this earth."

In his article on "Gandhi and Tolstoy", Anthony Parel says that Gandhi's indebtedness to Tolstoy has no parallels in modern Indian intellectual history. He regards Tolstoy as the foremost influence on Gandhi which belies the notion that there is no meeting of minds between the East and the West. He even argues that Gandhi had inherited the Tolstoyan moral legacy in the twentieth century. This moral legacy is best exemplified by the ideals enshrined in 'the sermon on the mount' found in the New Testament. Parel cites three works of Tolstoy to show what sort of influence they had on Gandhi. From *The Kingdom of God is Within You*, which Gandhi carried with him during his imprisonment, taught him that peace is a social good that can be realized not merely through spiritual self-renewal but through mobilization of public opinion in its favour, which was one of Gandhi's strong points in his campaigns against colonialism and oppression. In the *Letter to a Hindoo*, Tolstoy underscored the futility of violence. Even though the *Letter* originated as a result of the initiative taken by Taraknath Das, the credit for making it available to a wider audience goes to Gandhi. Tolstoy saw the enslavement of India as the direct result of her spiritual impoverishment. Unless Indians liberate themselves from the belief that violence can liberate them, they would not be able to redeem themselves from foreign yoke. Parel says that Tolstoy's exaltation of the power of the soul as against that of the body made an abiding impression on Gandhi. Parel contests the contention of some commentators that Gandhi was oblivious of art and aesthetics. He says that Tolstoy's *What is Art?* had a tremendous influence on him. Like Tolstoy, Gandhi wanted art to be used for promoting moral and humanistic values like peace, co-operation and solidarity rather than serving as a tool in the hands of the rich classes. Parel says that Charkha, Khadi and the loin cloth that Gandhi wore were artistic symbols which he consciously cultivated in solidarity with the common man.

Romesh Diwan and Shakti Bethea examine the nature of the post-modern malaise at the personal, interpersonal, familial and societal levels and argue that spirituality enacted in daily life is the antidote to it. They identify five aspects of spiritual living and contrasted the lives of two women to show how spiritually oriented life and post-modern material life differ. Then Diwan and Bethea seek to combine Gandhian economics with spirituality by making Ashram life based on the joint family principle an element of economic life. This is in tune with the current interest in institutional economics. The joint family and Ashrams, apart from serving as institutions for cultivating capacities to love, to give and to care, are also important economic institutions engaged in production and consumption of goods, investment and allocation of resources and outputs and evolving of strategies for productivity, efficiency, specialisation and growth. They then list six basic principles of Gandhian economics and contrast them with 'mainstream' economics in a very lucid fashion. In order to realise these economic principles, they say that we should be aware of what we desire to achieve, the path of achieving it and the position from which we begin. They challenge a number of myths underlying the capitalist order like 'There Is No Alternative' or TINA and calls for new economic alternatives of a Gandhian kind, which are far more practical than those of 'mainstream' economics.

Raghavendra Rao's "Gandhi on Modernity: A Revisionist Paradigm" seeks to uncover those aspects of Gandhi's thought which could be called modern situating him within an indigenous understanding of modernity. He banks on the space for alternative notions of modernity opened up by recent post-modern commentators, particularly the work of Stephen Toulmin, to bolster his argument. Toulmin sought to redeem modernity from post-modernist attack by highlighting certain positive features of the paradigm that existed during the renaissance period, which was later overtaken by the rational-scientific tradition. Rao says that in India there existed an indigenous paradigm of modernity which was similar to the humanistic paradigm of the renaissance period. Gandhi can be situated in this indigenous paradigm according to him. Rao then proceeds to identify the evolution of the indigenous paradigm and identifies its characteristic features. Its strength lays in its understanding of the human situation as involving a balance between reason and faith. Rao says that this balancing was found in Gandhi's thinking and action. Gandhi denies the notion of 'absolute subject-originality' in his work *Hind Swaraj*. Gandhi admitted the role of agency in history. In his version of modernity religion understood as fundamental moral principles had a key role to play. His vision of a pluralist nation-state is now widely advocated by theorists of nationalism as a possible solution to the question of self-determination in multi-ethnic societies. Whose interests does modernity serve?, asks Rao. He says that Gandhi had an answer to it – the toiling masses. The article makes a serious plea for re-opening of the Gandhi-modernity debate.

T.K.N. Unnithan looks at the possibility and desirability of a Gandhian world social order. World order has been a popular theme in the nineties of the last century, particularly in the aftermath of the collapse of the Soviet Union, even though a number of scholars associated with the World Order Models Project have been engaged in its elucidation and imagination since the sixties. But most commentators of world order seek to address it partially, concentrating mainly on some aspects of governance or social organization – often treating capitalism as an incontestable given. Any comprehensive view of world order must be based on a world view, which in turn must be preceded by a notion of self and man. In Gandhi's thought isomorphism among these three elements is more clearly visible. He did not see much hope in international organizations based on the principle of the inviolability of states. Seeing the state as an unproblematic entity was anathema. That is why Unnithan says that "Establishment of a world state by merely extending the characteristics of modern state" was not in line with his thinking. He opposed the creation of the United Nations for the same reason in as much it envisaged an association of states. He wanted a federation of states built around the principle of non-violence with the participating states also reflecting non-violent features in their internal organisation.

Usha Thakkar's article examines Gandhi's views on women in the context of social, economic and political issues. Gandhi was aware of the numerous unjust customs impeding the development of women and fought against them. He saw woman as an equal partner in marriage and could even go against the will of her husband if it was for a noble cause. He wanted women at the forefront of struggles against communalism and untouchability. Thakkar says that Gandhi had tremendous faith in women's inherent capacity for non-violence. He wanted women to reshape male-dominated politics according to their vision. Gandhi realized that women were more connected with service than power. He enlisted the support of women to popularise *swadeshi*. He advised women to be sisters rather than wives and mothers so that they will be able to serve the whole world. Gandhi enhanced the dignity of household work by asking his male followers to take up spinning and other daily chores, according to Thakkar.

Amalendu Guha, in his contribution "Development Paradigm Transition: From the Second to the Third Millennium", says that growth is not development, which can only come if human interest is given the primacy of attention. Economic development operating on the principle of efficiency had resulted in the outflow of resources from the peripheries to the centre. This can be tackled by organization of production and resource mobilisation at the local level using local resources to produce optimum locally useable goods and services. Further, it should generate local employment, ensure local distribution according to needs and lead to use of local savings by preventing its outflow to the urban centres. Guha argues that creation of such autonomous economic units in our localities is the only means for eradicating poverty. Instead of mass production we need production by the masses, which is slow but is more secure from the perspective of the poor. It also creates social values, which are currently lacking in the centralised mass production of both "private capitalist" and state capitalist systems. Guha advocates a decentralised system of production and distribution as an antidote to the competition for markets and profits embedded in mass and centralised production.

T.K. Oommen addresses the relationship between religion and nation-state. After providing a taxonomy of possible state-nation linkage scenarios, he emphasizes the inherent tension between nation and state, particularly in multi-national states like India. He speaks of the existence of not a hierarchy of loyalties with loyalty to the state assuming a pre-eminent position , but a plurality of loyalties. He also sees a struggle for supremacy between identity of nation and identity arising from either similarity in religious beliefs or racial origins. Oommen also explores the possible ways in which homogenisation can be brought about and the desirability of each of these modes before coming to the main argument in the paper. He argues that nationalism based on religion is untenable because of the de-territorial nature of the latter. Religions are also diverse and heterogeneous as visible from the denominational conflicts in Christianity, Islam and Sikhism. He contests the reasoning behind the *Hindutva* notion of 'one culture, many religions' by saying that the latter is a constitutive element of the former and therefore cultural homogenisation would amount to cultural annihilation. Oommen argues for religious pluralism and tolerance. He contests the secular credentials of the Indian state for ignoring the specificity of religious practices of the Adivasis and Dalits by labelling them as Hindus in blanket terms. Oommen laments that nationalism now "survives through demonization of the other". What we need is a more inclusive kind of nationalism, which can accommodate different religions as Gandhi always stood for. He ends the paper by laying down a number of conditionalities for the emergence and existence of religious pluralism. This includes de-linking state and nation, endorsing the notion of contextual and often horizontal rather than hierarchical loyalties and identities, dissociating nation and religion, and recognizing religious and cultural pluralism.

The question of sustainability is now widely debated in academic and activist circles. Many organizing principles of present society have been challenged in recent years on the basis of the sustainability argument. Drawing on reports of various international conferences organized under the aegis of the United Nations and other international bodies, John Mammen looks at the sphere of education and emphasizes the importance of making education attuned to living. Quoting Paulo Freire, he says that if education is to promote sustainable living, it should have an emancipatory content. In poor countries, liberatory education should precede development education, according to him.

We are confident that these essays will enrich the already existing vast literature on Gandhian studies. Some of these essays introduce new perspectives in understanding Gandhi and identify crucial areas for further research in this line. We thank all those who have contributed to this volume. Shri Kanagasabhapathy, Trichy, Tamil Nadu, deserves special thanks for his constant encouragement and help during the different stages of the production of this volume. The queries and good wishes of many colleagues and friends of Ravindra Varma, while the project was under way, have also served as key facilitating factors in the completion of the work. Last, but not least, we thank Mr. Sugunan of Lars Computer Centre, Athirampuzha, Kottayam, for prompt and efficient word processing.

Editors

PART - I

IMPRESSIONS

Ravi

N. Krishnaswamy

A special convocation was held during the centenary celebrations of the Madras University to confer honorary doctorates on a few eminent personalities. Dr.A.Lakshmanaswamy Mudaliar, the distinguished Vice-Chancellor was reading out the citations. Prime Minister Jawaharlal Nehru was the Chief Guest. There was the usual applause when, one by one, the names of those honoured were announced.

However, when the name of Dr. A. Ramaswamy Mudaliar was called out, a sudden hush descended on the audience. The Vice-Chancellor's opening remarks broke the silence: "It is extremely difficult Sir, to say anything complimentary about a person whom one has known from the moment of his birth". The thunderous clap that greeted these words literally drowned the rest of the citation, for the Mudaliars were twins!

Shri Ravindra Varma and I first met in the Alipuram Jail where we both were incarcerated for participating in the "Quit India Movement". We had literally been marched directly from our colleges in Madras to the prison. From 1942 to 2000 is a long, long period. Throughout these years, however, we have not merely been good friends but also close associates in several common endeavours – the Nationalist Student Movement, World Assembly of Youth and Gandhian constructive activities. Many who do not know us well have taken for granted that we are brothers, if not twins.

Ravi, as I have ever called him endearingly, is a man of many parts. Above all, he is a fine intellectual. He is not only a voracious reader, but also a clear-headed thinker. Great is his capacity to marshal facts and figures and present his arguments cogently, forcefully and convincingly. He is certainly an impressive speaker. However, his wry sense of British humour often fails to evoke adequate response. He sometimes feels frustrated and depressed that his speech has not gone down well with the audience forgetting that he has been "aiming where the head ought to be and not where it actually is". In his anxiety to present his case fully, he tries to cover too may points with fine words, and twists of phrases tumbling out of his mouth in rapid succession, stunning his listeners but leading to his exceeding the time-limit, especially when a quick and brief intervention is needed as during a Parliamentary debate or a radio or TV talk. He is at home in the company of the best intellectuals but feels uncomfortable among the plebeians, perhaps because he hails from the old royal family of Travancore.

If Ravi was His Imperial Majesty's guest in the Alipuram Jail, he also enjoyed the hospitality of their Highnesses the Maharaja of Mysore and Travancore for his role in the struggles for responsible government. I wonder if he himself has kept count of the number of times he has been imprisoned or for what periods. Thanks to Gandhi's unique technique of non-violent *Satyagraha*, however, after independence, Ravi has been an honoured visitor to many a palace including the Kawadiyar in Trivandrum.

Ravi has been an active politician for half a century but with a difference. Shy and modest, he has never been flamboyant or ever thrown his weight around. He has been a distinguished Member of the Lok Sabha and a Minister too at one time in the Union Cabinet. But he never sacrificed his principles nor supplicated before the powers-that-be to 'fawn or seek for power by doctrines fashioned to the varying hour'. Otherwise he would have been in Indira Gandhi's Cabinet even during her first stint as Prime Minister, instead of biding his time till 1977, when Morarji Desai included him in his Council of Ministers. If he was an active parliamentarian for three terms, he was also a competent Minister, conscientious and indefatigable.

Ravi is a great organiser who had shown commendable knowledge, talents and abilities in diverse fields – overground or underground. If he shone as a Secretary of many an organization, he sparkled as Chairman of a small group or a committee or even of a huge meeting. A good listener, he would rarely interrupt but would not hesitate to interject where necessary to call a speaker to order. He is at his best while summing up, leaving one and all satisfied. The old timers in the Ministry of Labour still recall with admiration the manner in which he conducted meetings. Is it any wonder then that the International Labour Organization compiled his ruling when he presided over the I.L.O Conference in Geneva in 1979, and many a Director has since relied upon them to guide successive Chairpersons in later years.

Ravi is as good a writer as he is a speaker. But he is not prolific. He writes only under internal or external compulsion. It is a pleasure to read his articles and fathom the depth of his thought. But, here again, his anxiety to be precise in his expression, makes him often use words and phrases whose meaning the ordinary reader will find it difficult to follow. "I do not write for idiots but for intelligent readers', replied an eminent Indian when a complaint was made by one of his closest aides. The only reply he got was: " You should not forget that a majority of the readers have but minimal knowledge of logic and language. If they cannot follow your writings, they will simply dismiss them as unintelligible".

Ravi's father, the late Dr. Goda Varma hailed as the father of Malayalam linguistics, was a Sanskrit scholar as well who had contributed greatly for bringing out the Sanskrit version of the Indian Constitution. He had even translated Omar Khayyam's writings into Sanskrit. Many other members of the family had been litterateurs. Ravi too is a linguist. Besides his mother tongue Malayalam, he is at home in English and Hindi. He knows Sanskrit, Tamil, Telugu, Bengali, Assamese and

Gujarati and has a nodding acquaintance with a few foreign languages too. He just does not 'pick up' a language but studies it carefully, trying to master complicated grammatical usages and unravel its finer nuances. His language is polished and precise. The average listener or reader would have to refer to a dictionary to grasp the significance of some of his words and phrases, a rather tedious task which no one likes to undertake except under compulsion of circumstances.

Ravi's handwriting is fine and beautiful. His letters are well-formed but small. I once committed the mistake of presenting him with a pen which had an extra-fine point. Over the years he has been specialising in micro-fine writing, compelling the reader to use a magnifying glass. No wonder then that he has become typists' nightmare.

An ancestor of Ravi was the eminent scholar and painter Ravi Varma. Ravi himself has a finely-developed aesthetic sense. He appreciates beauty and rhythm. When he and I had a couple of hours on our hand because our flight got delayed before take-off from Amsterdam, he immediately suggested that we rush to the Rembrandt Art Gallery; we still cherish some of the prints of the Master's great works like 'The Thinker'. Ravi managed to steal some time from his busy schedule to visit the well-known museums during his travels, whether in India or abroad.

Very few of even Ravi's friends know that he has a fine ear and a sound appreciation of both Carnatic and Hindustani music. There was a time when he himself used to sing, and sing well too. Bhajans and Rabindra Sangeet were his forte then. On rare occasions these days, in select company, he starts humming the strains of a *Bhor Bhairavi, Bhimplas* or *Malkauns.* He can sit for hours in a *Kavi Sammelan* or an Urdu *Mushaira* lost in rapturous joy.

For all his interest in public work, Ravi is basically an introvert. His occasional caustic remarks make people mistake him to be supercilious. When a Pakistani waxed eloquent on the 'benefits of British Rule in India' and called it a 'blessing in disguise' during an international conference in Brussels, Ravi was ready with his devastating repartee. "But the disguise was so thick that the blessing could not be seen!". Such sarcasm cost him many a friendship in the past. He is now comparatively mild, though a few flashes remind one of the old days.

Ravi's love of the English language, and many other British things, is unbounded. At one time he was even considered an Anglophile. During his travels abroad in his late thirties he used to sport a three-piece suit and a top-hat too. He was happy to swing his British umbrella folded thin as a swagger. He was once invited to address a meeting in France on Gandhi Jayanthi, to be presided over by our Ambassador K.M Panikkar. Ravi had spent a few days in London and was to fly down from there to Paris that morning. But a message came from his host just a few hours prior to the meeting that Ravi had caught the 'Asian Flu' and had been advised treatment and bed rest. The funny thing was that Ravi had earlier spent weeks in Delhi where the fever had raged like an epidemic but had avoided falling a prey to the painful illness. Hence, when he did make it to Paris a few days later, we could not resist teasing him by saying: "So, you would not accept even the Asian Flu unless it bears the label 'Made in England'. No more does he sport a coat and tie. He goes about wearing the typical Aligarhi Pyjama and sober-coloured Kurthas.

Though not an athletic type Ravi has kept himself in fairly good shape. He used to walk fast and take long walks too; he is a good swimmer, nowadays, the ailments of age act as a constant deterrent. He used to play cricket till his thirtieth year. Till recently, he used to keep himself well posted with tests and scores; the match-fixing scam must have diminished his interest in the game itself.

Fascinated by Gandhi from an early age, Ravi has made a deep study of Gandhian thought and is among the few authoritative interpreters of Gandhi's life, work and ideas. He built up the Gandhi Vichar Parishad (Institute of Gandhian Studies) from the scratch, and shaped it into a good institution for spreading the message of Gandhi and inculcating the Mahatma's ideas in the minds of youth, especially the university students. He has but recently relinquished his responsibilities in the Parishad to devote greater attention to the exacting work` of the National Labour Commission of which he is the Chairman. He is still the Chairman of the Gandhi Peace Foundation and the Vishwa Yuvak Kendra.

In recent years, Ravi has moved closer to Buddhism, especially Tibetan. He has not only been diligently studying the subject under the guidance of great teachers but has had the benefits of learning directly from H.H. The Dalai Lama himself. Ravi spends the very early hours of the morning in prayer and meditation.

In one of the thump-nail sketches which Churchill wrote in the early days of his political career, he said, "It is not difficult for a politician to know when to start climbing the ladder of power, but it is difficult to know when to descend". He himself had forgotten this when he stuck to power for too long and was forced to step down, following the controversy arising from his making public, without any provocation whatsoever, an unfortunate telegram he sent to Viscount Montgomery who was commanding the British forces in Europe during the last days of World War II. If the pull of power is difficult to resist, the desire simply to occupy positions without any great power or authority is often hard to abandon. The seeker after Truth and Light, however, has to learn to distinguish between *Maya* and Reality .

'Desire is the root-cause of all sufferings' was the refrain of the Sakyamuni. The same refrain is to found in other religions too in varying degrees. Gandhi drew heavily from different scriptures in shaping *satyagraha* as a way of life. Truth and non-violence were the cardinal principles on which his whole philosophy was based. The path lay through love and service.

The way to prepare oneself to be a *satayagrahi* was to practices the eleven *Vrats* (Vows), certainty extremely difficult and demanding. The evaluation and progress towards *Moksha* or *Nirvana* has to be made for himself by each individual, constantly aware of his thoughts and actions and monitoring them continuously.

However, the transformation from an active politician to a *Sadhaka* is none too easy. The politician can rarely say 'no' unambiguously and unequivocally to anyone. Every reasonable – and some times even unreasonable – request has to be met. Power has to be sought and secured, favours have to be given and compromises have to be made. The *Sadhaka,* on the other hand, has to systematically shed all unwanted baggage and lighten himself for the steep and perilous uphill climb.

The time has come for Ravi, who has just crossed not only the Bibilical age of three score and ten, but five more years too, to leave the penumbra and get ready to tread the Path illumined by Avalokiteshwara.

Natural Leader

(with abiding commitment to the principle of trying good means to achieve good ends)

Manoranjan Dutta

Ravindra Varma presents a profile of vision and imagination, adding much dynamism to the leadership of contemporary India. Following the World War II, the liquidation of the British Empire became a historic fact and India became independent of the British Raj in August 1947. India's student and youth movement played a very significant role in this process. Ravindra Varma led this movement.

We first met more than fifty years ago at a conference of students in New Delhi in the winter of 1946. Concerned student activists from so many states of India – West Bengal, Assam, Utkal, Bihar, Uttar Pradesh, Madhya Pradesh, Maharashtra, Karnataka, Kerala, Tamil Nadu, Andhra Pradesh, Gujarat, Punjab, Delhi, Rajasthan – came to attend the conference. I was a participant. Ravindra Varma walked up to the podium and made a historic presentation.

He pointed out that as the then Soviet Union joined the Western military alliance, a segment of India's students led by their leaders with commitment to India's Communist Party, aggressively adopted the slogan of the "People's war", convinced that the allied victory would ensure India's independence. A second segment of India's students, he continued, followed the leadership who accepted the thesis that India's freedom could be achieved by India's people, aided by international power led by the then powers of Germany-Italy-Japan, whose support was sought by Netaji Subhas C. Bose who baffled the watchful eye of the British Raj and left India to personally negotiate with the leaders of the alliance seeking military help for India's independence. At this juncture, Ravindra Varma presented an alternative format to organize India's student movement.

He forcefully argued that India's independence from the British Raj must be our goal with no compromise whatsoever, and that independence of the people of India must be won by themselves and for themselves. Independence of India earned with the foreign powers of either bloc – USA-UK-SOVIET UNION or Germany-Italy-Japan, would hardly be worth it. In the absence of necessary weapons and military power-base at the command of the people of India, the only way for India was to follow the non-violent movement of non-cooperation against the British Raj, as was the message of Mahatma Gandhi who preached the philosophy of trying good means to achieve good ends. Ravi went on to argue that to achieve India's independence – an end not to be disputed by any logic, we must develop proper means. Let the good end be achieved by good means. A pragmatic strategic case based on total non-availability of military resources for a violent overthrow of the British Raj was evident to many. A moral philosophy of matching good means and good ends also made an appeal to many of his listeners. India's socialist leader, Late Jayaprakash Narayan, Ravi cited, added his forceful voice to the non-violent, non-cooperation movement.

Ravindra Varma continued to argue that once we accept the thesis of non-violent, non-cooperation, we must work to build up an organization reaching out to students and youth in all states of India – men and women, irrespective of divisions based on religion, language, race and caste. Let the All India Students' Congress be constituted to provide the organisational umbrella. Varma added: once we have an agenda and an organization towards implementation of the agenda, we must elect the leadership so that India's student movement will be ready to accept the challenge.

I listened to Ravi with rapt attention and he most certainly appealed to me. Student activists from various states met in state-wise group meetings. Next day, the delegates at the conference voted to approve the agenda and the organizational structure proposed by Ravindra Varma. They also voted to elect him President of the All India Students' Congress (AISC). He bowed down and accepted the office. For many years thereupon, he did his best to do what he was empowered to do. I had the honour and privilege to join Ravi as a member of the AISC Working Committee.

Between 1946-1950, I had a very fruitful working relationship with Ravindra Varma, then President of AISC. For this period, I worked with him as a Working Committee member of AISC, and joined him at several All India Conferences of Students. I recall the eventful ones at the AISC plenary session at Bangalore, now in the state of Karnataka, at the West Bengal State Students' Conference in Bankura, at the Conference on National Union of Students in Bombay. During these years, I also worked with him at several special executive meetings, inclusive of AISC Working Committee meeting at Udaipur in Rajasthan, the two-day preparatory meeting for the National Union of Students at Simla in Punjab when the late Dr. Zakir Hussain, later President of India, chaired the two-day event, and at the Wardha meeting when Mahtama Gandhi received a select group of students at his *Ashram*. Ravi and I went on several joint trips to lecture at students' conferences in various states in India. On his behalf, I went to several special student/youth meetings. Let me recall three of them: one was at Bilaspur in Himachal Pradesh soon after the state was inaugurated; another at the Wagha Border in Punjab where Indian and Pakistani student leadership held a historic joint meeting for peace and friendship between India and Pakistan; yet another in Hyderabad immediately after the Nizam signed the instrument of accession of the erstwhile princely state of India.

It is a pleasure to recall our joint tour in Coochbehar and Darjeeling in West Bengal when we reviewed so many issues which challenged India's students and youth. It was always a learning process for me to engage in such discourses with Ravindra Varma. In early 1950s, the then Prime Minister, late Jawaharlal Nehru in his capacity as President of Indian National Congress, appointed the Indian Youth Congress Executive Board where Ravi was called upon to play a leadership role. I had the privilege to join him as a member of the Board.

In many and varied contexts I had the privilege of working with Ravindra Varma. His leadership ability was uniformly manifest. He persistently and with much diligence worked to engage his colleagues in the process. He often challenged us when we sat in a meeting. He also welcomed being challenged. Indeed, a two-way communication was the mode of his successful leadership. He always took time to do thorough homework to be prepared for a specific assignment and he wanted all of us with him to be so prepared. The thrill of being at a meeting with Mahatma Gandhi at his Sewagram Ashram was very much challenged by Ravi as he demanded each one of us who were with him at the meeting to be optimally prepared. At the Simla meeting with the late Dr. Zakir Hussain in the chair, Ravi demonstrated his superb ability to present the case for organizing India's National Union of Students (NUS). It was an innovative programme, and we all had to work hard to make our participation at the two-day meeting successful. We debated at cross-purpose; we argued and argued at length; finally we came to a common agenda. Much credit was due to Ravindra Varma.

Since I left for the United States in 1958, I met with Ravindra Varma four times – twice in Bombay when I had occasions to visit India, next time at my Martinsville residence in New Jersey when he was visiting the U.S., and then in 1979 in New Delhi when I was there joining Professor A. I. Nagar of Delhi University to co-chair the conference on " THE NEW PERSPECTIVE OF INDIA - UNITED STATES COOPERATION" and he was a member of the Indian Cabinet holding the Labour portfolio. For over one half of a century, we have been friends and we have elected not to take much of each other's time.

Ravindra Varma must have his place in India's history as one who salvaged the fractured student/youth movement in India during the difficult days of the World War II and the historic eventful days that followed India's independence in August 1947.

I also remember Ravi as a family man – a loving son and a loving father. I had an occasion to meet with his father, Profesor G. Varma; my wife Kanak and I also met with Ravi's two sons during one of our visits to Bombay.

It has been a high honour and great privilege for me to have Ravindra Varma as a friend. I have personally known many of his friends in so many states in India. One could disagree with Ravi for his/her ideological differences and/or political affiliations, and yet continue to be his intimate friend. He could disagree with any one of us without being disagreeable. My friendship with Ravi was enriched by the touch of his charming personality which combined firm thoroughness of decision-making with devoted commitment to friendship. The late Ramakrishna Bajaj of Bombay was one of his very close friends. Ravi introduced me to Ram, and, we three became very close friends. We worked together in India's student/youth movement under the umbrella of All India Students' Congress. We three would sit down and argue for one or another issue without prejudging the outcome. Let me recall one occasion. We three sat to debate if the All India Students' Congress should have a newsletter and we quickly agreed to vote "yes". The debate then progressed if the news bulletin would be in print or in old-fashioned pre-xerox, cyclostyle format. The cost of printing became an obvious issue. After hours of discussions, Ravi and I finally convinced Ramakrishna that a printed news bulletin was in order.

I sat with Ravi and other friends who were anxious to underscore the lapses of the student movement, challenging him for his office of president of the organization. Both at Udaipur and Bangalore meetings, we talked several late, late nights, and we agreed to remain friends with whatever decisions we made. Much of it must be attributed to Ravi's personality and his sense of commitment to the specific agenda. I believe that Ravindra Varma taught me that one must work hard to have a friend and that one must work hard not to lose one. It has been a great education for me.

Over the earlier years of our working together in the Indian student movement, we spent hours on many occasions reviewing issues of our concern for India and for young men and women of free India – members of our own generation at that point of India's history. Did India offer optimum educational opportunities to them? Did they have adequate students' hostel accommodation? Did they get balanced food facilities? Was there provision for their health care? How about their employment opportunities? Will Indian economy grow to provide them jobs? Will India develop advanced education in diverse fields of learning? As we watched the back-breaking work for the labour in the tea gardens in Darjeeling, we spent hours walking in the Darjeeling mall, covered with dense fog, sharing our dreams for the future of India. Will there be a technological revolution to help the Indian farmers, men and women working in tea plantations, in jute mills and steel factories, carrying loads/baggage on their back or head, pulling carts and non-automated rickshaws?

Ravi argued that until India would have the technological revolution with provisions for large scale capital investments, India's one and only option was to follow the teachings of the Gandhian economics of self-help and self-sufficient economic development. Application of indigenous tools – made with viable indigenous skill – would be one way to augment labour's marginal productivity and hence income. During one of his four post-1958 visits with me, he seemed to have suggested to me that India elected not to adopt the Gandhian economics, nor did India succeed in going for the high-tech industrial revolution by large-scale capital investment from indigenous sources, which could ensure economic growth and employment for India's millions. Not until very recently, India resolutely continued to vote against the option of importation of large-scale foreign investment. A sense of frustration overwhelmed Ravi, as I noted. In addition , the emerging disarray in the Indian political field seemed to have caused him much pain. Ravindra Varma elected to return to his commitment to the study of the Gandhian political philosophy and constructive work programmes.

During my latest visit to India in 1997, I made it a point to visit Trivandrum in the southern state of Kerala, the home state of Ravindra Varma. I missed him and I was disappointed . I wish I could have walked with him on the beach, washed by the colourful waves of Indian Ocean under the setting sun, reviewing how Gandhian economics could be given an intelligent and robust orientation with the magical new computer technology and how this electronic high-tech revolution could bring decentralized industrialization at an accelerated rate to the millions of villages where every seven of ten of India's one billion people continue to live and earn their livelihood.

I sincerely hope that Ravindra Varma will continue to be a mighty young man of vision and leadership far beyond his eventful 75. I join his hundreds of friends at home and abroad to wish him the very best for the new millennium as we celebrate his seventy fifth birth anniversary. What he has accomplished over the years will be on record.

A Jewel in the Gandhian Crown

Brij Mohan

One cannot possibly escape being accused of bias while writing about close associates with whom he has worked for more than five decades – almost a life-long association. So is my predicament when I think of making an assessment of Shri Ravindra Varma who has recently celebrated his seventy-fifth birthday. My acquaintance with Ravindra Varma dates back to the mid-forties, just a couple of years before the attainment of Independence when both of us were engaged in the freedom struggle. I was yet a beginner confined to local movements. While Ravindra Varma had already acquired the status of an all India leader as he was the President of the All India Students Congress. Even then, we youngsters looked upto Ravindra Varma as a leader whom we should emulate.

In fact, my active association with Ravindra Varma began in the mid - fifties when the Indian Youth Congress was recognised as a forum for the training of the youth for an active role in the parliamentary life of the country. After attainment of Independence the All India Students' Congress was disbanded, as Jawaharlal Nehru felt that the students should address themselves primarily to education before they can be drawn into political activity. The Youth Congress, though continued to function, was not active enough to play a major role among students as such.

Just around the time when the Congress adopted the socialistic pattern of society as its goal at the Avadi Session and the participation of the youth in the national re-construction works was keenly felt, Jawaharlal Nehru appointed a committee of three persons with Ravindra Varma as the

Chairman to draw up plans and programmes for the rejuvenation of the youth movement. The other members being Rama Krishna Bajaj and Hira Lal Bose. The report proposed by the committee was highly appreciated and served as the basis for the reorientation of the Indian Youth Congress. Obviously, Ravindra Varma was the choice for the presidentship in which capacity he functioned for three years. Ravindra Varma was highly acclaimed for the remarkable Presidential address he delivered in 1958 at the Lucknow Session of the Youth Congress which was inaugurated by Jawaharlal Nehru. Ravindra Varma was succeeded by Ramlal Parikh and then the mantle passed on to me in 1961. A point of interest is that Smt. Indira Gandhi had been placed in charge of the Youth Congress by the Congress Working Committee.

Ravindra Varma's arena of activities spread to the international sphere when he became the Indian representative in the World Assembly of Youth. It is a rare case when one person was elected as President of the World Assembly of Youth for three consecutive terms. It was during his term as President, the WAY acquired a personality of its own and extended its activities to most countries of the world including the Soviet Bloc.

During the 1950s and 60s Ravindra Varma was among those young Congressmen who were close to Jawaharlal Nehru and were functioning as the "Thinking Group" within the Congress. In fact, Ravindra Varma was at the top of the list. When he entered the Lok Sabha in 1962, he played a significant role and was marked for his clarity of thought and understanding of the parliamentary norms and traditions.

What impressed us youngsters most was Ravindra Varma's commitment to Gandhian ideals, persuasive logic, clarity of thought and orational skills. Whosoever came in contact with him became his ardent follower.

Personally, I owe it to him that he not only inspired me ideologically, he even sponsored me at the national plane because of which I could become a worthy successor to him in the Youth Congress. Even at present, he is deeply engaged in pursuing the Gandhian ideals as Chairman of the Gandhi Peace Foundation. Chairmanship of World Youth Centre, where he succeeded none else but late Morarji Desai, former Prime Minister of India, is yet another achievement. This organisation is known for its constructive and dynamic activities concerning world youths.

He was a minister in Morarji Bhai's Cabinet and very recently he has been appointed Chairman of the National Commission on Labour. In my opinion, he undertook these responsibilities only because of his humble and unassuming characteristic.

I wish him a long and eventful life of service to the country.

A Very Happy Association

A.K. Damodaran

I first met Ravi when he was very young, the youngest and the brightest of the group of students who gathered together in Nagpur at the end of April 1944 to discuss the formation of the Students' Congress. I was representing Cochin and among the other members of the group were Ramunni Menon, R. Achuthan, Appa Rao, Dinkar Sakrikar, Prabhakar Kunte, Girish Chandra Dixit and several others. Most of us were in our early twenties. Ravi was still technically a teenager. But I remember he took the lead in drafting the manifesto and institutional details of the new organisation. The conference was over in three days and we left Nagpur. It was my good fortune that Ravi and Ramunni organised a short tour for our little Malayali group to Wardha and Bombay after the meeting. This provided me an opportunity of coming to know Ravi quite well. There were conversations and conversations, mostly agreements and on some issues like the relative importance of Nehru and Gandhi in the National Movement, pleasant but vital differences of perceptions. The phrase "zero-sum game" had not been invented then and all of us could admire both the great men, and also Subhas Bose and Patel, without any feeling of exclusivity.

The tour was memorable. We spent a few days in Wardha and met Kamal Nayan Bajaj, Kishore Mashruwala and Arya Nayakam and his wonderful wife, Asha Devi. These meetings and their reminiscences restored in us something of our optimism about the future of the Freedom Movement. While in Wardha, we heard that Gandhi had been released on May 6th and had shifted to Bombay. In Bombay, Ravi and his friends there organised a day in the Juhu residence of Bapu. Even though it was the day of silence for him, we spent a memorable one hour with him, debating the might-have-beens of the 1942 Movement with Sarojini Naidu. There was also Vijaya Lakshmi Pandit, recently widowed, sitting silent like "patience on a monument". There was Susheela Nayyar who took an active part in the conversation. The same evening the four of us were conscripted to collect the offerings after Gandhiji's prayer meeting. There were several other meetings during our very brief stay in Bombay, all of them memorable. We met Achyut Patwardhan at his place of residence in the suburbs of Bombay leading the underground movement in the city. We met Yusuf Meherally in the hospital where he was lying literally on his death bed. He was brilliantly articulate as ever and we did not know then that he would be gone within a few weeks. We met two Gandhians, R.R. Diwakar and Choudhury Babu through Ravi's good offices. We met many distinguished journalists like Joachim Alva and Syed Brelvi. We then returned to Madras where I spent a few more days with my friends before I returned to Kerala. My personal association with active politics ended then and during the next several years my links with Ravi , Ramunni, Appa Rao and Krishnaswamy and the others were personal.

Out of that bunch quite a number of us became distinguished journalists or went back to various professions. Some of us sought comfort in the anonymity of a bureaucratic career. Only very few of us like Ravi, Kunte, Krishnaswamy and Appa Rao spent their whole lives in pursuit of their political visions. Among all of them, however, I would single out Ravi and Kitchu (Krishnaswamy) as the only two of their kind. They refused to go back to the University where they had brilliant, indeed dazzling, academic prospects and took the risk of giving up everything for a life in politics when the political situation in India was uncertain. Today, 50 years later, they are still continuing to be active.

I would like to spend a little space to some special aspects of Ravi's career. First, his background. He belongs arguably to the most distinguished literary family in modern Kerala. His father, Dr. Goda Varma, was a pioneer research scholar in the evolution of the Malayalam language. His maternal grandfather, A.R. Raja Raja Varma, was a great grammarian and translator and was known throughout our State as "Kerala Panini". Raja Raja Varma's uncle, Kerala Varma, was a superb poet and translator of Kalidasa, apart from being a patron of new young writers in Malayalam. He was known as Kerala Kalidasa. Ravi belongs to the royal family of Mavelikkara, which is connected in matrilineal terms with the Travancore Royal Family. There was a continuous relationship through adoption between the two branches, whenever there was a possibility of there being no heir in the royal family.

These details are mentioned just to indicate the sort of aristocratic comfortable background, which Ravi gave up when he joined politics. His father passed away very early and his family gracefully accepted their most brilliant member's courageous decision to get out into the world all alone.

Ravindra Varma's career as a political activist falls into four distinct stages. During the forties and the early fifties he was the charismatic leader of the Students' Congress and travelled all over India; he also helped in the running of the World University Service. The next stage is, perhaps, the most memorable. For about 10 years in the late fifties and the early sixties he was the President and chief organiser of the World Assembly of Youth. In this capacity he travelled all over the world establishing permanent links with the younger political figures in Europe, Africa and South East Asia. Krishnaswamy was equally active. Between the two of them they carried out a whole programme of propaganda of progressive nationalism linking together the developing nations with radical groups in the developed world. This was an achievement, which has hardly any parallel anywhere else except perhaps in some of the Marxist global organisations and the World Council of Churches.

After this exciting period as an international crusader Ravi returns to national politics. He was Member of Parliament from 1962 for several years. He took a major role in the split in the

Congress in 1969. He identified himself with Morarji Desai and the Congress (O). Then came the Emergency when Ravi was imprisoned with many of his colleagues. His health suffered permanent damage when a minor hernia operation was botched up. He has had to struggle with this problem for the last 25 years.

The rest is history. When the Janata Government was found, Ravi, as a Lok Sabha Member from Bihar, was made Labour Minister. That was a very distinguished period, which has to be written about by some expert on Trade Union Politics in India and outside. He represented India with his usual charm and authority in the Sessions of the I.L.O. In the 20 years since then he has been active in the Gandhian Movement in the Gandhi Peace Foundation, in the Vishwa Yuvak Kendra and in the Institute of Gandhian Studies in Wardha. Currently, he is very busy as Chairman of the National Labour Commission. We can all look forward to a major path-breaking report from the Commission during his tenure. All these years he has been writing on Gandhiji. As a friend and admirer of long standing I would like to conclude this by making a special request to him to write a major analytical monograph on Gandhiji, situating him in the global tradition of non-violence and the specific context of British colonialism in India with its distorted but real 'rule of the law' regime. He could also use it to look back, not "in anger" but in "wistful sadness", at all that has happened since Gandhiji and his heir, Jawaharlal Nehru, the prophet and the leader (a favourite phrase of Jawaharlal), tried to achieve and did not succeed, as is inevitable in the human condition. In Edwin Arnold's translation of the Geeta, there are some lovely lines:

> "He that laboureth rightly for love of me
> Shall finally attain:
> But if in this thy faint heart fails
> Bring me thy failure!"

The Young Ravindra Varma

A. P. Mahadevan

I first came to know Ravindra Varma as a young student of Madras Christian College, Tambaram where I did my Intermediate earlier and was serving as a Resident Tutor in 1942. Though not a robust person physically, Ravi was more than adequately compensated by his intellectual abilities. His academic achievements endeared him to the teachers and the leadership qualities that he exhibited at an early age naturally led him to the Presidentship of the College Union. He was extremely popular in this capacity and in the turbulent days of the early forties he led the students of the College in activities associated with our freedom struggle. As the late Diraviam was his contemporary at the College, he and Ravi became a formidable force to reckon with. They were responsible for instilling in the students a fervour for the national movement and fighting against the so-called progressive groups. I need not mention the names of these as history has recorded them. They were clamouring for support to a "Peoples war" and the bigoted leadership of the Muslim community. Thus, they contributed not a little to the great schism between the two major communities of the country. It was upto the national movement and the nationalist student leaders like Ravindra Varma to counter this vicious propaganda in the college campuses and among the student community. The success of their efforts was reflected in the ferment among the students. They were filled with a patriotic urge kindled by the heroic deeds of the freedom fighters all over the country . They were itching for a chance to plunge themselves into the national struggle.

Such an opportunity came their way when the Mahatma began his fast in the Aga Khan Palace in February 1943. Thousands of students all over the country courted arrest in a non-violent manner by disobeying the police regulations and demanding the immediate release of the Mahatma. Thus, it was that Ravi, K.V. Sankaran and I were arrested in front of the Magistrate's court in Egmore, Madras while demonstrating against the alien rule and sentenced to three months' rigorous imprisonment. While being taken by train to Alipuram Central Jail we were joined by several other comrades who had courted arrest in other parts of the city. These included Krishnaswamy, who from then on was to become a constant associate of Ravi in spreading the gospel of Gandhi. At Alipuram there was again an influx from other parts of the State. Our number swelled to 52 in the course of a few days.

Although initially lodged with older Congressmen, we were soon segregated from them to avoid being brainwashed with "dangerous thoughts" and assigned to a large hall where we spent our time under one roof. I was the lone exception in the group of being a tutor and not a student and thus earned the title of *Vadyar*. The period of incarceration was one of the happiest periods of our lives. We were indeed cut off from the outside world with no newspapers or letters but a lively and highly vocal group of youngsters in the late teens and early twenties could devise ways of occupying and enjoying themselves with prayer meetings, singing sessions and of course political discussions. Of the last pursuit Ravi and Diraviyam were the leading lights.

Coming out of the jail some of us fell by the wayside in so far as active participation in politics was concerned. Ravi was one of those who plunged themselves into the political and social arena and his achievements have indeed been colossal. Although I was watching Ravi's progress from a distance, our meetings were few and far between. I am sure that other contributors to this volume, who were associated with him subsequent to his first incarceration, would give a fuller picture of his political activities . Ravi had his apprenticeship in Gandhian thought and constructive work under the guidance of the veteran Gandhian Shri G. Ramachandran. No wonder he became disillusioned with the Congress Establishment and joined those who dreamt of a New India envisioned by the early selfless freedom fighters. Naturally, he was a prime target of the "Emergency" and naturally again a prime choice as a member of the Janata Cabinet. I had an occasion to meet him in his office in the Parliament House. I found him the same unassuming friendly and witty Ravi whom I had known as a student. The high office had not affected him in any manner.

Along with millions of our countrymen I shall always consider the fall of the Janata Government as the greatest tragedy that has befallen this nation since our independence. It was brought about by a combination of the pettiness of the highest of the land, shameful machinations of a few individuals and an insatiable lust for power of small men. One of the most undesirable consequences of the tragedy was that the country was denied the opportunity of prolonged service of able men like Ravi in the governance of the country. But great men do not let setbacks to hold them back from their goals. Ravi is still active in the service of the country in spheres, which he has chosen for himself, namely propagation of Gandhian ideals and social justice to labour. May I join his hosts of friends and associates in diverse fields in wishing him very many more years of healthy and active life to continue his service for others.

A Dedicated Gandhian

K. Janardhanan Pillai

I am sure rich tributes of distinguished personalities from India and abroad to Shri Ravindra Varma will be appearing in the festschrift volume in honour of his seventy fifth birthday. I am not one of them. But I presume I may be one among the few who knew him from his early days. Every great man has his own special background which is partly historical or traditional and partly his own creation. Shri Varmaji was born in a branch of the Travancore (part of Kerala) Royal family reputed for its cultural greatness. He is the son of Shri Goda Varma Raja, a distinguished educationalist. I came into touch with Shri Ravindra Varma when he was an intermediate student in Trivandrum. I was then organising study groups of college students to stress the importance of moral values and patriotic sentiments in them. Shri Varma became an active member playing an impressive role in discussions and in the work-cum-study camps held in villages. It was during these days that he came into touch with Dr. G. Ramachandran. Later, when the work spread to Tamil Nadu, he used to come from Madras, where he was studying, to participate in camps. This must have prompted him to take the initiative to constitute a student and youth department in the All India Congress Committee and to give leadership to it.

Later, when Shri Varma became involved in many activities as parliamentarian, minister, and in many international conferences of great importance he has been maintaining a high standard of moral integrity and intellectual excellence, which qualifies him to be a true Gandhian. His life is replete with great and noble achievements. In him we can see humility and dignity as inseparable.

Shri Varma has been making an invaluable contribution for the spread and implementation of Gandhian thought and Gandhian constructive programme by shouldering the responsibility of guiding the Institute of Gandhian Studies (Gandhi Vichar Parishad) in Wardha as its Chairman for many years now, and as an active member of the Executive Committee of the Gandhi Smarka Nidhi and as the Chairman of the Gandhi Peace Foundation.

Let us jointly pray for God's grace to bless him with many more years of physical well being and mental vigour to serve the cause of humanity and to establish a *Sarvodaya* social order.

A Human Dynamo

K. John Mammen

In this contribution to the festschrift volume to be brought out on the occasion of the seventy-fifth birth anniversary of Shri Ravindra Varma (hereafter referred to as Varmaji) I journey down the memory lane to the years 1953-55 when I was a research student at the newly founded Gandhi Vichar Parishad (GVP) which was located at Bajaj Wadi, Wardha and of which Shri Shankar Rao Deo was the Secretary and Varmaji was the Co-ordiantor devoting most of his time to look after the responsibilities of Shri Deo who was away from Wardha most of the time. I was offered a stipendiary research studentship for a study of the writings of Gandhiji and his associates on economic problems and research on a specific aspect thereof under Dr. J. C. Kumarappa, in July 1953 at the conclusion of a three month summer camp organized under the auspices of GVP at Wardha directed by Varmaji. I was a research student at the GVP for nearly two years during which period Varmaji and I stayed at the Bajaj Wadi and interacted very closely. He was my guide and esteemed friend.

At the three month camp Varmaji directed all activities and I recall vividly the comparative ease with which he interacted with a host of Gandhian leaders of national and international status who were visiting resource persons for the camp. Varmaji himself delivered a series of lectures at the camp, on a variety of topics.

I was thrilled by the quality of his attention-commanding lectures and his communicative and oratorical skills. This was the experience of all participants in the camp who were hand-picked from various Indian universities and most of whom subsequently occupied top positions in various walks of life (a name that readily comes to my mind is Shri J.N. Dixit who retired a few years back as India's Foreign Secretary). Varmaji prepared thoroughly for his lectures although he would cast a spell by the sheer magic of his oratorical skill extempore. The impression that I formed of Varmaji is that he took his tasks , assignments and responsibilities very seriously paying in-depth attention to details , sequences and rationale.

It was not all Gandhian studies and research at the GVP. Some of the fundamentalist diehard Gandhians of those days, who frequented Wardha, were surprised at our (including Varmaji) playing "Gandhian Cricket" at a makeshift pitch at Bajaj Wadi and playing ping-pong and shuttle cock at a club nearby. In cricket, spin-bowling was Varmaji's forte and I still recall Varmaji's eyes popping out when a novice to cricket that I was lifted a spinner by him for our version of a sixer. I also recall our going to Nagpur to witness S.J.O.C. P3 cricket match wherein Frank Worrell also played.

I had heard of Varmaji when I was a college student through the parents of one of his classmates (Dr. Eso John who subsequently held top managerial innings with IBM and was also Chairman of Madras Fertilizers and Parrys) that he was a stormy petrel at the Madras Christian College involving himself fully in the Independence Movement.

I had met Varmaji, briefly though, during the days of the Emergency declared by Smt. Indira Gandhi, for subverting which Varmaji played a key role, and also while he was a Minister for Labour of the Janata Government during the 1970's. I have also been in touch with him ever since. I remember how he readily accepted and published in Gandhi Marg a piece by me on 'Tagore, Gandhi and Amartya Sen' wherein I was critical of Sen for his apparent irreverent aside on Gandhiji in a New York Review of Books article. Varmaji always called a spade a spade and never compromised with his principles, come what may, and perhaps this may account for his "doings and undoings" in life! I often wondered how Varmaji could struggle so selflessly for addressing causes that were and are so dear to him. He was and is a fierce critic and he has no patience with the incompetent, the tricky, the time-servers and the opportunists.

I still remember a GT train journey during late 1954 to Wardha during which Varmaji emerged at Ballarshah station to join me at breakfast, an Idly-Dossa session that we had at his Bajaj Wadi residence and a community 'Onam Feast' we had at Bajaj Wadi which was put together with all of us including Varmaji at the GVP assisting and whose expertise in the culinary art was seriously suspect! Varmaji was (and I guess still is) a great mixer. He is indeed a man of many parts.

As I pen this memory piece I have before me an article in *The Hindu* (August 20, 1999) by the well-known Malayalam critic Prof. S. Guptan Nair on his student days at the well-known Thiruvananthapuram based Government Arts College, in which there is a reference to Varmaji who was junior to him. He mentions therein that G. Ravindra Varma was among "the jewels in the intermediate classes of that bygone era."

Despite all the crowns that life has presented him I still feel that Varmaji was cut out for much bigger statures early in life internationally since he had all the credentials for such positions, the opportunities for which he did not pursue. Now that Varmaji is the Chairman of the National Commission on Labour one may expect major recommendations in its report for a fair deal to India's toiling millions.

I would sign off this piece by mentioning that Varmaji always commenced his letters addressing me as "My dear John Mammen" and closed them invariably "Yours affectionately". He always strikes a special relationship with a friend and retains it strengthening its bond with passing years. Friends like Varmaji are rather rare these days.

Recalling Our Days in WAY

Piet Dijkstra

I came new to the Secretariat of the World Assembly of Youth (WAY) in Brussels at about the same time as Ravindra Varma. Ravi might have had connections with WAY in India. I had those via the Dutch National Youth Council.

Ravi did come from a country where at that time the majority of the population, as it is still now, lives in rural areas. One of the persons who opened my eyes to this world has been Ravindra Varma. We certainly shared Mahatma Gandhi's thinking that "India lives in its villages", although I can't remember whether we discussed this at length. My own thinking had been influenced by Gandhi's thinking about non-violence, when I had been a member of a small pacifist youth movement before the war.

One of the first occasions of our meeting each other and working together was the Council meeting in Accra in Ghana. Africa then was at the threshold of independence. Some of the countries had set their footsteps to a brighter future; other countries like the former Belgian colony of Congo were in turmoil and this influenced the atmosphere and the discussions during the meeting. It was then and there that Ravindra Varma highly impressed me by his stature and by his virtues, when he had to deal with a rather explosive situation. As Chairman, he demonstrated his skill in evolving an acceptable political resolution. He showed the same aptitude during the numerous meetings of the board of WAY and during international conferences organised by it.

The World Assembly of Youth had in him a President who could steer the organization through tempestuous situations and conflicts. Coming from a neutral country he left his mark on WAY as the international youth organization that stood for a democratic world and society and for the right of former colonies for freedom.

When Ravi had left WAY for serving his own country I had stayed on for a couple of years. After WAY I worked in various organizations in particular for development activities and adult education, like the International Council for Adult Education. This brought me from time to time to Asia and occasionally to India, a country which occupied a special place in me. We tried many times to meet, specially when Ravi was in Delhi, in politics. This however always failed.

Looking back at the period I worked with him in WAY, I consider this as of crucial importance: it taught me tolerance on a world-wide scale and the need to show responsibility for the forgotten world. Ravindra Varma has contributed to this.

I do regret that we did not have a chance to meet again. We might have discussed matters related to Mahatma Gandhi, now that we both – he in India and I in the Netherlands – are trying to make Gandhi's teachings better known. I hope and wish that Ravi will still be in a position to further exercise his influence.

An Inspiring Personality

S.K. Bandopadhaya

I came to know about Shri Ravindra Varma for the first time as the Vice President and thereafter the President of All India Students' Congress in the latter half of the 40s of the previous century. At that time I was a humble freedom fighter, under the aegis of the Indian National Congress in a remote area of Bihar. Naturally for us, workers and volunteers of the Congress, in such remote areas, an all India personality was coveted enough.

I saw him for the first time in December 1948, in close proximity of Acharya Kripalani, at the Jaipur Congress and I was really excited. But I had the privilege of coming in personal contact with him in the beginning of the 50s only.

I had the good fortune of hearing him for the first time, in a camp organised by the Gandhi Vichar Parishad, of which he was the guiding spirit. I was in those days a worker of the All India Spinners' Association and I must admit that I did get but very few opportunities of listening to such high standard expositions on Gandhiji and his socio-economic and political philosophy earlier. And that too from a young exponent of the Mahatma of almost our age! He was no doubt the unquestioned topmost intellectual amongst the younger generation of Gandhians of those days. In his ripe age also he retains the same position. This is no small wonder. His capacity to present such high calibre interpretations of Mahatma Gandhi, both in English and Hindi (and certainly in his mother-tongue Malayalam also) is second to none. To revert to my first experience of his speaking faculty, a worker from rural area like me was simply struck with awe hearing him quoting at ease the latest thinkers of many countries one after another, in support of his exposition.

Even though I came in his close contact after I joined the Gandhi Smarak Nidhi in 1984, from a distance I had appreciated the various roles he had been playing in both national and international scenario. I was particularly impressed with his role in upholding the rights of democracy and freedom of speech etc. during the black days of Emergency. I felt very much delighted when he won a seat in the Lok Sabha during the post-Emergency election and became a minister in central government. He was recognised as a very capable and successful minister, managing two very important portfolios during the Janata Party's rule. During all these years I did not miss any opportunity of reading his writings or speeches and found that they were as inspiring and thought-provoking as ever. I have no hesitation to add that in my humble life in the field of Gandhian constructive activities, on several occasions I have made use of his thoughts and ideas to carry conviction to my audience.

After joining the Gandhi Smarka Nidhi and being associated with the Gandhi Peace Foundation in that capacity, another dimension of his personality and capability came to my notice. This is his capacity to conduct meetings. He speaks to the point and that too very precisely. The quality of deliberations in any meeting he may preside over and even he may participate in is elevated, and fruitful results are obtained within the shortest possible time. Many others would, indeed, take much more time to conduct any such meeting fruitfully. He would allow other participants to have their full say, guiding them constructively wherever necessary. And he would do this with all humility, without giving any opportunity to anybody feeling belittled. While participating as a member of any group, he would contribute his valuable inputs and the whole affair would be over within the shortest possible time. He is equally successful in conducting both large meetings and small committee meetings in this manner.

An equally important quality of him, that I have marked in this process, is his command over any language he may be using.

Whenever there may be any difference of opinion in a meeting about the wording of any resolution, almost always, his views would be acceptable to all. I am relieved of all anxieties in drawing up the minutes of any meeting of any committee, once Raviji has vetted the same.

During this period I have also learnt a lot from him on various aspects of Gandhian philosophy. It is a real pleasure to listen to his high standard discourses with rapt attention, even though he were to speak for an hour or even more. When he stops, the listeners would feel that he has rather stopped very early.

Amidst his various engagements and activities, right from the management of several important institutions, contacts at high levels with both national and international figures, he finds time to write articles and monographs on various aspects of Gandhian thought. His writings have to be read by people to appreciate how deep is his knowledge in any topic related to Gandhi and his 'ism' and how capable he is in presenting and interpreting his subject. I have quite often insisted that his talks, articles and monographs should be published in suitable volumes so that such valuable materials are not lost to posterity. Particularly such useful materials, which are also valuable documentation of the evolution of both Gandhian thought and movement, are of immense value. Let us hope that some of his friends and admirers may take upon this responsibility to ensure that Raviji's articles are preserved as national heritage for our future generations.

Last but not least is the consideration of Raviji as a man. During the course of my half a century's experience in public life, I have come across quite a few eminent public figures. There is a type amongst them to whom one may not go very close because of some invisible barrier around them. We admire them from a distance. There are others, though fewer in number, with whom we can be very close. For, no such invisible barrier exists around them. Raviji undoubtedly tops amongst those who are in the second category. One has to see to believe how such an intellectual giant and a very successful administrator interacts with even a common worker. He is very personal and close to everybody, who may have come in touch with him. This is a unique humane character of Raviji, which I adore very much.

I am extremely fortunate that I am also one of his colleagues in the field of Gandhian activities and pray to God that He may bless him with a long life and good health so that he may be able to rise more and more with a view to carrying on his mission of service to the Gandhian cause, which has been very dear to him from his very young days.

A Politician with a Difference

Sadiq Ali

Ravindra Varma is a well-known name in the politics of the country. Earlier he was very much involved in youth activities both in India and abroad. These youth activities broadened his outlook. He impressed people with his intelligence. He could have been a fire-brand in the early days but he also believed in discipline and orderly behaviour.

After India became free there was no question of his living a humdrum life. All his old contacts drove him into active all India politics. He had the calibre of making a successful politician. He could easily specialise in a few subjects. He was articulate and an effective speaker. Language was no problem for him. He was a multilingual. In any case he could express himself eloquently in English, Hindi and Malayalam. He made almost an immediate mark in Parliament. He soon had ministerial responsibilities, which he discharged with tact, ability and efficiency.

We all know the part he played in the ill-starred emergency. He was arrested and put behind bars. There he had opportunities of being influenced by fellow prisoners and influencing them in turn.

He has an analytical and critical intellect. He can hold his own with any group of intellectuals.

Indian politics has been no easy or smooth affair. There were stormy periods during which it was difficult for decisions to be taken or take a definite line. Mr. Varma kept cool and rendered sane and responsible advice.

Mr. Varma held important offices in the organisation of Congress (O) and other parties. He made a distinctive mark when he became a Minister in the Government of India.

A time came when he got disillusioned with politics. He took to the Gandhian way. He almost mastered Gandhian thought. In life he came more and more under the influence of Buddhism.

My Teacher

Sanjay Matey

I have had the rare privilege to be the student of the Diploma Programme of the Institute of Gandhian Studies, Wardha, in the first batch of 1988-89 when Shri Ravindra Varma was its Director. I also had the fortune to work with him at the Institute until August 1994.

Varmaji, as we called him endearingly, is one of the finest exponents of Gandhian thought. Although I had studied Gandhian ideas as part of my Masters degree, it was only after listening to Varmaji that I came to know about the dynamic, intricate and practical aspects of Gandhian thought. Varmaji's analytical approach helped me to examine Gandhi's ideas critically, and the years spent in his company have really stood me in good stead in my life and work in later years.

Varmaji is a workaholic. I have seen him getting up at 3.30 a.m and working for 14-15 hours a day even when he was in his mid-sixties. He is the most punctual, disciplined, hardworking and profound scholar of Gandhian thought that I have ever come across. He has been a major source of inspiration and influence in my life.

On this occasion, I pray to God for Varmaji's health so that he may continue to serve the nation and the cause of spreading Gandhian studies for many years.

A Unique Personality*

Neema Vaishnav

Words are insufficient to express my feelings of admiration, affection and indebtedness for a person like Ravindra Varma who has earned high reputation and regard in the national and international arena. Varmaji is my teacher and spiritual guide. I call him Dadaji in view of my family ties with him. Although I would have loved to call him my father, I hesitate to do so because I have not done anything for him entitling me to the status of his daughter.

I became acquainted with Varmaji a decade ago. In 1992-93 I stayed at the Institute of Gandhian Studies, Wardha, doing the Diploma Programme. After returning to Kausani, I started a course in Gandhian thought with the help of the Institute for the benefit of youth and social workers in the Uttarakhand region. Since part of the programme is held at Wardha, I keep visiting the Institute every year, thereby giving me an opportunity to be with Varmaji. With every visit I got to know him better and each time I returned to Kausani, I had the satisfaction of having broadened my own knowledge and vision.

Varmaji is a multi-dimensional personality. I have not been able to identify some of his talents and qualities due to my own limitations. He is a clear-headed thinker and teacher. Ideas flow one after the other like a chain when he delivers a talk. He makes it a point to prepare himself well and organise his thoughts very systematically before he delivers even a public speech. He is quite particular that we should not be blind followers of Gandhi. His critical insights actually enabled us to

---

* Translated from Hindi

better appreciate the meaning and practical implications of Gandhian thought. I found him to be a practitioner of Gandhian ideas in his personal and social life. Even as a politician, Varmaji made his mark as a competent and self-less leader deeply committed to Gandhian values.

Meeting Varmaji has been a major turning point in my life. Although a father himself, I found him behaving more like a mother, a fact which being a woman I can sense better. I wish and pray that God may give him health so that he may continue his work and inspire people like me for many more years to come.

PART - II

ESSAYS

1

Social and Environmental Violence : A Buddhist Perspective

Sulak Sivaraksa

Ravindra Varma is a Gandhian scholar, thinker and activist of rare distinction. He represents the generation of Gandhians who formed a crucial linkage between the era of Gandhi and the post-independent India. Given the historical circumstances and the political developments since 1947 it has been far more challenging to preserve and advocate the Gandhian values and ideas in India. Gandhi did what he could in his own lifetime and he could have done much more had the people around him and the Congress leadership understood him better. Yet he possessed a dream which needed millions to respond. Ravindra Varma is one of those who responded to the call of Gandhi and remained true to his dreams and commitment.

I have been asked to write on some economic aspects of social and environmental violence, approaching the subject from a Buddhist perspective. Indeed, this invitation offers a wide range of choices, but I shall try to keep my subject matter fairly general and straightforward. The present economic reality, widely known as neo-liberal capitalism, prizes the accumulation of profits over human well-being and environmental sustainability. As such, it is criminal and hence definitely not the way to regulate or organize the global society. The present trend however is of increasingly giving the agents and institutions of capital a free hand to do so.

The main beneficiaries of this violent and highly unjust system are invariably transnational corporations (though some critics prefer to call them transnational tyrannies), big financial investors and their supporters. Roughly two-thirds of what is known today as world trade are simply intra-firm or inter-firm trade. Small wonder that they are virtually the present-day 'masters of the universe', increasingly accumulating special rights, influence and power vis-a-vis the mass of humanity. An open secret is that the wealthiest 20 per cent of the world's population receive 83 per cent of the world's total income – a fact that no longer creates consternation or moral outrage in the mainstream; rather it is taken as a healthy phenomenon that will contribute to human progress. Moreover, the environment is being plundered to quench the greed – which happens to be a bottomless pit – of the few. Inevitably, this creates a two-tiered system both within and between countries; a small opulent minority builds their castles on the suffering and impoverishment of the absolute majority of humanity. A large segment of humanity enjoys freedom with no opportunities and has the freedom to starve but not freedom from poverty. While I am writing, thousands of children are probably dying from easily preventable diseases. Millions more are malnourished or starving. It is against this backdrop that we need to discuss some of the economic aspects of social and environmental violence from a Buddhist perspective.

Let us first deal with the production side of the capitalist equation. What is its main driving force and value system? How do they impact social organization and the environment? Undeniably, the fuel that keeps the capitalist engine running is profit: the more of it, the better, the argument goes. Hence, corporations must be free to pursue it at all costs. The ends justify the means. It is also argued that the profit generated by the system will eventually trickle down to benefit the mass of humanity. The available evidence points otherwise. To be fair, capitalism does generate some benefits to humanity, but they are completely unintended by-products of the system.

In mainstream discourse, profit is said to derive solely from entrepreneurship – a concept that acts as a soda-bicarbonate for intellectual and moral indigestion. In reality, the easiest and cheaper way to reap massive profits is exploitation or ostracism: one is rich by keeping or making others poor, directly or otherwise. The masters then seek solace in the tenuous assumption that the global economy utilises the best and disposes the rest. Furthermore, the environment is seen as a sub-system of international capitalism, not vice versa. Hence, it is to be raped in order to lubricate the wheels of the capitalist machine. Put differently, the insatiable quest for profit upheld by capitalism really reflects greed, hatred, moral callousness and wanton criminal negligence towards the well-being of the people and environment. The name of the game is getting ahead even at one another's expense, to rise to the top of the pecking order. If one frequents any bookstore one is likely to find business books with interesting titles such as *Divide and Rule* and *Colonizing the Market*. This nefarious aggressiveness is being known as "free competition" in mainstream parlance. Those, that succeeded to the top, are lauded as "efficient". If allowed to have a firm grip on the people, these values will necessarily generate a grotesque society of violent, selfish, anti-social environmental-plunderers. A founding father of the free market system, Adam Smith himself, derided acquisitiveness, selfishness and greed as "the vile maxims of the masters of mankind"; of course, this is expected out of a child of the Enlightenment.

However, let us now turn to Buddhism and profit. Capitalism may be an efficient and rational socio-economic system, but its morality is highly dubious. To put it less charitably, the morality of capitalism is conspicuous by it absence. The so-called triumph of capitalism in the late twentieth century in fact exploded the moral world, removing all moral (and increasingly legal) restraints to the accumulation of profits.

Unlike (neo-liberal) capitalism, Buddhism respects and upholds the primacy of all sentient beings – not of non-corporeal corporations. Also, Buddhism critically differs from capitalism in that it does not make a virtue out of self-interest, greed and self-aggrandizement out of the masters' vile maxims. Unfortunately, the masters' vile maxims are gaining ascendancy in, for example, educational institutions and the mass media. The logic is simple: the more the guardians of the brutal system, the more stable it will be.

Buddhism denounces and renounces greed, because it is seen as leading one down the perfidious road of aggression and hatred – in a word, of suffering. Greed can never lead to satisfaction, individually or collectively. Thus, Buddhism seeks to show how to be content with changing oneself, that is, self-cultivation, and emphasises the importance of caring about, promoting and benefiting from one another's well-being. Whereas capitalism treats a person as only half-human (the economic dimension e.g., greed, hatred) and selfishness is cultivated to the exclusion of other considerations, Buddhism approaches a human person holistically. The mind and heart must be cultivated, and diversity must be nourished in social relations and in human relations with nature. A human person is an "inter-being".

At the individual level, this means the practising of *inter alia,* the Four sublime Abodes (*Brahma Vihara*). They are as follows :

A) ***Metta*** or living-kindness towards oneself and others. Yes, we all desire to be happy and have every right to do so. Nevertheless, through practising the precepts and meditation, a different state of happiness can be achieved. It is a state of happiness where the mind is harmonious with oneself as well as with others. It renders assistance and benefits without ill-will and without the malice of anger and competition. Once one is tranquil and happy, these qualities will be spread to others as well.

B) ***Karuna*** or compassion can only be cultivated when one recognises the suffering of others and, consequently, is driven to bring that suffering to an end. Undoubtedly, a rich person who does not care about the miserable conditions of the poor lacks this quality. It is terribly difficult for him or her to develop into a better person. All those who lock themselves up in ivory towers in the midst of a shockingly unjust world cannot be called compassionate. In Mahayana Buddhism, one vows to become a Bodhisattva and forgoes one's own nirvana until all sentient beings are free from suffering. In other words, one cannot remain indifferent. Rather, one must endeavour to help others and alleviate or mitigate their suffering as much as one can. The essential characteristic of any healthy community/society is its principle of inclusion. As we become more attuned to compassion as the instrumentality of social organization, we can embrace the community.

C) ***Mudita*** or sympathetic joy is a mental condition whereby one genuinely rejoices when others are happy or successful in a number of ways. One feels this without the flame of envy even when a competitor gets ahead.

D) ***Upekkha*** or equanimity refers to the state in which the mind is cultivated until it becomes evenly balanced and neutral. Whether one faces success or failure, whether one is confronted with prosperity or adversity, one is not "moved" by it.

The Four Sublime Abodes are to be developed step by step from the first to the last. Even when one is not perfect, one must set one's mind towards this goal. Otherwise, in one way or the other, one's dealing with the self or with others will tend to be harmful. Moving towards happiness and tranquillity rather than towards worldly success and material progress, a Buddhist is then in a position to develop his or her community – the family, neighbourhood, village, etc. An individual who is awakened by these realities is called *Purisodya.* Once this awakening is gradually shared with others ultimately the whole nation may be awakened to the threats posed by capitalism, including its ethos.

Moreover, in a time of *moral emergency* like now, the Buddhist teaching of the Four Wheels may serve as useful antidotes to the detrimental values of capitalism. As a cart moves steadily on four wheels, likewise human development should rest – and this point cannot be overemphasized – on the four *Dhammas*, namely, Sharing, Pleasant Speech, Constructive Action and Equality.

A) One must share (*dana*) what one has with others – be it goods, wealth, knowledge, time, labour, etc. Capitalism, on the other hand, upholds the dictum "all for myself and nothing for other people", in Adam Smith's telling phrase. Powerful transnational corporations control the access to essential commodities such as food, drugs and technology. Yes, they are all made available to us – for a high sum , of course. To a large extent, *dana* is still practised in most village cultures. We should strengthen the concept of *dana* and spread it to counteract the invasion of materialism and the ethos of competition by sharing, by leading less commercialised lifestyles.

B) Pleasant Speech *(piyavaca)* not only refers to polite talk but also to speaking truthfully and sincerely. Its basic assumption is that everyone is equal. On the contrary, consumerism or the culture of capitalism, which will be dealt in greater detail below, posits that less commercialised lifestyles are inferior. People must be *deceived* to consume goods and services that they do not really need in the name of 'high standard of living'.

C) Constructive Action (*atthacariya*) means working for one another's benefit. Here again it is antithetical to the dynamics of the corporations. A corporation does not work to benefit its employees or the town or city it is situated in. Rather, it is only geared towards enriching the large shareholders. For instance, it seems that every time a corporation "downsizes", the price of its shares would skyrocket. Thereby new rules must be promulgated whereby investors that have high stakes in the well-being of their localities are rewarded.

D) And finally Equality (*samanattata*) means that Buddhism does not recognize classes or castes, does not encourage one group to dominate or exploit the other. The global economy however creates a small caste of "winners" and mass hordes of "losers". The winners take all, and their action is deemed perfectly legitimate under the banner of "free trade" and "free competition". Hence, we urgently require "fair trade" not free trade.

In Buddhism, one is taught to be aware of the three root causes of suffering: greed, hatred and delusion – the very things that capitalism promotes. They are great barriers to openness, compassion and responsibility – in short, to the Buddhist conception of freedom, which is threefold. First, all people should be free from insecurities and dangers that threaten their existence such as poverty, disease, famine, etc. Second is social freedom. All people should be free from human oppression and exploitation; such a sate presupposes tolerance. Solidarity, and benevolence. And lastly is the freedom of the inner life. This means the freedom from mental suffering, from impurities of the mind that propel people to commit all kinds of evils.

To achieve such states, the practising of *dana* (sharing or generosity), *sila* (moral precepts) and *bhavana* (mindfulness) is essential.

Examining the practice of *dana* one can clearly see that giving is more important than receiving or taking. Giving enables us to restructure our consciousness; that is, away from selfishness towards selflessness. Additionally, we should be content with simple lifestyle, a lifestyle that is not obsessed with the accumulation of wealth at the expense of others. *As Mahatma Gandhi pointed out, we should all live simply so that others can simply live.* We must also be willing to share our wealth, knowledge, talents, time, etc. to benefit those that are less fortunate. Once we have restructured our minds to be more humble and less selfish, we will then be able to start transforming society to be more just, peaceful, and environmentally sustainable. Needless to say, *dana* is a radical departure from capitalism and consumerism.

The practice of *sila* is still useful in transforming the self and society. The Five Precepts entail the following: a commitment to abstain from taking life and from taking what has not been given; and refraining from sexual misconduct, false speech and intoxicants that cloud the mind. It can be argued that the global economy at least violates the first two precepts.

If we understand liberation as an impulse that seeks to enhance life in all forms, then the Buddhist *ahimsa* (non-killing) concept becomes a precondition for societal liberation and world peace. To generate peace and bring about liberation requires eliminating, or at least reducing, violence. The first precept deals with direct violence, but may also encompass structural violence. Structural violence may be defined as "institutionalised forms of violence involving, for example, women, children, minority groups, low income countries, or the rest of nature". It is the culmination of greed, hatred, and delusion. Though less visible and hence less accountable, structural violence sets the ground for direct violence: Violence does not require direct confrontation. The structures of the global economy make possible exploitation and oppression on a scale that defies comment – actions that necessarily involve the loss of lives. These structures inclined the masters to violate the poor and the environment. Partly because of vested interests, the rich and powerful do not see these structures and their actions as violent. Besides, they have a number of ideas that help legitimise and redeem these structures such as progress and development. Increasingly, trade laws are legalizing the exploitation and plunder of transnational corporations.

Furthermore, the global economic structures facilitate the concentration of wealth, capital, and especially resources in the hands of the masters, denying them to the masses. Certainly, the masses' permission of such conduct is found wanting – hence the violation of the second precept.

And if one perceives consumerism as deliberately deceptive, then one can also accuse the global economy of promoting false speech.

Modern education deals almost exclusively with the minds, not the hearts, of students. The most able (e.g., aggressive, competitive etc.) are recognized and rewarded, although they need not be 'good' in the moral sense or aware of societal ills. Indeed, many of the rich and powerful are unhappy. Directly or otherwise, their exalted positions are built on mass poverty and ecological devastation. This is in part a result of ignorance (*avijja*) or delusion (*moha*). Realizing the threat of ignorance or delusion, Buddhism encourages the cultivation of right mindfulness, which directly leads to inner peace and heightened awareness of social realities.

In order to build inner peace along with an understanding of social reality, one uses *bhavana,* the third Buddhist component to realize freedom. Often described as meditation, *bhavana* is better understood as 'cultivation' or 'self-training'. Contrary to popular belief, it does not merely mean sitting in solitude and engaging in some special form of internal contemplation. *Bhavana* really entails investigating, reflecting, learning, nourishing the mind in order to develop oneself towards enlightenment. In short, it is the practice of living daily as mindfully as possible. Thus, one can engage in it even while performing daily routines.

Traditionally, the first part of *bhavana* aims at achieving tranquillity *(samatha),* at planting seeds of peace within. The second is comprised of the technique for understanding the true situation of one's psycho-physical constitution and of the world. This is known as *vipasanna* or insight mediation, which can further be developed into analytical thinking by way of causal relations or problem solving. With the ego detached, it becomes an internal factor of wisdom. Critical self-awareness leads to selflessness.

The Buddha said that tranquillity is the most important prerequisite for self-cultivation and self-criticism, for the true understanding (*pranja*) of the self. It should be pointed out that understanding is different from intellectual knowledge, since it is filtered through both the heart and the mind. Understanding helps the individual to recognize his or her limits and to be more humble. At the same time, it promotes loving kindness and compassion: the individual will be in a better position to witness the suffering of others and to help eliminate the cause of suffering. Of course, when one tackles the cause of suffering, particularly in an oppressive social system, one usually gets hurt. Here *bhavana* facilitates the understanding of such danger as well as the forgiving of the oppressor. The oppressive system is hated and will be destroyed, but the oppressor will neither be despised nor executed. If one is aware of one's anger, then one can envelop it with mindfulness, thereby transforming it into compassion. Thich Nhat Hanh says that anger is like a closed flower; the flower will only bloom when deeply penetrated by the sunlight of *bhavana.* The constant radiation of compassion and understanding will eventually crack anger, enabling one to perceive its depth and roots. Likewise, *bhavana* will fully open the flower buds of greed, hatred and delusion.

So far, I have only offered a Buddhist glimpse at the production side of the capitalist system. I have tried to answer (cursorily, of course) the question 'What makes the masters tick?' by examining their vested interest, mentality and value system, and have analysed some of their negative impacts on society and the environment. And contrasting Buddhism with capitalism, I have offered some suggestions on how to make *Dhamma* matter in everyday life, that is, how to correct the ills of capitalism and achieve liberation, individually and collectively.

Let us now turn to the second half of the equation : consumption. The master's vile maxims still dictate the nature of consumption in capitalism. (Therefore the Buddhist critique presented above is also relevant here.) After all, production and consumption form a vicious circle. Mincing no words, consumption is likewise driven by greed, acquisitiveness and selfishness – albeit in a slightly different context. Here consumerism or insatiable consumption is equated with ultimate happiness and freedom, with self-realization. As David Arnott, an English Buddhist, explains, "By participating in the sacrament of purchase, sacrificing money, we can buy an object that is not so much an object as a focus of images which grants us a place in the system of images we hold sacred. For a while when we buy a car we also buy the power, prestige, sexuality, success, which the advertisements have succeeded in identifying with the car, or whatever the commodity is. Consumerism works by identifying the sense of unsatisfactoriness or lack (*dukka*) we all hold at a deep level of mind and then producing an object guaranteed to satisfy that 'need'".

If transnational corporations are able to appease their greed for profits then consumers will be able to consume 'happiness and satisfaction' with greed, the argument goes. Both sides will benefit. Wonderful! In reality, greed, in whatever context, can only breed suffering. Furthermore, the enormous pressure that this vicious circle puts on the environment is all too apparent.

The culture of economic globalisation and consumerism directly nourishes the unlimited greed of soulless transnational corporations. It will take quite a talent to miss this observation: markets dependent on consumption and controlled by powerful corporations cannot do otherwise. The consumers cannot be expected to know what they want; the demand must be manipulated or generated. The unconscious of the consumer must be 'told' what to purchase. Therefore, whereas the political and economic dimensions of globalisation are marginalizing many people worldwide, particularly the poor, consumerism seeks the active participation of all classes. As a form of greed, consumerism obscures the path to personal liberation.

In many respects, consumerism is able to dominate much of contemporary society because individuals have become alienated from their culture and from each other. The sense of community that led people to share scarce resources and work cooperatively has been supplanted by the vile maxims of the masters of mankind, by an anger or competitiveness that causes people to seek acquisitions at the expense of their neighbours. In sum, consumerism is a consequence of using greed and violence to regulate socio-economic relations.

At the most profound level, consumerism owes its vitality to the delusion of the autonomous individualized self, a self that exists independently of social relations and of human relations with nature; a human person is thrown into the world. For the Buddha, it was clear that the 'self' constituted only a pattern of persistently changing experiences that had no more substance or permanence than those experiences.

We are deluded into seeking some transcendental subject, something that defines experience yet lies beyond the experience. We are exhorted to know ourselves and yet the 'self' in this dualistic system remains unknowable. For the Buddhists, this delusion is the fundamental cause of suffering. Ontologically, we become estranged aspects of our experiences of others and ourselves. Hence, we are precluded from any meaningful conception of identity.

Consumerism provides an artificial means of defining our existence by suggesting that identity is realized through the process of acquisition. Put differently, consumerism is a perverse corollary of the Cartesian proof of personal existence: "I shop therefore I am."

I have often referred to consumerism as a demonic religion because of the manner in which individuals become mired in a cycle of behaviour that is fundamentally self-defeating: the insatiable desire for goods ultimately leads to despair or boredom.

However the Buddhist practice of mindfulness may help the individual to realize gradually that "I breathe therefore I am." Put another way, *bhavana* will help us synchronize our heads with our hearts. The primary result will not be greater intellectual power, which is amoral and compartmentalized. Rather, we will achieve real understanding or *prajna*. The less selfish we are, the more our *prajna* will merge with *karuna* or compassion. *Prajna* and *karuna* are important for leading an alternative lifestyle, for overcoming consumerism. The two foster spirituality, which goes hand in hand with the engendering of harmony within ourselves, our society and our natural habitat. In turn, this would help bring about social justice, fraternity and ecological balance.

The deterioration of the community as a significant social, economic and political system is both a cause and a consequence of consumerism in the contemporary world. Traditional communities in both the North and South were predicated upon recognition of the interrelationship of all beings and the responsibilities that arise from that kind of relationship. Industrialization tended to undermine the conditions upon which traditional communities were constituted – no doubt a process that is still happening in the industrializing parts of the world. The exaltation of wealth and possessions (i.e., the legitimisation of greed, hatred and delusion) often led to the disintegration of these communities. Therefore the individual, isolated within the society, anchors to the new sense of purpose configured by the corporate culture.

Under market capitalism, individuals and communities are required to be completely dependent on the market for goods and services, which in turn must be consumed in ever-increasing quantities: the more the better. A new television set for everyone, a new car for everyone, and so on. Prosperity is defined as "more having". Again, the adverse environmental implications are clear. In large part, economic growth is predicated on this dependent lifestyle: the greater the degree of market dependency, the greater the chance of having a high growth rate.

Control over one's own sustenance must be abolished: let the market and the technocrats take care of it. No, you must not grow your own food. Rather, you must shop in supermarkets (i.e., feed the multinationals). The availability of food is not a problem as long as one can afford to buy them: every person on his or her own. The only freedom is the freedom of consumption – or conversely, the freedom to starve. Along with this new pattern of behaviour comes a new set of attitudes, which has already been discussed above. They are necessary and complementary to each other. Social organization or relation is necessarily fragmented, atomistic and violent. The more people are concerned with amassing personal possessions at all costs, the less they would care about 'the losers' of the unjust system and about the state of the natural environment, the less they will be able to embark on concerted efforts to challenge the transnational tyrannies. Thus, contrary to popular belief, economic globalisation thrives on fragmentation – on indifference or lack of compassion. Fragmentation offers the best environment for the flourishing of monoculturism, including that of the mind and heart. From a Buddhist perspective, this is not propitious at all for individual and collective liberation.

In Buddhism, prosperity is defined as "more being". As such, it cannot be realized atomistically, only collectively and with an emphasis on spirituality. The Buddhist spiritual community is known as *sangha.* A *sangha* should be small, autonomous and decentralized. The objective of the *sangha* is to live together in harmony with oneself, with the community and with one's natural surroundings; that is, not to exploit oneself, and other sentient beings. In other words, members of the *sangha* would have the time to cultivate seeds of peace within and to develop critical self-awareness. The realization of one's optimal potentiality would, in turn, help enhance the understanding of the self and the world. The lifestyle pursued should be simple, content, self-reliant, compassionate, generous and mindful. Such qualities are necessary in order to restructure one's consciousness and overcome greed, hatred, delusion. What can be a greater threat to consumerism than voluntary simple lifestyle and self-reliance?

The Buddha used the term *sangha* to refer to his community of celibate renunciants who left home in pursuit of the ultimate truth. It was perhaps first experimented in Vajji, a small republic in India that existed approximately six centuries before Christ. The Vajjian *sangha* was democratic; its members fully participated to decide matters unanimously and harmoniously. In this way, the democratic model of liberty, fraternity and equality was developed non-violently some 2,500 years before the French Revolution.

The Buddha predicted that the Vajji republic would remain ever prosperous if its leaders met regularly, resolved conflicts peacefully, decided on matters unanimously, respected women and elders, conserved the natural environment and sacred monuments, maintained a simple lifestyle, and accepted guidance from spiritual persons.

Ultimately, the Vajji republic was destroyed, but not because of the military might of the great Magadha Empire, which was an absolute monarchy. Rather, the external powers stirred disunity among the Vajji leaders, sowing jealously among them and luring them with the illusory happiness of a luxurious lifestyle.

To this day, *sangha* members, whether high or low born, are treated equally. Seniority is based on the day he or she joined the body. Each member has only three pieces of robes, an alms bowl, and a few other essentials. Superfluous objects are either owned by the community or jointly with another member.

The basic philosophy of the *sangha* can be applied to the contemporary world. For instance, Gandhi's vision of the village republic is quite similar to the Buddha's *sangha.* More recently, the promising Sustainable and Self-Reliant Communities Movement worldwide also shares a similar view.

In Thailand, to cite an example, there are vital signs that the Vajjian ideals are being revived, deliberately or otherwise. A sizable number of monks, nuns, engaged Buddhists and activists are mindful of the dangers posed by consumerism and transnational corporations. They are helping to promote a new form of literacy to the poor and marginalized, one that is based on empowerment, participatory community economics and sustainable development, one that will also really contribute to the culture of peace and poverty eradication. For example, many of the poor are being morally and spiritually empowered to overcome drugs addiction, gambling and superstition. Many, including their communities, are rediscovering confidence, identity and wisdom in traditional cultures. Cultural diversity is being affirmed; this is an important bulwark against the global monoculture that is destroying alternative ways of life. Many no longer feel dispirited and inferior; how extreme marginalisation and oppression lead to apathy and fatalism is well known. Hence, they are more actively participating in the civil society, an important prerequisite for a meaningful democracy. A sizeable number is engaging in voluntary simple lifestyles that are based on self-reliance and self-sufficiency. For instance, they earn their livelihoods by small-scale traditional farming, seek solace or entertainment in nature and traditional plays, dances and songs, and no longer use chemical fertilizers.

To sum up, in the Buddhist context, liberating and sustainable lifestyles are possible if people live in small communities, surrounded by natural habitats; the achievement of human freedom in community is possible when the individual's interest is in harmony with those of the whole. Buddhadasa Bhikku put it well, "The entire cosmos is a cooperative. The sun, the moon and the stars live together as a cooperative. The same is true for humans and animals, trees and soil. Our bodily parts function as a cooperative. When we realize that the world is a mutual, interdependent, cooperative enterprise, that human beings are all mutual friends in the process of birth, old age, suffering, and death, then we can build a noble, even heavenly environment. If our lives are not based on this truth, then we shall all perish."

An unintended benefit of globalisation is that it enables the oppressed and marginalized peoples worldwide to support each other's struggle, to create transnational alliances that will help check the growing power and influence of the transnational tyrannies. Ironically, while economic neo-liberalism is creating massive socio-economic inequalities, formal political democracy is spreading worldwide. Without mindfulness and compassion this combination is a recipe for social and political mayhem or instability. With Dhammic sensibility far-reaching socio-economic and political changes are possible – a globalisation based on cooperation, as opposed to competition, can be unleashed.

There are opportunities for great and constructive changes. But we, as concerned global citizens, must first reclaim our respective civil society and minds as well as the international society, all of which have long been colonized by **greed** (e.g. consumerism, profits and capital), **hatred** (e.g. violence, distrust of mass participation, centralization, secrecy, militarism, etc.) and **delusion** (e.g. expertism and scientism).

No single action is sufficient to meet this challenge. Rather, there must be concerted efforts to turn back the tide. Opposition to the global economy must be waged, but alternatives to it must also be laid out or experimented with. Reforms or changes need to be simultaneously made at the individual, local, national and international levels.

For example, the activities of transnational corporations must be vigilantly inspected and made accountable to the public. The hidden agendas of the transnational capitalist class in the forms of free trade or investors' rights agreements must be constantly exposed and subverted. Governments must increase their roles in regulating the market for the sake of public well-being and environmental conservation; the public and the environment must not be left to the mercy of the transnational oligopolies. Democratic participation by the public must be encouraged, not restricted to only casting ballots in elections. Alternative media must be set up to voice the concerns of the subaltern groups. Experiments with economic localization must be supported; this means independence from the global economy. Alternative lifestyles (e.g. voluntary simple lifestyles) must be sought and promoted to combat consumerism, lest cultural diversity and the environment are destroyed. Through time unregulated capital will homogenize all cultures like it had successfully broken down political, social, economic and geographical barriers since its emergence 500 years ago. In the 21st century, the clash between cultures and capital is more likely than the so-called clash of civilizations. Vajjian values such as compassion, mindfulness, self-contentment, selflessness and cooperation must replace selfishness, delusion, acquisitiveness, competitiveness and hatred.

With patience, diligence, compassion, as well as solidarity we will be able to stymie, if not completely overcome, the exploitation of the mighty transnational corporations, the World Bank, the World Trade Organization, the International Monetary Fund, etc. Undoubtedly, this is no small feat. The best and brightest work for them, and they are equipped with the latest technologies. Furthermore, their mass media lure and tempt us daily into the demonic religion of consumerism, indoctrinating us with the "I-shop-therefore-I-am" equation. But, however powerful they are, with the Buddhist practice of mindfulness, we will be able to experience the false as the false, to see the truth in the falseness of capitalism.

2

Gandhi's Lessons for the Twenty-first Century*

Gene Sharp

It is over fifty years since Mohandas-Karamchand Gandhi was assassinated. With the dawn of the twenty-first century, it is an appropriate time to reflect. Does this extraordinary man from the past have any lessons for us for the future?

The twentieth century was a strange one. Without question it was a century of great violence. Two World Wars. Hundreds of other large and small wars. Nuclear biological and chemical weapons. Massive colonialism. Nazi and Communist totalitarianism. Military and political dictatorships. Repeated genocide. Destruction of indigenous peoples. Terror in the name of justice. Slaughters of non-violent demonstrators. Popular powerlessness. And more and more terrible things.

Yet, something different also was and is still happening.

The twentieth century was also a time of major developments in the practice of non-violent struggle against the various expressions of political violence.

---

* It is a revision of a lecture presented at the annual Mahatma Gandhi Lectures on Non-violence at McMaster University, Hamilton, Ontario, Canada, on 9 October 1997.

Gandhi was a central figure in the non-violent struggles of the last century. He stood out above all the other individuals in the many non-violent struggles against oppression and violence during the past ten decades. It is appropriate to ask what lasting lessons he held for us – we who face multiple conflicts and suffer the combined pains of popular powerlessness and pervasive violence.

There are people who would contend that he had no lessons for the future. It is claimed by them that he belonged to an earlier era only, and is now irrelevant.

It is said that Gandhi operated under unique and favourable circumstances that no longer exist. The British were supposedly all gentle men who never harmed Indians, and that supposedly explains the past viability of non-violent action in India – they ignore the massacre of Jallianwalla Bagh in Amritsar and other brutalities committed by British "gentlemen".

It is also claimed that Gandhi's accomplishments are primarily attributable to his being a "mahatma". However, before 1920 few called him a holy man, yet he led non-violent struggles. His political influence in later years, minimally, clearly had major additional sources. It should also be remembered that Gandhi often rejected the "mahatma" title.

It is appropriate to acknowledge that Gandhi was a truly remarkable person with significant spiritual attributes. It is understandable that millions of people express their reverence for him by bestowing the title of "mahatma" on him.

However, the use of the title can often help to make Gandhi's life and work irrelevant to us by excessive reverence instead of thoughtful respect.

Naming Gandhi a "mahatma" has become a way to dismiss his life and work without much thought. By honouring Gandhi without listening to him we become vaccinated against taking him seriously. "Gandhi was great, but we are not mahatmas. So you cannot expect much of us".

It is claimed by many that Gandhi was an ascetic eccentric who was able to stir attention under passing historical circumstances, but is without relevance a half century later.

Others belittle Gandhi by merely using his name to support their personal opinions, it often seems, without ever studying his thinking and actions.

I do not share the views of any of those detractors. Also, I believe neither that moral principles and political wisdom began and ended with Gandhi, nor that he could make no mistakes.

In my view Gandhi's thought and work are of great relevance today and they will be so throughout the twenty-first century.

His conviction that people should be able to control their lives and society remains valid. His insights and actions showing how people can be the masters of their societies are of great relevance in a world of so much violence, oppression and dictatorship.

This does not mean that it is always easy to understand this man and to interpret his actions. His views were developing and often changing throughout his life. Sometimes his statements seem to be contradictory.

For those who benefit by emphasizing Gandhi's spiritual views and achievements, that is fine. However, those perspectives must not be allowed to cloud Gandhi's wider relevance.

One source of confusion is that we often do not recognize that Gandhi knowingly operated on two levels for different purposes. On one level were his own personal religious beliefs. On the second level were society and politics. Gandhi often operated on these two levels independently, without either dominating the other.

His personal religious beliefs and spiritual and ascetic practices were intended for his own life and that of a handful of devotees in his ashram who wished to share them. Gandhi never thought it adequate to live for his own sake, not even to focus primarily on his own spiritual development. His life was to serve others. His social and political views were offered to the mass of humanity.

That distinction was crucial in his insights into how to make the world more non-violent. Gandhi rejected the practice of only personal non-violence as inadequate and felt strongly obligated to apply non-violent means in the society and politics. He therefore fought political battles, challenging the Empire on which the sun never set.

He wrote, "That non-violence which, only an individual can use, is not of much use in terms of society. Man is a social being. His accomplishments to be of use must be such as any person with sufficient diligence can attain. That which can be exercised only among friends is of value only as a spark of non-violence. It cannot merit the appellation of *ahimsa*" [1]

Gandhi knew that he and his group of believers in *ahimsa* would always remain minuscule. (*Ahimsa* was to Gandhi not only ethical non-violence, but non-injury in thought, word and deed.) In order to have a wider impact he had to operate on the political level with many people who would never accept that belief. He chose, therefore, to operate socially and politically with political leaders and masses of people in the struggle to uplift the masses of India and to win India's independence from the British Empire.

Gandhi was committed to social and political transformation.

To do this he pioneered unconventional means of action that are of lasting significance and relevance. The major tools he chose for this were the constructive programme and pragmatic non-violent struggle. He called non-violent struggle *Satyagraha* – adherence to Truth.

Let us look briefly at the constructive programme first.

Some years after his return to India Gandhi conceptualized and began to organize constructive work as a major tool for transforming society. He formulated a constructive programme for rebuilding society from the bottom up outside the State structure. The constructive programme was an attempt to build the beginnings of a new more decentralized popularly controlled social order while the old system still existed.

For the constructive programme in India he outlined eighteen components, including communal unity, village sanitation, women's rights, and work with the peasantry and labour. Such work was to be conducted by voluntary efforts and encouragement of self-help. These components usually had separate organizations to promote and conduct them. In addition to non-violent struggle, therefore, the needed work for social change included building, constructing, nurturing, and healing.

We need to look at our own multiple, complex and deep social problems and think whether, and if so how, such constructive programmes can be developed that would be viable and effective in our very different societies. Many current activities and programmes are likely to be already compatible with this concept.

Gandhi's greatest contribution to social and political transformation, however doubtless, was the development and application of non-violent struggle. This included various forms of non-violent protest, non-cooperation and intervention, applied with skill and discipline.

Many years ago I used to think that Gandhi had uniquely united non-violence and politics. Many people have believed that he had invented a new type of struggle that was both powerful and non-violent. We now know that is not true, even in his work in South Africa and India.

At the meeting at the Empire Theatre in Johannesburg in 1906 Gandhi courageously vowed defiance of anti-Asiatic legislation. However, other participants – both Hindu and Muslim – were already familiar with and supportive of disobedience against oppressive legislation.

Furthermore, as Gandhi himself pointed out, he had been learning from non-violent struggle elsewhere in the world as well as in India. In the pages of his journal *Indian Opinion*, he cited important non-violent struggles in Russia, China and Bengal. He was also familiar with non-violent struggles in Ireland, religious disobedience in England and tax resistance in the American colonies. He knew of earlier disobedience by Indians in South Africa and of tax resistance by Africans in South Africa. He cited the African resistance as a reason why the Indians in South Africa could also resist in these ways.

Human experience with non-violent struggle is in fact much more extensive than most people have thought. Non-violent protests, resistance and defiance have occurred in all parts of the world, in all periods of history, in many cultures, and against all types of oppression and regimes.

Since Gandhi's death, non-violent struggles have grown dramatically in prominence and political impact. Recall, for example, the Solidarity struggles in Poland 1980-1989, the 1986 people power revolution in the Philippines, the mass resistance struggles in South Africa, brave but not yet successful struggles in Burma and China, the independence struggles of Latvia, Lithuania and Estonia, the defeat of the hard-line coup in Moscow in 1991, the liberation of East Germany in 1989 and 1990 and Czechoslovakia in 1989, as well as others.

The non-violent struggles before Gandhi and after Gandhi help to place him in historical perspective, and so to see better his continuing significance.

Gandhi faced a major question. If one believes in *ahimsa*, what does one do to make society and the world more non-violent?

Gandhi also faced the parallel question of how existing oppression was to be lifted.

A standard response from believers in principled non-violence has been to seek to induce others also to believe in that type of non-violence.

Remarkably, even after Gandhi became a believer in *ahimsa* as a religious and moral principle, he did not engage in a campaign to win individual converts to that belief. Instead, he sought to gain support from people and groups that did *not* accept that belief for applying non-violent forms of struggle in the conflicts that faced his people.

As they did not accept *ahimsa,* they would only accept non-violent action over both passivity and violence if they became convinced that the non-violent option was practical, that is that it would "work".

Therefore, Gandhi consciously chose to offer non-violent struggle as a practical way to act in acute conflicts. Stated more baldly, Gandhi presented non-violent struggle as an expedient, without apology, either at the time or later. "Yes, I adhere to my opinion that I did well to present to the Congress non-violence as an expedient [he wrote in 1942]. I could not have done otherwise, if I was to introduce it into politics. In South Africa too I introduced it as an expedient.....But I have no sense of disappointment in me over the results obtained. If I had started with men who accepted non-violence as a creed, I might have ended with myself. Imperfect as I am, I started with imperfect men and women and sailed on an uncharted ocean. Thank God that, though the boat has not reached its haven, it has proved fairly stormproof."[2] Gandhi told students in August 1947 that, "He had all along laboured under an illusion. But he was never sorry for it. He realized that if his vision were not covered by that illusion, India would never have reached the point which it had today"[3]

At a meeting of the All India Congress Committee in January 1942 Gandhi insisted with no regrets on the political nature of non-violent action as he had presented it to India. He also rejected the views of those who dismissed his policy as being "religious". "I placed it before Congress as a political method, to be employed for the solution of the political questions. It may be a novel method, but it does not on that account lose its political character...As a political method, it can always be changed, modified, altered, and even given up in preference to another. If, therefore, I say to you that our policy should not be given up today, I am talking political wisdom. It is political insight. It has served us in the past, it has enabled us to cover many stages towards independence, and it is as a politician that I suggest to you that it is a grave mistake to contemplate its abandonment. If I have carried the Congress with me all these years, it is in my capacity as a politician. It is hardly fair to describe my method as religious, because it is new."[4]

Despite Gandhi's dissatisfaction with shortcomings of the Indian practice of non-violent action, he affirmed the importance of corporate and mass struggle, by which ordinary people could themselves correct the problems they faced, and thereby achieve a sense of their own power.

Gandhi's practice in South Africa and India, and his comments about problems in other parts of the world, project a particular conception of how to make the world more non-violent.

The way was not to gain individual conversions to moral or religious non-violence (although he probably welcomed such believers). Instead, the way to make the world more non-violent was to initiate a pattern of specific substitutions of non-violent struggle in place of violence in individual conflicts.

Those struggles had to be waged overwhelmingly by people who did not believe ethically or religiously in *ahimsa*. The participants, however, had to be willing – as they were in South Africa and India – to conduct the struggle non-violently and to adhere to non-violent discipline for the course of the struggle. In that way the struggles against oppression could be fought non-violently by masses of people, and the level of violence in the world somewhat reduced.

Gandhi also recognized the importance of strategy – skillfulness in the choice and use of means and methods to increase the possibilities of success – in non-violent struggle. He contributed significantly to the refinement of strategy and the practice of careful strategic planning for this type of conflict.

How are we, then, to evaluate Gandhi and his challenge for the twenty-first century?

Although Gandhi was not the originator of non-violent struggle, he was a major historical player in its refinement and development. He brought greatly increased strategic sophistication to the technique. He charted ways in which people – both intellectuals and the masses – who did not share his full beliefs could join in the non-violent struggles and could become empowered. He challenged the most vast empire the world had ever seen – and won.

What, then, are Gandhi's lessons for us in this new century? They appear to me to be the following:

- Justice and freedom require empowering the oppressed and redistributing power in society.
- Peace is not achieved by stifling conflicts in which important issues are at stake, but by using non-violent struggle to fight out those conflicts to a resolution.
- Mass non-violent struggle in politics is possible as a substitute both for passivity and violence.

- Masses of people, who will never accept non-violence as a moral principle, will at times practise pragmatic non-violent struggle.
- The key to widespread adoption of non-violent means lies in formulating and implementing strategies of non-violent struggle to serve as substitutes for violence for serving specific purposes.
- Non-violent struggles can be made significantly more effective if wise strategies with implementing tactics are developed and applied.
- Non-violent struggle can be developed, refined, adapted and adopted to be a substitute for violence as the final means of applying pressure and power in society and politics by a series of specific replacements.

The implications of this conscious choice of non-violent struggle in place of violence are profound.

The fundamental problem of all humane politics is how to act effectively to achieve goals and to advance and defend human values and human dignity.

Gandhi's important contributions to the development of strategy in non-violent struggle help to answer that problem and need to be continued and expanded. There are significant reasons to believe that greater strategic sophistication can improve the effectiveness of future non-violent struggle, well beyond our present understanding.

Normally, most people and policy makers view violence as the ultimate sanction – the final means of applying pressure and wielding power to gain one's objectives. In thought and action Gandhi challenged that view during his own time and continues to challenge that view in our time. How far can we succeed in replacing violent sanctions with non-violent ones?

What will be the ultimate sanction of humane politics by the end of the twenty-first century? Can non-violent pressure and struggle become to a much greater degree an ultimate sanction during the coming hundred years? Can non-violent power replace violence in conflict after conflict? Efforts to achieve that development are vitally important and are a fitting tribute to Gandhi.

Stimulated in part by the struggles in India, but also by recognition of other major non-violent conflicts in other parts of the world, scholars from several disciplines and countries have during the past century made major contributions to knowledge about this phenomenon.[5] This work, which proceeded on a relatively small scale throughout the twentieth century, has significantly increased our understanding of this phenomenon. That, in turn, makes non-violent struggle more understandable and more likely to be considered a realistic option for people facing the need to wage serious conflicts.

In recent decades other studies of conflicts, violence and peace-war issues, sometimes combined with studies of non-violent action , have been used in college, and even high school, courses and programmes. Where non-violent struggle receives significant attention, these educational efforts also assist the general expansion of knowledge about non-violent alternatives It is very important that all such courses and programmes be of high quality and be conducted with rigorous academic standards. Far too often people and groups espousing interest in peace and "non-violence" have been happy to explore feelings and intuition in situations where vigorous applications of their intellects have been required. Lack of intellectual rigour not only produces poor results but helps to discredit efforts to promote academic and policy consideration of non-violent alternatives.

It is also important that carefully focused research be continued on non-violent struggle and that pioneering policy and strategic studies be conducted on the future application of non-violent struggle in diverse conflict situations.

While concentrating attention on Gandhi and India, we also need to remember and learn from the many people who have waged non-violent struggle in many other parts of the world.

These include Russian strikers, Norwegian teachers, Berlin wives of Jews, Lithuanian patriots, Chinese and Burmese students, Polish workers, Guatemalan teachers, South African demonstrators, African-American bus boycotters, French conscripts, Mexican and Irish hunger strikers, Filipino mutineers and nuns, Serbian marchers and Kosova resisters. And, of course, many many others. Gandhi and the brave Indians, who participated in the struggles he led or inspired, rank very high among these.

We are now at a new stage in the development of non-violent struggle. Examples and challenges have been offered to us. It is now possible to refine the technique of non-violent struggle, to plan strategies that are more effective, and to learn how to increase the chances of success while reducing the causalities of conflict. We need to explore how non-violent struggle can be adopted and applied as an alternative to both passivity and violence in a wide range of conflicts that involve issues of great importance. These include the following:

- What is the possible role of non-violent struggle in dismantling dictatorships?
- What is the possible role of non-violent struggle in blocking new coups d tat so as to prevent new dictatorships?
- What is the possible role of non-violent struggle in defence against foreign aggression and occupations?
- What is the possible role of non-violent struggle in efforts by indigenous peoples to preserve their existence and ways of life?
- What is the possible role of non-violent struggle in lifting the oppression of ethnic, religious and racial groups?
- What is the possible role of non-violent struggle in lifting economic exploitation and correcting economic injustices?
- And what additional situations merit consideration of non-violent struggle as a tool of empowerment and liberation?

With such conflict situations in mind, we need to plan carefully, and then move step by step forward to respond to Gandhi's challenge to the twenty–first century.

If we do so, the chances are significantly greater that brave men and women and responsible political leaders will join the effort and increasingly apply non-violent struggle in the conflicts of the coming decades. The result can be major reductions in violence, dictatorships, cruelties and oppression, and a growth of freedom, justice and peace.

Gandhi's challenge remains. It is to reshape politics. Are we ready to take up that challenge?

Notes and References

1. Gene Sharp, *Gandhi as a Political Strategist, with Essays on Ethics and Politics,* Boston: Porter Sargent, 1979, p. 110; *Harijan,* 14 December 1947.
2. Sharp, *Gandhi as a Political Strategist,* pp. 103-104; *Harijan*, 12 April 1942.
3. Sharp, *Gandhi as a Political Strategist*, p. 104; *Harijan*, 29 July 1947.
4. Sharp, *Gandhi as a Political Strategist*, p. 116; D.G. Tendulkar, *Mahatma: Life of Mohandas Karamchand Gandhi* (new edition in eight volumes), New Delhi: Ministry of Information and Broadcasting, Government of India, 1960-1963, vol. VI, pp.40-41.
5. For detailed references on these and many other references on non-violent struggle, see Ronald McCarthy and Gene Sharp, with the assistance of Brad Bennett, *Non-violent Action: A Research Guide.* 739 pp. New York: Garland, 1997.

3

Honouring Gandhi and Gandhians

Peter van den Dungen

The history of the twentieth century has aptly been described as one of extremes – an age when humanity plunged into the depths of barbarity and depravity (symbolised in the names of Auschwitz and Hiroshima, chosen from a catalogue that is depressingly long). But the same century redeemed itself partly through the emancipation of all those who suffered oppression and discrimination, including workers, women and non-whites. Hundreds of millions of people throughout the world have gained or regained their freedom and dignity – a process which is by no means complete, and which can never be final. While the century can boast a gallery of history's most terrible henchmen comprising Hitler, Stalin and Pol Pot, it can also claim saintly figures such as Gandhi, Schweitzer and Mother Teresa. If we were to include also the living in the latter group, there is no shortage of candidates – from Desmond Tutu to Nelson Mandela, and from Aung San Suu Kyi to the Dalai Lama.

It is no accident that these 'heroes of humanity', whose thoughts have enlightened us, and whose actions continue to inspire and encourage, have all been singled out by what is commonly regarded as the world's most respected and best-known award for service to humanity, viz. the Nobel Peace Prize. Indeed, the history of the twentieth century is also the history of the noble men and women who are its laureates, and of the organisations, movements and campaigns – from the International Committee of the Red Cross to the United Nations Peace-Keeping Forces, and from Amnesty International to the

International Campaign to Ban Landmines – which have greatly contributed to making the world less violent and more peaceful.

This year, in 2001, the Nobel Peace Prize will celebrate its centenary. While the institution – which the Prize has undoubtedly become – has indeed a record it can be proud of, a few of its decisions, whether of omission or commission, are widely regarded as unfortunate, first and foremost the absence from the Nobel peace pantheon of the century's greatest philosopher and practitioner of non-violence. There is almost universal agreement on this issue, so much so, it is possible to argue, that this view even extends to the members of the Norwegian Nobel Committee who were serving on it in 1948 when Gandhi's nomination was intensely discussed. According to the statutes of the Nobel Foundation then in force, a posthumous award was possible under certain circumstances. The Committee made various enquiries but the negative replies which it received from the Swedish prize-awarding bodies on posthumous awards (except in the case where a laureate died after the Committee had made its decision) dissuaded it from going ahead with making such an award (even so, one of its five members still favoured it).[1] The clearest public evidence that the prize for 1948 would have gone to Gandhi if he had been alive is to be found in the careful phrase through which the Committee explained its decision of reserving the prize for that year (and not allocating it in the following year, as has often happened) since there was 'no suitable living candidate.'[2] The present secretary of the Committee and director of the Norwegian Nobel Institute, Professor Geir Lundestad, has written that in his opinion Gandhi has been the 'one major omission'.[3] A similar view was also expressed by August Schou, the director at the time.[4]

The (accidental) non-award of the century's highest honour to its greatest peace figure has of course in no way affected Gandhi's standing. He continues to exercise a profound influence on all those who are concerned with issues of war and peace, conflict and violence, injustice and oppression – in short, on everyone who is involved in social change as well as the related question of how we should lead our lives and relate to the living world around us. This is evidenced by the fact that his writings are still widely read and studied, as well as being published and reprinted. New biographies and analyses of his ideas and campaigns continue to appear. Not only in his native country but throughout the world, institutions are named after him, gardens and parks are dedicated to him, and sculptures of him are unveiled. As a symbol of peace, Gandhi is without peer and is likely to remain so.

If in the realm of the exact sciences and our understanding of the physical world, the century has been shaped by Einstein, so Gandhi has opened the horizons of our social, political and spiritual world. It is no wonder that *Time* magazine selected them as its men of the century (together with F.D. Roosevelt, with whom Gandhi was runner-up to Einstein as Person of the Century). *Time* commented: 'His work and his spirit awakened the 20th century to ideas that serve as a moral beacon for all epochs. … He stamped his ideas on history, igniting three of the century's great revolutions – against colonialism, racism and violence. … He shines as a conscience for the world … proclaiming the power of love, peace and freedom.'[5]

Against this background, it is not surprising to find that his name is also honoured and commemorated in the naming of several awards for peace and non-violence. There is poetic justice in the fact that he, who was never honoured with the prime peace award, has given his name to more peace awards than any other figure. The next most popular names commemorate the life and work of Woodrow Wilson, Carl von Ossietzky, Albert Schweitzer and Andrei Sakharov (Nobel peace laureates all – for the years 1919, 1935, 1952 and 1975, respectively).

It is not the least of the beneficial (and no doubt, unanticipated) effects of the Nobel Peace Prize that it has inspired the creation of many other awards for peace. Depending on the definition of peace used, several hundred such regular, often annual, awards exist, instituted by a great diversity of bodies, including private, official and international ones.[6] The work of peace and non-violence needs encouragement, support (both moral and practical-financial) and publicity – and for achieving these goals, awards, honours and prizes are appropriate instruments. It is wrong when the object of obtaining them becomes the motive for one's actions, or when the belief arises that one is entitled to such honours. It is a different matter altogether, however, if – unexpected and certainly unsought – they are bestowed on a deserving laureate (whether this be an individual, organisation or campaign).

Some have speculated that Gandhi, if he had been awarded the Nobel Peace Prize, would have refused it, or would not have bothered to come to Oslo to receive it and participate in the ceremony. His absence at the 1947 Indian independence celebration is quoted in support of this contention.[7] The present author is unable to judge and must defer in this matter to others who are more familiar with Gandhi's personality and social philosophy. It is interesting to note, however, that such speculation is perhaps somewhat weakened by the fact that the great spiritual leaders of our time who have been honoured with the Nobel Peace Prize, notably the Dalai Lama and Mother Teresa, were not at all 'rejectionist' in their attitude (even though Mother Teresa requested that the banquet traditionally offered by the Norwegian Nobel Committee on the eve of the ceremony not take place and the money thus saved be used to support her cause).[8]

The Dalai Lama considers himself to be a follower of the Mahatma and, as a young man, was deeply inspired by Gandhi's adoption of non-violence during India's struggle for freedom. His non-violent campaign for freedom and rights in his own country, Tibet, resulted in the award of the Nobel Peace Prize to him in 1989. The Dalai Lama has explained its significance for him and for his people as follows: 'the award ... filled Tibetans with hope. It meant that, though we have not drawn attention to our plight by means of violence, we have not been forgotten. It also meant that the values we cherish, in particular our respect for all forms of life and the belief in the power of truth, are today recognised and acclaimed'.[9] In the hypothetical case referred to, Gandhi's reasoning might well have been along the same lines.

What cannot be denied is the profound influence which he has exercised on virtually all leaders of non-violent movements in the 20th century, many of whom have been singled out with the Nobel Peace Prize. About his own award, the Dalai Lama has said, 'I consider it also a tribute to Mahatma Gandhi, whose example remains an inspiration to so many'.[10] This is yet another irony about the non-award of the Nobel Prize to him, viz. the fact that so many of his later followers have become Nobel laureates.

Of the several awards which incorporate Gandhi's name, the one which was instituted by the government of India in 1995 on the occasion of the 125th anniversary of his birth is undoubtedly the most important one. This is not only because of the considerable prize money, but also because it is an *official* award, instituted by the *Indian* government, and specifically commemorating the birth of *Gandhi*. The composition of the five-person jury underlines the importance which the government attaches to the award since it comprises, as permanent ex-officio members, the highest authorities in the country, viz. the Prime Minister and the Chief Justice, as well as the Leader of the Opposition in the Lok Sabha. One of the 'two other eminent persons' who make up the jury has been a former President of India. The 'international' dimension of the prize – which can be awarded to non-Indians – is also reflected in the jury through the presence of a prominent non-Indian national whose life and work have been influenced by Gandhi. For the first award, this position was filled by Nobel Peace laureate and former Archbishop of South Africa, Desmond Tutu. The combination of these factors is likely to make the Gandhi International Peace Prize among the most important of all peace awards. From a purely monetary standpoint – inevitably the first or even only criterion by which the general public judges the standing of an award – this Prize (of Rs one crore, or some $ 280,000, depending on the rate of exchange) is second only to the Nobel Peace Prize in the field of annual peace prizes.

The award is given 'for social, economic and political transformation through non-violence and other Gandhian methods'. The late Dr. Julius Nyerere, former president of Tanzania, was presented with the 1995 inaugural award on 27th June 1996 to coincide with the official conclusion of the celebrations of the 125th anniversary of the birth of the Mahatma. In his acceptance speech, he expressed a sentiment that will have found strong echoes around the world – 'I have come here ... to thank you that you gave us Gandhi'. Similarly, inspiring words were spoken by the most recent winner, Baba Amte, upon learning that he had been chosen for the 1999 award: 'I am now entering my 86th year and I find that Mahatma Gandhi is more relevant in the 21st century than he was in our time. If we listen to the words of Gandhi, then it will be an era of conciliations and not confrontations.'

Anniversaries of one kind or another are frequently used to institute new peace awards, sometimes as part of a wider celebration. This is also the case for the second Gandhi peace award that will be briefly introduced, the Gandhi International Peace Award.[11] It was inaugurated in London in 1998 during a ceremony marking the 50th anniversary of the death of Gandhi. The event was organised by the Gandhi Foundation, set up in 1983 to spread knowledge of Gandhi's teachings. This followed in the wake of the highly acclaimed Gandhi film created and directed by Richard (now Lord) Attenborough who brought Gandhi before a large audience as never before. Commenting on the celebration, the religious affairs correspondent of *The Times* reported that of the various messages and readings (by actors from the Oscar-winning film), 'the most moving part was the readings from Gandhi himself ... The power of his words to move, even today, was extraordinary'.[12] The award – in the form of a bronze statuette mounted on a wooden (oak) globe, designed by the French sculptor Philippe Tallis – is presented when the Gandhi Annual Lecture is held, usually in the House of Lords in October (to coincide with the anniversary of Gandhi's birth). It is presented only to those who have rendered outstanding service to the cause of peace, particularly in the following areas: (1) Conflict resolution, conciliation and mediation; (2) Efforts to reduce and ultimately eliminate the international arms trade; (3) Contribution towards Gandhian influence on new economic thinking; (4) Endeavours to reduce violence in all walks of life. The Foundation gives preference to 'unsung heroes' in these areas whose services have not been publicly recognised elsewhere.[13]

The award was presented for the first time in 1998 to Eirwen Harbottle, on behalf of her late husband Brigadier Michael Harbottle, former chief of staff of the UN peacekeeping forces in Cyprus, and founder of Generals for Peace and Disarmament. Together with his wife, he established the Centre for International Peacebuilding. In October 1999, the second award was presented to Nicholas Gillett in recognition of his peace work over many decades. A Quaker, his personal quest for peace had started eighty years ago when he 'was sent into the street to collect money to help the children starving in Germany just after the end of the First World War'.[14] A life-long peace activist, educator and fund-raiser for peace causes, he has recalled how his refusal of tax for nuclear defence 'brought a loss of precious furniture, but more importantly tears to the eyes of the official who presided over it'. In his acceptance speech he argued the need for lateral thinking without which the world would continue to fail to mitigate, let alone abolish, war and weapons. Without such thinking, the radical and so necessary changes in the way in which we make decisions about policies and methods would not come about. He also commented on the difficulties peacemakers and their organisations are constantly confronted with because of underfunding – partly because in many countries peace is on 'the wrong side of the charity laws'.[15] Peace awards, when they include a substantial monetary component, are able to contribute to the alleviation of precisely this vital problem.[16]

Another, very different, result of peace awards is the increased responsibility that the recipient commonly experiences and the need to live up to the honour bestowed. This is illustrated in the message that UN Secretary-General Kofi Annan delivered upon receiving the first Gandhi/King Award for Non-violence in

January 1999. He said, 'This award carries the names of two of the most exceptional leaders of our century, indeed of all times. It is a great distinction, but it also represents an even greater challenge. ... In accepting this award, I pledge never to forget the sacrifices that Gandhi and King made for humanity. Their message and their example – their inspiring summons on all people to turn away from violence and towards a future of dignity and justice – will continue to guide the United Nations in its global mission of peace'.[17] The award was created by the Interfaith Centre in New York; a year before, Annan had helped the Centre in launching its 'Season for Non-violence'.

The three Gandhi awards mentioned above were all created in the second half of the 1990s; it is likely that several more will be created in the years to come. Perhaps the first award to be named after Gandhi (at least outside India) is the Gandhi Peace Award, first given in 1960 and conceived by Dr. Jerome Davies in the USA. He founded a charitable, non-political but religious and educational organisation, 'Promoting Enduring Peace Inc.' Laureates are selected on the basis of their contribution to world peace and international good will in the tradition of Gandhi's philosophy of love and non-violence. The award consists of a citation which sets forth the reason for the award and a bronze medallion with the profile of the Mahatma on one side with the statement, 'Love Ever Suffers, Never Revenges Itself', while the other side shows the names of the award and award-winner. The first recipients were Eleanor Roosevelt and Rev. Edwin T. Dahlberg. The award has been given in most years since then, sometimes more than one a year, at a ceremony held in New Haven, Connecticut. Among the recipients are Linus Pauling, A. J. Muste, Norman Thomas, Dr. Benjamin Spock, U Thant, Dorothy Day, Daniel Ellsberg and Cesar Chavez. 'Promoting Enduring Peace Inc.' is currently in the process of reorganisation and its Gandhi Peace Award has been suspended as a result. The 1995 award went to Edith Ballantyne, president of the Women's International League for Peace and Freedom.

One of the most venerable educational institutions in the United States, The College of William & Mary (established in

1693 in Williamsburg, Virginia), has been awarding a Mahatma Gandhi Freedom Award since 1981. The ceremony is part of the Mahatma Gandhi Freedom Lecture Series which the College inaugurated that year. The first Gandhi lecture was delivered by the late Philippine Senator Benigno Aquino. The Gandhi Lecturer/Awardee is chosen from the ranks of scholars and public figures who, by personal example, have given meaning and substance to peace and freedom, consistent with the ideals and principles of Gandhi. Few could have anticipated at the time that a few years later Aquino would also follow Gandhi in being assassinated and becoming a national hero in his country. The Gandhi lecture/award was a further development of the large annual International Dinner/Programme which the College had launched in 1975 in order to promote international understanding, both in the College and in the wider community. A key figure in these events was Mario P. Zamora, Professor of Anthropology at the College. Bangladesh's ambassador to the United States, H. R. Choudhury, received the award in 1984; in 1993 it was presented to Dr. Lourdes Arizpe, a leading Mexican anthropologist. In the intervening years, awards were made to several prominent politicians and educators from India and the Philippines, as well as to distinguished anthropologists from the United States and the United Kingdom. It seems that following Dr. Zamora's death in 1993, the Mahatma Gandhi Freedom Award and the annual events programme of which it formed a part have been discontinued.[18]

The field of peace awards is characterised by little permanence and much change – awards 'come and go', except for the few that are securely established. It remains to be seen how many of the countless awards, that have been instituted in recent years and decades, will continue into the new century, let alone live long enough to celebrate their centenary as the Nobel Peace Prize is about to. Peace prizes named after Gandhi are also subject to the same vagaries. While two American Gandhi peace awards were discontinued in the mid-1990s, a new award named after Gandhi was created at the same time on the other side of the Atlantic – the Mahatma M. K. Gandhi Prize for Non-violent Peace. This is awarded by the similarly named Mahatma M. K.

Gandhi Foundation for Non-violent Peace, a non-governmental organisation established in 1989 in Oslo, Norway by Amalendu Guha. It awards two prizes every year, one to an outstanding peace researcher, and one to a peace activist. The first awards were made in 1993 to Professor Kenneth Boulding (USA) and the Buddhist monk Vishuddhananda Mahathero (Bangladesh). The latter walked with Gandhi in 1946 to restore inter-communal and inter-religious harmony in Noakhali (the then undivided Bengal, now Bangladesh). Some special awards were made in 1994 on the occasion of the celebration of the 125th anniversary of the birth of the Mahatma, including one to Johan Galtung 'for his contribution towards interpreting and developing the Gandhian peace philosophy and way to achieve peace.'[19] Several state presidents and heads of government, such as Jimmy Carter, Gro Harlem Brundtland, Nelson Mandela, Mikhail Gorbachev and Sheikh Hasina of Bangladesh have also received the award. Norway's most prominent student of Gandhi (next to Galtung), Arne Naess, received the prize in 1996, together with Aung San Suu Kyi. In 1996, the Foundation awarded a special Gandhi Prize in Tokyo to Tenjio Watanabe, the Buddhist monk who is known as the Gandhi of Japan and whose life-long work has been inspired by Buddha's and Gandhi's philosophy for achieving social peace and harmony through non-violent methods. Among the philanthropic work for which he was honoured is the establishment of the Centre for Widows and Orphans in Bangladesh. Daisaku Ikeda, President of Soka University in Japan and of Soka Gakkai International was the recipient of the prize in 2000.[20]

The intention of organisations that institute peace awards is frequently not only to honour and encourage the recipient but at the same time to publicise and promote the work that is being honoured and the social philosophy that underlies it. Awards named after Gandhi aim, almost by definition, to popularise his life and work and thereby spread the ethics of non-violence. This is the objective of GANDHISERVE, an internet-based non-profit enterprise that offers an online information service about the Mahatma and seeks to promote the sale of both traditional and modern information sources, such as publications, audio/

videotapes and CD-rom's. The organisation intends to use any profit for the support of quality media on Gandhi by establishing an annual Gandhi Media Award. This venture was initiated by the German Gandhi expert Peter Rühe who has been engaged in the promotion of Gandhi's life and work for almost twenty years. His experience made him realise how difficult it is to work for a good cause – 'Although my work is recognised and appreciated around the globe it remains extremely difficult to get any other than moral support.'[21] This was also a theme in Nicholas Gillett's acceptance speech, as noted above, much of whose work has involved fund-raising for peace.

A fair number of the many awards for peace (and the related concepts of non-violence, tolerance, human rights and development) that exist today have been instituted by UNESCO. The creation of several of these awards was made possible through their endowment by private initiative. This is the case, for instance, for two of the most significant prizes that the organisation awards, viz. the Prize for Peace Education, and the Félix Houphouët-Boigny Peace Prize. The first is based on a capital donation of $ 1 million by the Japan Shipbuilding Industry Foundation, the second on an initial capital of 40 million French francs provided by the Félix Houphouët-Boigny Foundation in Côte d'Ivoire. While most of UNESCO's prizes comprise a monetary component, this is not the case for UNESCO's Gandhi Medal. UNESCO Director-General Federico Mayor presented Nelson Mandela with the Medal in July 1996, describing him as 'a symbol of peace, wise leadership, tolerance and farsightedness', and pointing out the importance of South Africa in the life of the Mahatma.[22]

Although not named after Gandhi, in the context of UNESCO prizes for peace, it is appropriate to refer also to the UNESCO-Madanjeet Singh Prize for the Promotion of Tolerance and Non-violence, especially since it was established in 1995 on the occasion of the United Nations Year for Tolerance and the 125th anniversary of Gandhi's birth. It is given to honour significant activities in the scientific, artistic, cultural or communication field aimed at the promotion of a spirit of tolerance and non-violence. The prize derives from funds that are donated by Madanjeet Singh amounting to $ 40,000 every two years. The donor is an Indian artist, writer, diplomat and international civil servant with UNESCO, who currently serves as a special adviser to the Director General. The prize is awarded biennially, on International Day for Tolerance (16th November). It was, for the first time, presented in 1996 to the organisation 'Pro-femmes Twese Hamwe', a collective of 32 women's organisations in Rwanda, formed after the 1994 massacres that inflicted particular suffering on women and children. Together, the collective launched an Action Campaign for Peace to work towards social justice and respect for women's rights, and against impunity for those responsible for genocide.[23] In 1998, the prize was shared between the Joint Action Committee (JAC) for Peoples Rights of Pakistan and Narayan Desai of India. The JAC is an informal coalition of over 30 NGOs and individuals founded in 1990 whose work has primarily focused on women, promoting religious tolerance and social non-violence. The Committee has also campaigned against the nuclear arms race. Desai heads the Institute for Total Revolution; he is a noted war resister and was Chair of the War Resisters' International (WRI) from 1988 to 1991.[24]

The last award to be presented here is also the most explicit regarding its aim – the Jamnalal Bajaj International Award for Promoting Gandhian Values Outside India. The annual award is made by the Jamnalal Bajaj Foundation in Mumbai, established in 1977 in memory of Jamnalal Bajaj with the objects of serving the ideals for which he had dedicated his life and helping to promote the kind of constructive activities in which he himself was deeply involved during his life time. Bajaj was a close associate of Gandhi, who called him his 'fifth son.' From 1920 until his untimely death in 1942, he was treasurer of the Indian National Congress. He took an active part in the freedom struggle and devoted himself to most of the activities included in the Constructive Programme propounded by Gandhi. The Foundation supports rural development projects and projects for the upliftment and welfare of women and children. It also gives three annual awards in India (each of the value of Rs. 100,000) to individuals for outstanding contributions in the fields of constructive work and the other areas mentioned.

The International Award was instituted in 1988 to commemorate the centenary of the birth of Jamnalal Bajaj. It consists of a trophy and a citation, and carries today a cash amount of Rs. 2 lakhs or its equivalent in foreign currency. The object of the Award is 'to recognise outstanding contributions (made outside India) to any of the following: (1) Promotion of peace and harmony among people and friendliness among nations through application of Gandhian philosophy of truth and non-violence; (2) Ending exploitation in any form and seeking solution of social, cultural, economic and political problems through Gandhian principles and constructive programmes; and (3) Innovative work in social organisation with a view to promoting Gandhian values of purity of means and ends by awakening moral conscience, fostering community self-reliance and bringing about harmony of human life with nature.'[25] In the operation of its scheme of awards, the Foundation is guided by a Council of Advisers under the chairmanship of a former Vice-President of India, and comprising prominent persons from various walks of life. The inaugural award in 1988 was presented by Prime Minister Rajiv Gandhi to Pierre Parodi, head of the Ark of Lanza del Vasto in France. In his address entitled 'In Praise of Gandhi,' Parodi approvingly quoted Nehru's words following Gandhi's death: 'A light has gone. I am wrong to say "has gone". In a thousand years this same light will still shine ... For us it represents life and eternal truth; it reminds us of the straight path and protects us from falsehood.'[26] Parodi recalled the hope that Gandhi represented for his mentor, Lanza del Vasto, when several countries in Europe were ravaged by fascism and Nazism in the 1930s. For Christians, Gandhi's way of living was in complete harmony with the evangelical message, and he 'showed us that such a life was possible even at the present time and in the midst of the worst difficulties.' For Parodi in the 1980s, just as for Lanza del Vasto in the 1930s, 'the life and struggle of Mohandas Gandhi remains for hundreds of thousands of people a light and hope. This light increases proportionately as the failure of our civilization becomes more evident.' Among later recipients of the award are Homer Jack (USA, 1992) and Adolfo de Obieta (known as the Argentinian Gandhi, 1996).

It is very likely the case that in India several other awards exist for the promotion of Gandhian values than the two that have been mentioned above. Some of them may have been instituted by followers of the Mahatma, others by educational or grassroots movements that derive their inspiration from him. Since such awards are meant for activists of such movements, or for pupils at local schools, or for citizens in certain districts, knowledge about such awards will often be limited to those concerned. It is, therefore, obvious that the survey of peace awards named after Gandhi presented above is bound to be incomplete and needs to be supplemented by the kinds of awards hinted at and which are less visible to the outside world (but therefore not devoid of merit). Owing to lack of time, the present author was unable to research the Mahatma Gandhi Peace Award, instituted by the Bharatiya Vidya Bhavan, India's foremost educational and cultural organisation. In 1994 it was presented to Coretta Scott King and to Sri Chinmoy.

A fuller picture would also have to take into account occasional or ad hoc prizes, for instance in the form of school essay contests that are designed to stimulate knowledge of Gandhi and inculcate Gandhian values. An interesting example is the essay competition on 'Life and Works of Mahatma Gandhi', organised by the Indian Embassy in Peru for schoolchildren of 14 -17 years on the occasion of the celebrations of the 125th anniversary of Gandhi's birth. The contest generated over seventy submissions of high quality in the Spanish language. A prize ceremony took place at the Chancery in October 1995, with the participation of those pupils who had entered the competition, their parents and teachers. According to a brief report on the event, 'The contest helped increasing the awareness of the thoughts of Mahatma Gandhi in the young Peruvian minds and bringing them closer to India.'[27]

The present contribution has focused on peace awards that commemorate in their naming Gandhi. They comprise only a fraction of the total number of peace awards (see above). For a full appreciation of the relationship between them and Gandhi, and specifically of the way in which at least some of these other awards are also honouring Gandhi and Gandhians, it would be necessary to study the terms of reference of each award, particularly the purposes for which the award is made. One of the most interesting and innovative of all awards in this regard is the Right Livelihood Awards, first given in 1980. The Awards, which are also known as the 'Alternative Nobel Prizes', are presented annually by the Right Livelihood Award Foundation, a charity registered in Sweden. That its philosophy is strongly influenced by Gandhi is indicated by the emphasis on such notions as holistic living, respect for the environment, self-reliant development, indigenous rights, non-violence and spiritual values.[28] It is not so much individuals as projects and campaigns that are honoured by the Foundation. The annual award of $ 250,000 is normally shared between four recipients. The author believes it is legitimate to claim (and does not believe he is in danger of engaging in some kind of Gandhi-imperialism) that the Right Livelihood Award can be regarded as a Gandhian award, and that it honours today's followers of the Mahatma. Similar observations can, no doubt, be made for other peace prizes.

The laureates of Gandhian peace awards commonly pay tribute both to the inspiration that Gandhi's life has given them, and to their co-workers in the cause in which they have been engaged and with whom they have often shared hardship and oppression. They frequently justify their acceptance of an honour or award by regarding it as applying to a whole group of people whose representative the awardee is. Indeed, the simple pleasure inherent in the receiving of an award – and the gratification and encouragement that go with it – is subject to the multiplier effect and therefore difficult to calculate (It must also be admitted that prizes can be divisive, even among the friends of peace and non-violence, but this is fortunately the exception). Finally, it is important to recognise that peace not only has its *awards* (in which many share) but also its own *rewards*. A recent study of peace activists has found that 'peace action evolves into an ethical career that is inseparable from personal identity and day-to-day life.'[29] The peace movement is 'not only a collective effort to diminish violence in the world, but also [becomes] a vehicle for personal evolution.'[30] This evolution is best summed up in the term personal development or personal growth, and involves such features as self-empowerment, emotional maturity, life style changes, a more conscious living, finding a deeper meaning and purpose in life, and achieving greater inner peace – in short, becoming a more complete person. In this way, 'inner peace and world peace are interconnected goals and the movement is the incubator for those possibilities.'[31] Gandhi summed it up well when he said, 'We must become the change we seek.'

As noted above, Gandhi was only runner-up in *Time* magazine's 'Person of the Century' contest. Yet, this is what Einstein, its nominee for this accolade, said about Gandhi: 'Generations to come will scarcely believe that such a one as this ever in flesh and blood walked upon this earth.' Let us also return for a moment to Nobel, whose inventive genius gave us dynamite. His conviction that the development of the means of destruction would force humanity to abandon war one day, Gandhi countered with the seemingly paradoxical insight that 'Non-violence is the greatest force at the disposal of mankind It is mightier than the mightiest weapon of destruction devised by the ingenuity of man.'[32] The 20th century has provided ample evidence that Gandhi was right.[33] It may be thought appropriate that there is only one Nobel Peace Prize, but many Gandhi peace awards.

The above contribution, modest as it is, is meant as a tribute to a noted Gandhian scholar and activist whose friends and colleagues are honouring his 75th anniversary with a *Festschrift*. Even more important than the material present is the idea behind it since it expresses the esteem and love in which the person honoured is being held. Instinctively, from our own experience, and without requiring the insights from 'human needs' or any other theory about human development, we know that every human being craves love and esteem. They manifest themselves in myriad guises and their fulfilment, which can come in as many different ways, is the natural concomitant of a life well lived. The present writer is pleased to be able to join with others in conveying his gratitude and respectful greetings to Shri Ravindra Varma.

Notes and References

1. Details concerning this matter have only recently become available since the archival material relating to the 1948 nominations and award could not be consulted before 1998 under the fifty-year rule which the Nobel Foundation in Stockholm applies. Even though there are no minutes of the Committee's deliberations, there is sufficient evidence on this issue to allow a reliable reconstruction of the course of events surrounding Gandhi's nomination. For details, see Øyvind Tønneson, 'Mahatma Gandhi, the Missing Laureate', http://www.nobel.se/essays/gandhi/index.html [accessed on 29th May 2000]. Tønneson indicates that Gandhi was nominated five times for the Nobel Peace Prize (1937, 1938, 1939, 1947, 1948), making it to the shortlist on three occasions (1937, 1947, 1948). However, mention should be made also of Thomas Weber's scholarly study, 'Gandhi and the Nobel Peace Prize', pp. 29-47 in *South Asia*, Vol. 12, No. 1, June 1989 which contains already some of this information. Tønneson's essay has been reprinted in *Frontline*, Vol. 17, No. 4, 3rd March 2000, pp. 94-97. See also the following correspondence in the issues for 14th April and 12th May.

2. See Tønneson, o.c., and also Irwin Abrams, *The Nobel Peace Prize and the Laureates*. Boston: G. K. Hall, 1988, p. 137. Tønneson is able to correct the speculation by Abrams about Count Bernadotte.

3. Geir Lundestad, 'The Meaning of the Nobel Peace Prize', pp. 7-10 in Karl Holl & Anne C. Kjelling (eds.), *The Nobel Peace Prize and the Laureates*. Frankfurt am Main: Peter Lang, 1994, at p. 8.

4. See Weber, o.c., p. 30.

5. *Time* Magazine, 31st December 1999, 'Person of the Century. Runners-Up – Mohandas Gandhi', pp. 86-91. This article by Johanna McGeary is followed by an appreciation on 'the liberator of India' by the 'liberator of South Africa': Nelson Mandela, 'The Sacred Warrior', pp. 94-96. Gandhi was *Time*'s 'Man of the Year' for 1930. Cf. Weber, o.c., p. 33.

6. For an overview, see the present author's 'Peace Prizes', pp. 795-808 in Lester Kurtz (ed.), *Encyclopedia of Violence, Peace & Conflict*. San Diego, CA: Academic Press, 1999, Vol. 2. and *The Nobel Peace Prize and the Global Proliferation of Peace Prizes in the 20th Century*. Oslo: The Norwegian Nobel Institute Series, Vol. 1, No. 5, 2000.

7. See, e.g., the special feature article 'Nobelprijs voor de Vrede bestaat een eeuw' [Nobel Peace Prize a century old] in the leading Dutch newspaper, *NRC Handelsblad*, 24th December 1999, pp. 4-5. On Gandhi's reaction to a 1934 newspaper editorial that he should be nominated for the prize see Weber, o.c., p. 33.

8. Abrams, o.c., pp. 227-8.

9. The Dalai Lama, 'Mahatma Gandhi', p. 12 in *The Awardee* ('A bi-annual publication of the Ramon Magsaysay Award Foundation', Manila), January-June 1999, p. 12.

10. Ibid.

11. This award should not be confused with the official Indian prize mentioned above; such confusion is likely given the fact that the two honours are only differentiated in their naming by the interchangeable terms 'prize' and 'award'.

12. Ruth Gledhill, 'The truth about Gandhi', *The Times* (Weekend), 7th February 1998.

13. Personal communication by Surur Hoda, Secretary General of The Gandhi Foundation, 2nd June 2000.

14. 'Nicholas Gillett – Second recipient of the Gandhi International Peace Award', pp. 11-12 in *The Gandhian Way*, No. 61, Autumn 1999.

15. Nicholas Gillett, 'Peace movements – a fresh look', pp. 4-6 in *The Friend*, 28th January 2000.

16. Just as Baba Amte donated his award to the leprosy ashram which he established and for which he is well-known, so nearly fifty years before him Albert Schweitzer welcomed the award of the 1952 Nobel Peace Prize since it allowed him to build and equip the hospital for lepers that he had dreamed of. Such examples can easily be multiplied and are the rule rather than the exception.

17. See UN Press Release SG/SM/6880 of 29th January 1999.

18. Personal communication by Ann Gaudreaux, Office of University Relations, The College of William and Mary, 5th June 2000.

19. Cf. 'Mahatma M. K. Gandhi Foundation for Non-violent Peace Awards', pp. 46-7 in *International Peace Research Newsletter*, Vol. 34, No. 1, March 1996 and ibid., Vol. 34, No. 4, December 1996, pp. 34-5.

20. Details of the Foundation and its Prize are given in an Information document of the Foundation (issued in May 2000). In it, Ikeda is referred to as 'known as the Gandhi of Japan.' No mention is made of Tenjío Watanabe.

21. Peter Rühe, 'Following the Footprints of Mahatma Gandhi in India', pp. 112-5 in *Exhibiting Peace: The Proceedings of the Third International Conference of Peace Museums*. Kyoto: Kyoto Museum for World Peace at Ritsumeikan University, 1999, at p. 115. See also GANDHISERVE's 'Mahatma Gandhi Research and Media Service' at <www.gandhiserve.com>

22. See the brief report in *UNESCO Sources*, No. 82, September 1996, p. 5. The medal is available in gold, silver and bronze, and can also be bought by members of the general public.

23. Cf. 'UNESCO Tolerance Prize Goes to Rwandan Women's Collective', p. 50 in *UN Chronicle*, No. 4, 1996.

24. Cf. 'International prizes: WRI members receive international recognition', p. 5 in *Peace News*, November 1998.

25. This information is quoted from the Foundation's brochure on the International Award.

26. Pierre Parodi, 'In Praise of Gandhi', pp. 3-4 in The Gandhi Foundation [UK], Newsletter No. 20, Summer 1989.

27. Cf. 'Essay Competition on Mahatma Gandhi', p. 49 in *International Peace Research Newsletter*, Vol. 34, No. 1, March 1996.

28. The Foundation's letterhead incorporates the following quotation from Gandhi, 'The world has enough for everyone's need but not for everyone's greed.'

29. James Downton Jr. & Paul Wehr, *The Persistent Activist: How Peace Commitment Develops and Survives*. Boulder, CO: Westview Press, 1997, p. X.

30. Ibid., p. 118.

31. Ibid., p. 126.

32. Quotations taken from Walter Isaacson, 'Person of the Century: Who mattered – and why', pp. 20-32 in *Time*, o.c., at p. 24.

33. As Isaacson has written, 'In a century marked by brutality, Gandhi perfected a different method of bringing about change, one that would turn out (surprisingly) to have more lasting impact', ibid.

4

Gandhi and Tolstoy

Anthony J. Parel

There is no parallel in modern Indian intellectual history to what Gandhi says he owed to Leo Tolstoy. Neither Nehru nor Tagore, nor for that matter Aurobindo Ghose, acknowledged their intellectual indebtedness to particular thinkers in such detail and with such humility as had done Mahatma Gandhi. Tolstoy (1828-1910), Ruskin (1819-1900) and Rajchandbhai (1868-1901), according to his own testimony, had the greatest formative influence on him[1] . The first two of these influenced him through their books, and the third 'through intimate personal contact'.

Compared to Ruskin, Tolstoy exercised the greater influence on him. As we look at Appendix 1 of *Hind Swaraj* we notice that of the twenty books listed there, two were by Ruskin, but as many as six were by Tolstoy. Three of these – *Letter to a Hindoo*, *The Kingdom of God is Within You*, and *What is Art?* – he considered so important that either he himself translated them or he had others translate them into Gujarati. Add to this his adaptation into Gujarati of *Ivan the Fool,* we get an idea of the high esteem in which he held Tolstoy.

A study of Gandhi-Tolstoy relationship has a great lesson for us even today. It is that where universal ideas are concerned, cultural origins do not matter: they transcend all cultural boundaries. There is a warning here to all those who think that there can be no significant meeting of minds between India and the West. And there is also a challenge to those in both the East and West who believe that in today's world one's own culture is self-sufficient. A close scrutiny of Gandhi-Tolstoy relationship is valuable for yet another reason. It is a model of how one should go about assimilating ideas taken from other cultures. Gandhi read Tolstoy carefully but critically, and he assimilated only those elements in his works which he thought were necessary for the development of his own original philosophy. Gandhi did not become a Tolstoyan any more than he became a Ruskinian, although without studying Tolstoy and Ruskin he could not have become what he actually became.

The relationship between Gandhi and Tolstoy was a one-sided affair. For one thing, they were separated in age by forty-one years. By the time Gandhi came to know Tolstoy, which was in 1894, he was just an unknown Indian lawyer finding his way in South Africa, while Tolstoy had already reached the zenith of his fame. Their correspondence started only in 1909, a year before Tolstoy's death. They exchanged seven letters in all, four from Gandhi and three from Tolstoy. Tolstoy came to know Gandhi only through *Hind Swaraj* (1909), and Doke's biography, *M. K. Gandhi: An Indian Patriot in South Africa* (1909). Though the duration of their contact was very short, it nevertheless proved to be very significant. Tolstoy had enough time to recognise the historic importance of *Hind Swaraj*, and of what Gandhi was doing in South Africa. Thanks to that contact, Gandhi came to be seen as an inheritor of the Tolstoy moral legacy into the twentieth century.

Looking back on this historic relationship, we see three works of Tolstoy as being especially significant. They are, in the order of importance, *What is Art?*, *Letter to a Hindoo,* and *The Kingdom of God is Within You*. They deal with three enduring themes in Gandhian philosophy, namely, the place and function of art in life, the problem of violence and its resolution, and the need for a spirituality based on a practical love of God and fellow human beings. I shall comment on each of these works in turn.

We begin with *The Kingdom of God is Within You* (Tolstoy, 1935). He read it in 1894, the year in which it first appeared in English translation.[2] As he states in his *Autobiography*, the book 'overwhelmed' him. It remained his *vade mecum* during his South African days. It was a required reading for members of Phoenix Settlement and Tolstoy Farm. It was his constant companion during all three of his prison stays in South Africa. He took it with him on his first prison term in January 1908[3]; and again, on the second prison term, October-December 1908, at the end of which he presented his copy as a gift to M. G. Nelson, the jail warder, with a signed personal inscription: 'For the many kindnesses within the law during his incarceration at Volksrust.'[4] Again, it was with him during the third prison term, February-May 1909. Here we have an amusing story of how he actually carried the book to the jail cell: 'I was handcuffed...the warder locked up the handcuffs rather tight... The Chief Warder saw this. I had obtained his permission to carry a book *The Kingdom of God is Within You* with me to read on the way. Thinking probably that I felt ashamed of the handcuffs, he asked me to hold the book with both hands, so that the handcuffs might not be seen. I was rather amused at this. To me the handcuffs were a matter of honour. It happened by chance that the title of the book which I was carrying, if rendered in Gujarati, would be: *Khuad-no Darbar Tara antar-man-CChe.*'[5]

The underlying theme of the book is the question of violence and its peaceful resolution. Its basic insight, which remains valid even today, is that peace is a social good, and that there can be no peace on earth unless there is a genuine spiritual self-renewal among individuals, supported by a strong public opinion favouring peace. By spiritual self-renewal Tolstoy meant a new understanding of the meaning of pure religion. The essence of pure religion, in his view, lays 'in man's faculty of foreseeing prophetically' the true meaning of life.[6] As far as the resolution of violence was concerned, what was needed, he felt, was a new appreciation of the relevance of the ethic of the Sermon on the Mount. He stated the problem as follows: 'how to settle the conflicts between people who now consider a thing evil that others consider good, and vice versa? To say that evil is what I consider evil although my adversary consider it good, is not a solution to the difficulty. There can be but two solutions: either to find an absolute and indubitable criterion of evil, or not to resist evil by violence.

'The first course has been tried since the beginning of history, and as we all know has so far led to no satisfactory results.

'The second course – not to resist with violence what we consider evil, until we have found some universal criterion – the solution proposed by Christ.'[7]

The rest of the book is taken up with a spirited defence of this fundamental thesis. It starts with an analyses of the various solutions offered to the problem of violence. In the first place, there was the solution offered by Western Christianity. He found it inadequate and incompatible with the teachings of the Sermon on the Mount. For Western Christian philosophy both justified the state and tolerated the theory of just wars. In his opinion, however, 'Christianity in its true sense puts an end to the state.'[8] The profession of pure Christianity required the rejection of the legitimacy of the state. His critique of Western Christianity comes down to this: 'which is more necessary for the good of humanity, which better secures men's welfare, the political form of life, or its downfall and its replacement by Christianity?'[9] There was no doubt in his mind as to what the answer would be: the state had to go, and the ethic of the Sermon on the Mount had to be reinstated. This ethic could not be practised, however, so long as one accepted the institutions of the modern state. It could only be practised in small communities of pure believers who withdrew from politics, and who would refuse to cooperate with the state in any shape or form. Gandhi, it may be noted in passing, did not accept Tolstoy's anti-statist pacifism.

Tolstoy next turned his attention to the solution to violence proposed by scientific humanism. It was Tolstoy's considered opinion that modern social philosophies were infected by this humanism in one way or another. The schools of philosophy mentioned are those of Positivism, Communism and Socialism.[10] August Comte, David Strauss, Herbert Spencer and Ernest

Renan came for special mention.[11] Modern social philosophies had one thing in common. They believed that the laws of human life were governed by 'the same laws as those of animal life'. They did not believe in the soul and a spiritual life properly so called. They believed that 'the chief activity' of humans, who wished to serve society, had to be directed 'to the amelioration of external political, social, and above all else, economic conditions' of life.[12] Such modifications were brought about in a variety of ways – by legislation, the diffusion of public education and propaganda in favour of Positivism, Socialism, etc. 'Let all those external alterations be realised,' countered Tolstoy, 'and the position of humanity would not be bettered.'[13] The position of humanity would be bettered only when real internal spiritual progress took place in larger and larger numbers of individual citizens. There was no sign that spiritual progress was taking place. On the contrary, scientific humanism showed its real colours as it became the theoretical lubricant for the machinery of modern wars, of colonialism and the genocidal extermination of 'whole races of men called savages' that took place during the periods of colonisation.[14]

Tolstoy has nothing but scorn for scientific humanism, especially since it was being presented as an alternative to pure religion. It substituted, he pointed out, 'the love and service of humanity for the love and service of God.'[15] True religion, had its source in the love of God. Authentic love of the neighbour had its basis in the soul, while love of humanity which scientific humanism professed turned out to be 'only a theoretical deduction by analogy.'[16] 'They propose love of humanity alone without a love of God'–they want 'the fruit without the root'.[17] Tolstoy next turned to a discussion of what pure religion was and how it alone could lead to true inner progress. Pure religion had its source in the unconditional love of God, from which flowed the true love of fellow human beings. And human life, taken at the individual level, was a process of striving to achieve the fullness of this love. Taking the notion of asymptote from mathematics, he explained the process as follows: 'Human life is an asymptote of divine perfection towards which it always tends and approaches, but which can only be reached by it in infinity.'[18] The love of God guides human beings not by external rules but 'by an inward consciousness of the possibility of reaching divine perfection.'[19] This growth in inner perfection is the necessary spiritual condition that would make life at the social and political level less violent. The reality of this development he called the kingdom of God. It is a metaphor signifying 'a new system of life free from violence'.[20] This kingdom is found within each individual human being. It can flourish only if we live 'according to the light in us'.[21] The development of such an inner kingdom was the end of all true religions. And its attainment depend on human effort. 'The Kingdom of God can only be reached by effort, and only those who make such effort reach it.'[22] And effort here meant the effort to rise above external conditions and to follow the truth that is revealing itself within. The ability to cultivate the kingdom within was an ability which all human beings possessed. 'The sole meaning of human life lies in serving the world by promoting the establishment of the Kingdom of God. This service can be accomplished only by the recognition and avowal of the truth by each separate individual.'[23]

The kingdom within, then, provides the most effective solution to the problem of violence: it provides a solution superior to that provided by the state and by scientific humanism. This more or less is Tolstoy's basic contention in the book.

But was Tolstoy being too idealistic and utopian here? The thought must surely have crossed his mind. That is why, I think, he introduced a second means to non-violence. He called this second means public opinion. He devoted two long chapters, chs. 10 and 11, to this subject. 'The moral progress of humanity is accomplished,' he writes, 'not only by a recognition of truth, but also by the establishment of a public opinion.'[24] In his view public opinion was more influential than even legislation, which without the support of public opinion would fail in any case. In the modern world nothing lasting could be done without the support of public opinion. It was 'the fundamental factor that moves men and nations'; it was 'the resultant of all the spiritual forces' available at any given time to a given people.[25] It followed that corresponding to the rise of a higher consciousness of the pure ethics of non-violence, there should be public opinion favourable to peace and opposed to war.

Thus, the argument of the book ends on a very positive and practical note: non-violence needs not only spirituality but also the backing of a strong public opinion. It is not enough to have high ideals; one should also know how to create public opinion favouring them. In this regard Gandhi was a master creator of public opinion. If he learnt anything from Tolstoy, it was that he had to change public opinion in India in favour of his causes, whether in regard to foreign rule or untouchability. And only when public opinion comes to the aid of non-violence, could non-violence become a major force in contemporary life.

Letter to a Hindoo

The background to the *Letter* is as interesting as its contents. It was written in response to two letters from Taraknath Das (1884-1958). The first was written on 24 May 1908, from University Station, Seattle, Washington state, and the second, on 15 July 1908, from Norwich University, Northfield, Vermont. A former member of the Bengal terrorist organisation, the Anusilan Samiti, Das had emigrated to the United States in 1906. There shedding terrorism, he began, among other things, a penny monthly, *The Free Hindusthan* (1908), promoting the cause of the extremist brand of Indian nationalism. It was modelled on *The Indian Sociologist* of London and Paris, started in 1905 by Shyamji Krishnavarma. Das was influenced by both the spirit of extremist nationalism as well as by the scientific humanism of Herbert Spencer. Following the example of *The Indian Sociologist*, and professing faith in Spencerism, his monthly carried two quotations from Spencer on its masterhead: 'Every man is free to do that which he wills, provided he infringes not the equal freedom of any other man', and 'Resistance to aggression is not simply justifiable but imperative. Non resistance hurts both altruism and egoism.'

Das completed his academic studies in the United States, taking his B.A. and M. A. from Washington University in Seattle, and his Ph. D. in 1924 from Georgetown University in Washington, D. C. In 1924, he married Mary K. Morse and embarked upon a very distinguished academic career, during which he served the cause of India in the United States with great zeal and distinction. It is ironic, however, that the entry for him in *Who's Who in America* for the 1950s makes no mention at all of his extremist nationalist background, nor of the *Letter to a Hindoo*, nor even of his historic contact with Tolstoy.

Be that as it may, it was due to Das's initiative, however, that we have at our disposal *A Letter to a Hindoo* .[26] His two letters to Tolstoy gave a brief description of the terrible plight of India under colonial rule. Their purpose was to seek Tolstoy's support for India's cause.

Tolstoy took Das's letters very seriously. It took him seven months, 29 drafts and 413 manuscript pages to prepare the *Letter* which is only about 6,000-word long.[27] That a writer of Tolstoy's stature would devote so much time and effort to compose this document is in itself a sign of its historical importance.

Even though the *Letter* originated as a result of Das's initiative, it probably would never have become famous, had it not been for Mahatma Gandhi. For a copy of a typescript of the *Letter* fell into his hands in 1909 while he was in London. To verify its authenticity he wrote directly to Tolstoy. He had also asked permission, if the document proved to be authentic, to have it published in both English and Gujarati. The permission was readily granted, and Gandhi did the work of editing and translating at the same time that he was writing *Hind Swaraj*, on board the ship Kildonan Castle. The text of the *Letter* was first published by Gandhi in South Africa, in three successive issues of *Indian Opinion* – 25 December 1909, 1 and 8 January 1910. Das published it four months later, in April 1910, in a Boston monthly *Twentieth Century Magazine*, not under the title under which it is known today, but under a title Das himself gave to it, viz., 'A Message to Young India, by Count Leo Tolstoy'. This was followed by a highly critical response from Das himself, under the title , 'Young India's Reply to Count Tolstoy.' It was no secret that Das and his friends did not like what Tolstoy had to say. Indeed, they were shocked by his utter repudiation of violence as a means of obtaining Indian freedom.

It is against the context of this hostile reception by Das and the friendly welcome by Gandhi that we have to assess the historic relevance of the *Letter*.

The *Letter* makes three basic points. The first is that 'the chief, if not the sole' cause, of the enslavement of India is the absence of a pure religious consciousness in all nations, including India. Nations no longer believe in a spiritual element in their lives, an element which manifests itself in the love of God and fellow human beings. Modern men rather seem to believe in scientific humanism, according to which life is a struggle in which only the fittest survive. It is the tacit rejection of the principle of love of God and the tacit acceptance of a Darwinian humanism that is really at the basis of violence of every kind, including the violence underlying colonialism.

Secondly, Indians are implicated in their own enslavement. This is perhaps the one point that stirred the ire of Das and his colleagues. For Tolstoy pointed to them that they were repeating 'the amazing stupidity' indoctrinated in them by their European teachers such as Herbert Spencer that force could be resisted only with force. He further pointed out that Indian society itself was built on violence. That was why, the English were able to enslave them by their greater violence. 'If the English have enslaved the people of India it is just because the latter recognised and still recognise force as the fundamental principle of the social order.'[28] It is because of this acceptance of violence that they were willing to submit themselves to their little rajahs, and on their behalf to fight against one another. Under these circumstances, for Indians to complain about the English was like alcoholics complaining about wine-merchants. If you want to get rid of the wine-merchants, the first thing you have to do is to stop drinking. But you say that you cannot do that because alcohol keeps up your energy. The conclusion is clear. 'If the people of India are enslaved by violence it is only because they themselves live and have lived by violence and do not recognise the eternal law of love inherent in humanity.'[29] This was indeed bitter medicine for Indian nationalists of the extremist persuasion. Tolstoy's conclusion was that India's liberation laid with Indians liberating themselves from the belief that violence could liberate them. They should begin to believe in the power of the soul and in that of a public opinion favourable to non-violence.

Gandhi, in his Preface to the *Letter*, endorsed the central truth of Tolstoy's indictment. That truth was that Indians ought realise that 'We are our own slaves, not of the British. This should be engraved in our minds.'[30] That is to say, Indians have 'to understand and act upon the irresistible power of the soul over the body, of love, which is an attribute of the soul, over the brute or body force generated by the stirring up in us of evil passions.'[31] One can already hear in Gandhi's Preface the echoes of *Hind Swaraj*. He had good reason for putting the *Letter* in Appendix I of that work.

What is Art?

The first question that will cross the mind of anyone who looks into Appendix 1 of *Hind Swaraj* is this: Why would Gandhi include in it two works on art by two of Europe's greatest art critics, Ruskin and Tolstoy? I am referring of course to Ruskin's *The Political Economy of Art* or, in its revised title, *A Joy for Ever*, and to Tolstoy's *What is Art?*[32] What have Western art and art criticism to do with India and its swaraj? What made Gandhi think that all serious students of his philosophy should read these works as well?

Critics and art historians have not always been kind to Gandhi when it came to the question of his understanding of the relationship of art to society. Madan G. Gandhi's *Gandhian Aesthetics* is an honourable exception. It at least legitimises the discussion of the subject, even though it does not go far enough in its analysis of the works of Ruskin and Tolstoy. Apart from Madan Gandhi, critics have been generally dismissive of Gandhi's aesthetic significance. Partha Mitter, for example, gives him the short shrift: 'in Gandhi's programme there was no room for art, with the possible exception of Nandalal Bose's decoration of the Haripura Congress venue, done at Gandhi's behest.'[33] Gandhi fares no better in Bhikhu Parekh's estimation. His 'moralistic vision', states Parekh, prevented him from seeing the significance of the other aspects of life, including the aesthetic.[34] The fact remains, however, that Gandhi had a deep and continuing interest in art in general, and Indian art in particular. He greatly admired Ananda Coomaraswamy's *Essays in National Idealism* (1909), recommending it to his colleagues in South Africa and to his followers in India.[35] The reference to the works of Ruskin and Tolstoy clearly suggests that his interest was practical as well as theoretical. He thought of *What is Art?* so highly that he had Valji Desai translate it into Gujarati. 'If you translated Tolstoy's *What is Art?* for publication and read proofs you will get Rs. 100...I shall get the work done through you', he wrote to Desai in 1916.[36] That is not all. A decade later, in 1927, we see Gandhi recommending the same book to Sushila, his daughter-in-law, living in South Africa. The context in which the recommendation occurs reveals how knowledgeable he was on the subject. 'Sushila is right when she says that in the realm of art there can be no distinction between indigenous and foreign, but her statement calls for some reflection. Lovers of art take a superficial view of art and use it as cover for many weaknesses. We should, therefore, examine what we mean by art... I have read conflicting opinions about many paintings and statues expressed by art critics who have become famous in the world. We should, therefore, think what art means. The book *What is Art?* has been translated into Gujarati. Sushila should read it. If you cannot get it there, please write to me.'[37] In rounding off this brief introduction to Gandhi's competence in art and aesthetics, it is useful to bear in mind that the friendly controversy between himself and Tagore had an underlying aesthetic element in it. The question was, to what extent art was immune from the political questions of the day, and to what extent were the political questions of the day to impinge on art. Then there is the well-known 1924 interview given to G. Ramachandran in which he gave his basic position on art and aesthetics, and also his reasons for not wanting to write a book on the subject.[38] Finally, there is the 1931 discussion on art between him and Romain Rolland, an extensive account of which is found in *Romain Rolland and Gandhi Correspondence.*[39] *What is Art?*, which according to Aylmer Maude, Tolstoy's biographer and translator, was one of his 'greatest contributions to the welfare of mankind', is both a work of art history and art theory. As a historical work, it reviews the history of European art from the Italian Renaissance to the last decades of the nineteenth century. As a theoretical work, it proposes a definition of art, its place in human life and its relationship to human brotherhood and non-violence.

From the Gandhian perspective, the theory of art underlying the work is more relevant than its analysis of European art history. The most basic theoretical issue, of course, is Tolstoy's conception of what art is. Art is an activity of human life, as important as the activity of speech and as generally diffused. It is a means of communicating feelings which the artist has experienced. 'To evoke in oneself a feeling one has once experienced and having evoked it in oneself by means of movements, lines, colours, sounds, or forms expressed in words, so to transmit that feeling that others experience the same feeling – this is the activity of art.'[40] The more the art manages to transmit feelings, the better the art. The ability to inflect others in this way will depend on the individuality, the clarity, and the sincerity of the art.[41] The artist produces art because of the artist's 'inner need to express' the feeling that has accumulated.[42]

Tolstoy distinguishes between universal art and art catering to the tastes of the ruling classes. Universal art expresses feelings related to the ultimate meaning of life. This meaning is expressed by the religious perception of each age.[43] Such perception is very clearly expressed by a few advanced individuals in each society, and more or less vividly perceived by rest of society.[44] The religious perception of our times, according to Tolstoy, is the consciousness of 'growth of brotherhood' among peoples.[45]

Upper-class art, by contrast, panders to the tastes of the rich and the powerful. It stimulates their pride, sexual desires and a general discontent with life. Pride of life is the theme of art that glorifies kings and queens, and people in positions of power. Sexual desires and general discontent with life began to dominate works of fiction in modern times. The purpose of this sort of art is pleasure and amusement.[46] Art of this sort is very expensive and inaccessible to the average people. There is a conscious effort, in recent times, for which he blames Neitzsche and his followers, to separate beauty from goodness, and to claim autonomy for art from the norms of goodness.

According to Tolstoy, the task of art in our times is to strengthen the feelings of human solidarity cutting across all major human divides – race, religion and economic status. Aided by science, and guided by religion, art should promote the goal of 'peaceful co-operation' of human beings. This co-operation is now being achieved through law, police, charitable institutions, factory inspection. Art should come to the aid here: 'Art should cause violence to be set aside.'[47] The feeling of human solidarity is now attained by only 'the best members' in each society; but art should make that feeling 'the customary feeling and instinct of all men.'[48]

Remarkably, *What is Art?* ends on a note close to that articulated by *The Kingdom of God is Within You:* 'The destiny of art in our time is to transmit from the realm of reason to that realm of feeling the truth that well-being of men consists in their being united together, and to set up, in place of existing reign of force, that kingdom of God – that is, of love – which we all recognise to be the highest aim of human life.'[49]

To what extent Gandhi himself implemented the notion of art found in Tolstoy (and Ruskin) is a question we cannot go into here for reasons of space. It must be said, however, that Tolstoy did strike a sympathetic chord in Gandhi's inner consciousness.

Living in a pluralistic society, he saw how art could bring different peoples together. He was able to invent and popularise universal symbols such as the charkha and khadi. His loincloth itself was an artistic symbol of the first order. It expressed 'the agony' of his soul for the poverty of the masses. It was a symbol of his solidarity with them.[50] A bare body and bare head, he said, were signs of mourning for India's plight.[51] It was painful for him to eat or dress as rich people do, so long as the poor did not have enough to eat and enough to cover their bodies with.[52] And he made it clear again and again that by donning the loincloth he was not glorifying poverty, but criticising it, not starting a loincloth civilisation, but trying to correct some of the injustices of existing Indian civilisation.[53] Some of his most famous writings came from the depth of his inner feelings. This was certainly the case with *Hind Swaraj*; 'I have written because I could not restrain myself', he wrote in the Foreword. And at the very heart of its arguments for *swaraj,* he makes a plea for the need to experience *swaraj*. 'The *swaraj* that I wish to picture before you and me is such that, after we have once realised it, we will endeavour to the end of our lifetime to persuade others to do likewise. But such swaraj has to be experienced by each one for himself.'[54]

Whatever critics and art historians might say, those who knew Gandhi personally well or those who were artists themselves, saw the artist, the unique artist, in him. Here perhaps E. M. Forster expresses the idea better than most. Speaking of Gandhi he said that he was with the great artists, though art was not his medium.[55] And Tagore in the end came to understand him, as he said, as he would an artist.[56] Nehru called him 'the perfect artist'. 'All his manifold activities became progressively a symphony, and every word he spoke and every gesture that he made fitted into this, and so unconsciously he became the perfect artist, for he had learnt the art of living, though the way of life he had adopted was very different from the world's ways.'[57]

Of the three works of Tolstoy that we have discussed here, *What is Art*? I think is the most significant. For it gives us a unique entry into Gandhi's mind and feelings. We see him inventing new symbols, using them to shape public opinion, and to move people to action. And of course, the values those symbols represented were universal values to peace, human solidarity and material well-being.

Notes and References

1. *The Collected Works of Mahatma Gandhi* (CWMG), Vol. 32, New Delhi, 1969, p. 4.
2. Pyarelal, *Mahatma Gandhi* , Vol. 1, Ahmedabad, 1986, p.627.
3. *CWMG*, Vol.8, 1962, p. 159.
4. *Ibid.,* Vol.9, 1968, p.115
5. *Ibid.*, p.240
6. Leo Tolstoy, *The Kingdom of God and Peace Essays*, Trans. Aylmer Maud, Oxford, 1935, p. 104.
7. *Ibid.*, p.58
8. *Ibid.*, p.281.
9. *Ibid.*, p.282
10. *Ibid.*, p. 127.
11. *Ibid.*, p.108
12. *Ibid.*, pp.401-2
13. *Ibid.*, p.411.
14. *Ibid.*, p. 450.
15. *Ibid.*, p.122.
16. *Ibid.*, p. 123.
17. *Ibid.*, p. 127.
18. *Ibid.*, p. 117.
19. *Ibid.*, p. 118.
20. *Ibid.*, p.332
21. *Ibid.*, p.334

22. *Ibid.*, p. 428.
23. *Ibid.*, p.444.
24. *Ibid.*, p. 281.
25. *Ibid.*, p. 309.
26. Leo Tolstoy , *Letter to a Hindoo* , Christian Bartlof (ed.), Berlin, 1997.
27. Christain Bartlof " Tolstoy and Gandhi" in Antony Copley and George Paxton eds. *Gandhi and the Contemporary World*, Chennai, 1997, p.197.
28. Tolstoy, 1997, *op.cit.*, p. 25.
29. *Ibid.*, pp.25-6
30. *CWMG,* Vol. 10, 1963, p.2.
31. *Ibid.*, p.5.
32. Leo Tolstoy, *What is Art?* Trans. Aylmer Maud, Oxford, 1929.
33. Partha Mitter, *Art and Nationalism in Colonial India 1850-1922*, Cambridge, 1994, p.379.
34. Bhikhu Parekh, Gandhi, Oxford, 1997, p.99.
35. *CWMG*, Vol. 10, 1963, p. 356; Vol.14, 1965, p.13.
36. *Ibid.,* Supplem. Vol. 1, 1989, p.103.
37. *Ibid.,* Vol. 35, 1969, p.363.
38. *Ibid.,* Vol.25, 1964, pp. 247-50.
39. Romain Rolland, *Romain Rolland and Gandhi Correspondence*, New Delhi, 1976, Passim.
40. Tolstoy, 1929, *op.cit.*, p. 129; p.123.
41. *Ibid.*, p. 227.
42. *Ibid.*, p. 266.
43. *Ibid.*, p.127.
44. *Ibid.*, p. 232
45. *Ibid.*, p.235, p.263.
46. *Ibid.*, p.135; pp.153-54.

47. *Ibid.*, p. 287.
48. *Ibid.*, p.288.
49. *Ibid.*
50. *CWMG*, Vol. 46, 1971, p. 55.
51. *Ibid.*, Vol.21, 1966, p. 181.
52. *Ibid.*, Vol.24, 1967, p.456.
53. *Ibid.*, Vol.46, 1971, p.55.
54. *Ibid.*, Vol., 24, 1967, p.72.
55. E.M. Foster, "Mahatma Gandhi" in S. Radhakrishnan (ed.), *Mahatma Gandhi : Reflections on His Life and Work*, Bombay, 1956, p.315.
56. R.K. Prabhu and R. Kelelkar, *Truth Called Them Differently : Tagore- Gandhi Controversy*, Ahmedabad, 1961, p. 132.
57. Jawaharlal Nehru, "The Perfect Artist" in S. Radhakrishnan (ed.), *op.cit.*, p.354.

5

Spiritual Living, Gandhian Economics and Well-being

Romesh Diwan and *Shakti Bethea*

Introduction

The Gandhian approach to economics stems from a cultural tradition in which spirituality is the guiding factor in life. With spiritual values as the starting point and focus, it is assumed that the resulting social and economic system will reflect those values, conceptually and practically, in order to maximize human well-being. If classical, materially-based economic conceptualisations, of both the Marxist and Capitalist varieties, can be seen as spanning the left and right quadrants of the horizontal or X-axis, then Gandhian economics can be seen as spanning the vertical or Y-axis. It thus intersects with and includes material approaches to economics, yet adds a larger spiritual dimension within which to define and create well-being.

Such spiritually-based well-being creates social capital,[1] the communal trust enjoyed by a society which facilitates coordination and cooperation for mutual benefit. Social capital, in addition to human and physical capital, is essential to a satisfying quality of life. In a Gandhian sense, production of social capital is dependent on the creation and maintenance of a strong community, which is, by definition, spiritually-oriented. Through community, spiritual values are implemented in daily life, thus contributing to human well-being and a high quality of life. In exploring the connections between spiritual values, well-being and Gandhian economics, it will be useful to define some of the key concepts.

Conceptual Definitions

1. Well-being

The literature on human well-being is large and spans many disciplines in the social, physical and behavioural sciences. Classical economic conceptualisations generally include only the material, and occasionally the mental dimension of well-being. However, to be truly comprehensive, the concept of well-being must include the spiritual dimension as well. This expanded concept of well-being thus contains the three essential components of material, mental and spiritual well-being, which are integrally, rather than hierarchically, related. The concept of well-being also implies a condition of "enoughness,"[2] in which resources are adequate to fill the needs of all but the greed of none.[3] Well-being can thus be defined as a state of enoughness, of human needs being satisfied, on the material, mental and spiritual levels of human experience.

2. Spiritual Values

In surveying the beliefs of spiritually-oriented cultures throughout time and across geographical boundaries,[4] one single, common assertion emerges: the immutable unity or oneness of life at all levels and in all manifestations.[5] This unity of life axiom then provides the philosophical foundation, guiding and informing human decisions and actions at the material, mental and spiritual levels. All universal spiritual values and the actions following from them are thus grounded in respect for and preservation of the integral oneness of life.

3. Gandhian Economics

Gandhian Economics is both a theoretical and practical conceptualisation of economics based on spiritual values and the definition of wealth as relational, rather than solely material. Relational wealth is largely independent of material scarcity or abundance and potentially exists at all levels of human experience, provided sufficient time and others with whom to share love and care.[6] Such spiritually-based relational wealth creates social capital which, like other forms of capital, is productive in an economic sense and enhances well-being.[7] Gandhian economics thus provides a framework within which well-being can be articulated economically, created in a practical sense and sustained in communities.

Current Malaise

1. Background

During the past two decades, economists[8] and other social scientists have documented an increasingly debilitating malaise among the world's high-income, post-industrial countries. Despite a booming economy characterized by low interest rates, a "bull" market, low unemployment and high consumer confidence, there is widespread evidence that the relatively affluent citizens of these prosperous countries experience growing emptiness, isolation, alienation and lack of meaning or purpose.[9] This pervasive state of post-modern anomie thus reveals that a successful economic system alone has not been sufficient to provide a satisfying lifestyle.

2. Manifestations of Malaise

This pernicious malaise occurs at all levels, from the personal to the interpersonal to the familial and, ultimately, to the societal level. And while manifesting differently at each of these levels of analysis, the underlying malaise persists despite infusions of massive amounts of public and private funding. As legislative bodies, social service and law enforcement agencies have been quick to point out, throwing money at the problem has done little or nothing to diminish its symptoms.[10]

At the individual or personal level, this malaise manifests as greatly increased rates of depression, substance abuse and stress-related health problems. The three leading causes of death in the United States, heart disease, cancer and stroke, are strongly stress-related, while suicide and alcohol-related liver disease are among the top 10 killers. Seventy-five to 90 per cent of visits to doctors' offices stem from stress, with stress-related illnesses becoming so prevalent that the nation's healthcare budget has now caught up with and overtaken the federal defence budget. In 1996, for instance, the healthcare budget exceeded one trillion dollars.[11]

At the interpersonal level, this malaise manifests in increased litigation and aggression, ranging from road rage to rampant workplace violence.[12] The annual cost to the economy is huge, as employers find themselves increasingly unable to keep up with costs associated with loss of productivity, employee absenteeism, skyrocketing insurance claims, costly lawsuits, property damage and high turnover and training expenses directly brought about by workplace violence.[13] The National Institute for Occupational Safety and Health (1997) reports an average of 20 murders in the workplace each week, while, in the same week, 18,000 more employees are victims of nonfatal workplace assaults. Such nonfatal workplace assaults annually result in over 876,000 lost workdays and $16 million in lost wages. Homicide is the second leading cause of death on the job, and is the leading cause of workplace death for women.

In marriages and families, this post-modern malaise is marked by a divorce rate of over 50 per cent and a tremendous escalation in child abuse and domestic violence. Despite a booming economy, the incidence of children living in poverty has not decreased, even though poverty among senior citizens has been cut by more than half. In 1996, the incidence of children living in poverty had climbed to 37 per cent in eight states, with 40 per cent of Latino and African American children below the poverty level. Overall, 44 per cent of America's poor children live in households with incomes no more than half the poverty threshold. Women are representing an increasingly high proportion of the poor, with the rate of poor households headed by women more than doubling from 25 per cent to 54 per cent between 1960 and 1996.

Child abuse and domestic violence against women are also

on the increase. Gelles notes that, with the exception of the police and military, the family is the most violent group in society.[14] In 1997, the FBI reported an estimate of at least 600,000 women who were victims of domestic violence. As opposed to just 3 per cent of men, 30 per cent of women who are homicide victims die at the hands of their current or former spouses. In addition, about 1 million cases of child abuse are reported each year, with several thousand cases involving death.[15] At the societal level, this malaise manifests as unprecedented apathy and withdrawal from electoral processes and an overall increase in violent crime and crimes against property. In the 1996 presidential election, less than half of registered voters cast a vote well below the comparable level in most other industrialized nations. Those segments of society at highest risk are the least likely to vote: most low-income people do not vote at all, with Hispanics voting at less than half the rate of whites. There is an inverse relationship between income level and participation in electoral processes, which sociologists attribute to alienation rather than simple indifference.[16] And even though violent crime has tapered off in the past several years, the FBI reports an overall rise in crime rates since 1960, with police addressing around 8 million serious crimes each year.[17]

3. Post-Industrial Materialism

This post-modern malaise and its manifestations at the personal, interpersonal, familial and societal levels have become a major focus of concern, not only for economists but also for policy makers, social and physical scientists, lawmakers and scholars from diverse disciplines. It has become clear to many studying the problem that answers are not to be found in taking a strictly material approach, such as that proffered by classical economics.[18] On the contrary, such a material approach appears to actually exacerbate problems by overlooking their underlying causes and by failing to address crucial existential dimensions of the resulting malaise.

It is ironic that those who are most immersed in material wealth are among the most disenfranchised. In fact, a century after Durkheim's[19] pioneering study on suicide, the rate of suicide among the wealthy continues to exceed that of less well-off groups by a factor of four. Material wealth not only fails to provide protection against alienation and despair, it actually appears to increase the risk, as shown by suicide statistics.[20]

Even though material wealth does not guarantee a successful or satisfying lifestyle, its pursuit has nevertheless become an addictive cycle which is self-perpetuating. This vicious cycle constantly builds through self-reinforcing, but ultimately hollow promises of fulfilment. Rather than satisfying the yearning for fulfilment, then, consumption becomes an end in itself, as seen in all addictive processes. Addictive consumption perpetuates anomie, much the same way in which overeating of nutritionally depleted, high-calorie synthetic foods creates an insatiable craving for more and more of the empty calories.

Potential Solutions to Malaise

1. Spiritual Beliefs

In response to the shortcomings of a strictly material approach to creating a satisfying lifestyle, a growing number of leaders[21] and ordinary people[22] in the post-industrial countries have begun to seek and explore spiritual solutions which might alleviate, and eventually heal, the deadening post-modern malaise. It is this intense interest in and enactment of a spiritual approach to living which is the focus of this chapter.

What distinguishes a spiritual from a strictly material approach to living? In surveying the beliefs and practices of recognized spiritually-oriented cultures throughout history,[23] one single, common factor emerges: assertion of the underlying unity, connectedness, or oneness of all life, from the microcosm to the macrocosm.[24] This universally-held belief in the unity of all life, then, provides the philosophical foundation for the enactment of spiritual principles in every facet of life.[25] The success of a spiritual approach in addressing post-industrial malaise ultimately lies in such a translation of theory into action.

In the latter part of this chapter, we will explore Gandhian economics as an approach to bringing together theoretical principles and spiritual living in the everyday world. But, first, let us consider the implications of a belief in the ultimate oneness of life for a more spiritual way of living.

Spiritual living, simply put, is the choice to relate, make decisions, and act based on the principle of the unity of life. Such a choice does not negate the material dimension of life but, rather, relegates material concerns to a secondary position.[26] Table 1 provides a comparison of the tenets of the material and spiritual approaches to living:

Table 1: A Comparison of Material and Spiritual Approaches to Living

Material Approach	**Spiritual Approach**
Wealth defined as acquisition of material goods	Wealth defined by richness of relationships and quality time
Consumption is an end in itself	Consumption is to satisfy need
Consumption becomes addictive and unfulfilling	Consumption is not excessive and fully satisfies needs
Rewards of consumption justify exploitation of others and the Earth	Consumption is balanced by replenishment of resources

In placing the spiritual dimension first, priorities are automatically shifted from satisfying greed to satisfying need;[27] from competition to partnership;[28] from economic systems based on scarcity and inequality to those based on abundance and shared wealth.[29] Further, if spiritual values are to contribute to human well-being, it is necessary that they be *embodied* by people and *enacted* through social structures and systems. Such an implementation of spiritual values in everyday life provides the needed grounding of theory into action, making social change possible and contributing to the development of ecological enhancement and social capital. Being of a spiritual nature, such enhancements would automatically result in an increase in human well-being.

2. Essential Elements of Spiritual Living

In keeping with the unity of life axiom, it is possible to specify several universal elements of spiritual living. These elements have been articulated in some form within all spiritual traditions throughout time and across cultures. The most obvious is "do unto others as you would have others do unto you." If all life is fundamentally connected and whole, then it is impossible to cause harm to another (including non-human life and the Earth itself) without also harming oneself. Truth is a necessary but not sufficient condition for the practice of "doing unto others." In a spiritual framework, it is obvious that words or actions should never be undertaken unless they first stem from truth. However, in addition to fulfilling the primary criterion of truth, words and actions must meet two other criteria: they must be not only kind, but also necessary.[30] Pausing to consider words and actions in light of both the Golden Rule and the criteria of truth, kindness and necessity would introduce the spiritual elements of mindfulness and care into everyday human interactions.

A recognition of the underlying unity of life also leads to appreciation and respect for all forms of life, and for the unique part each plays in creating the greater balance which sustains life. Accordingly, regardless of its degree of biological simplicity or complexity, the essentiality of each life form as a vital thread in the larger fabric of life is respected. Such appreciation for the existence of all life forms ultimately results in a choice to end artificially-constructed hierarchies, in which life forms are ranked and treated according to their immediate desirability or usefulness to humans. Of course, there is the recognition that all life ultimately exists by consuming other life forms. Yet, without the imposition of unnatural hierarchy and its resulting exploitation of some life forms for the benefit of others, the underlying unity of life may be preserved. Then, all life forms may be allowed to exist, to maintain their place in the larger fabric of life, until they evolve to other forms according to natural, rather than artificially-imposed, processes. Such allowance for life to evolve within its own integrity would ultimately lead to the correction of those social, economic and environmental injustices which threaten to undermine the sustenance of life on the planet.

The extension of respect to all life forms allows us to articulate a third element of spiritual living: a commitment to non-violence. Rather than being a fact of life, violence is, at essence, a human choice.[31] We can distinguish between violence and the simple act of killing a life form for food by examining the connotations inherent in Webster's definition of violence: as opposed to simply killing, violence implies an extreme level of force which is "discordant, abusive, destructive and not natural."[32] While all life consumes other life forms in order to live, it is only humans who exceed the level of force necessary to bring about the desired result.[33] Because humans alone possess the ability to make such a choice, the factor of intentionality is introduced.[34] Killing solely for food is done out of biological need, while the impulse to behave in a violent manner stems from choice, regardless of whether that choice is made consciously or unconsciously. In eschewing violent actions, then, it is possible to satisfy human need without the additional infliction of unnecessary waste, abuse and suffering. Because it is need-based rather than driven by greed, a spiritual lifestyle is always founded on non-violence. Ultimately, such a sustained choice for non-violence would result in sustainable economic systems in which enough truly is enough.[35]

A fourth, and equally important, element of spiritual life is the recognition that ends cannot ultimately be separated from means.[36] If all life is indeed one, and exists in a state of dynamic and immutable unity, then it becomes impossible to employ violent or otherwise undesirable means without eventually creating undesirable ends. The untenable problem of attempting to separate means from ends is succinctly expressed in the song lyrics, "Why are we killing people who are killing people to show that killing people is wrong?"[37] If spiritual living is to be a viable antidote to post-industrial malaise, then a commitment to honour the unity of life is translated into a refusal to treat violence with violence, hatred with hatred, greed and exploitation with retaliation in-kind. [38] The foundation of a spiritual life lies, not in adding to the suffering and injustice in the world, but in choosing actions which help to restore the integrity of that greater whole. Living in health and abundance then becomes eminently more important and satisfying than being right, winning at others' expense, or destroying the balance of life by constantly taking without giving back. The maintenance of unity and integrity is itself a coming together of means and ends, and a necessary part of spiritual life.

Finally, a fifth crucial element of spiritual living, which flows from the first four, is the translation of these aspects of spirituality into a lifestyle of connection, sharing and service; in other words, into creating and sustaining *community*. As awareness of the unity of life grows, humans naturally experience the need to express and share connectedness with others by materially living in ways that more closely reflect that underlying unity. The enjoyment of material abundance is superficial and fleeting without others to share it. In fact, since wealth is highly correlated with weaker social ties, it is actually a risk factor for alienation and social isolation. All spiritual systems recognize the difficulty of implementing the foregoing elements of spiritual living into everyday life. For this reason, they encourage the creation and maintenance of community within which individuals can be supported in making spiritually-oriented choices and actions. In economic literature, community plays a nurturing function which leads to productivity and, thus, social capital formation and enhanced well-being. It is only in community that individuals, families and groups are able to experience the nurturing, belonging, safety, sharing of material resources and higher meaning or purpose which make human well-being possible. Thus, it is within a context of community that the spiritual principle of the unity of life can best be embodied and lived.

While the foregoing principles of spiritual living are

articulated in some manner in all major spiritual traditions, they are ultimately only of value when successfully applied to daily living. In a later section, we will discuss the theory and application of these principles as articulated in Gandhian economics. First, however, let us explore some of the ways in which spiritual living and materialism differ.

3. Contrasting Material and Spiritual Lifestyles: Real-Life Examples

To appreciate the difference between a primarily spiritually-oriented lifestyle and the more typical materially-oriented lifestyle, let us now compare two real-life examples. We can start by looking in on a day in the life of a career-oriented woman living in the upper-middle class suburb of a major metropolitan area. We will call this ambitious young woman Jamie.

Jamie wakes up at 5:00 a.m. to an alarm clock featuring a choice of 36 different tones. Still in bed, she uses her remote control to turn on the TV, catching the morning's news on CNN. As she dresses in the corporate uniform of power-suit and expensive yet look-alike jewellery, her coffee maker has already measured, ground, brewed her coffee, and dispensed it into a thermally insulated carafe. Her computer has turned itself on and is busy organizing her schedule for the day. As she pulls out of the garage in her new, leased BMW, Jamie voice-activates the car's CD player, which, through sixteen speakers, blares a motivational speech by an entrepreneurial billionaire. Jamie is energized by the get-rich guru's powerful and persuasive message when she arrives at the office at 6:30 a.m.

Her morning consists of meetings, checking voice mail, returning e-mail messages and coordinating a high-pressure teleconference. At noon, she breaks for power lunch at a trendy restaurant, not tasting or enjoying the food because she is completely focused on impressing her client and winning a large contract. Already seriously overextended on credit cards, she worries about her year-end bonus if the contract doesn't come through. A trace of resentment creeps in as she realizes that her superiors will get most of the credit for her hard work. She doubts that they even notice the long hours she puts in, though, since they are all equally busy competing for recognition and success.

That afternoon, there are more interminable meetings in her corporation's elegantly appointed, artificially-lit, climate-controlled boardroom. Jamie briefly wonders what the weather is like, trying to remember the last time she even noticed anything outside of her office. Mid-afternoon, she checks stock prices, extremely upset to find that a new speculative stock she had purchased has fallen 23 points. She takes a tranquilliser, applies more make-up to conceal the dark circles under her eyes and practises the successful image-projection technique taught by the billionaire get-rich guru, barely regaining her professional demeanour before the next meeting.

The meeting runs late, increasing Jamie's anxiety as she excuses herself from the office for a "dental appointment." Her blood pressure has elevated to 210/130 by the time she arrives at her therapist's office across town. In addition to the time strain, these bi-weekly therapy sessions are becoming a financial burden. Yet, with her history of suicidal depression and an out-of-control eating disorder, Jamie dares not cut back on therapy. Before she even sits down, she is in tears, recounting the monotonous litany of fear, loneliness and deprivation, despite her tremendous investment of time, energy and money to maintain appearances to the contrary. Her panic and anxiety disorder is under better control thanks to an increased dosage of the tranquilliser, but that concern is now replaced with the looming threat of another drug dependency. Jamie has never felt more hopeless or alone as she fights rush-hour traffic to get back to the office for a mandatory staff meeting. Her blood pressure rises again as she realizes that she will be singled out in the meeting for losing an important account with a difficult but high-paying client.

The staff meeting is worse than she had imagined, requiring

her to double up on her tranquilliser. Even though her doctor approved a dosage increase last week, she has already exceeded her daily amount and is stressed about how she will justify asking for refills prematurely. Noticing that her energy is flagging, she buys three candy bars and a diet soda from the vending machine on her floor. She consumes the junk food mindlessly before sneaking a cigarette in the bathroom. Even though the office building is strictly non-smoking, she has learned that there are few people around to notice at that time of night. At 10:30 p.m., Jamie drives to her private, 24-hour health club, where she works out on machines while watching CNN. There is no way she can justify the club's monthly membership fee, yet she knows that working out is the only way she can compensate for the weight gain caused by an active eating disorder. She wonders whether her attractive professional trainer is single, immediately telling herself to forget it because she has no time for a romantic relationship, anyway. In fact, she guiltily recalls that she has not even responded to the numerous concerned phone messages from her mother in the past month. If she can't stay in touch with her own mother, whom she considers to be her best friend, how can she possibly maintain her other friendships? Rather than experience these painful feelings, she turns her mind to eating and the prospect of taking another pill.

On the way home from the health club, Jamie swings through a fast food restaurant, again not tasting the food as she obsesses about whether she will land the big contract. Eating alone always makes her feel lonely, yet her calendar is much too full to schedule dinner with a friend any time in the next three months. As she turns onto her street, Jamie pulls out the garage door opener, which will enable her to find her house in the sea of identical ones in the new development. She tries to remember whether she has ever seen any of her neighbours, since everyone in the neighbourhood seems to come and go from their garages by car. Arriving home, she is reassured that the computer has turned on the lights, deactivated the alarm system, and turned on the TV for the late-late news. She notices that she has many messages on her phone answering machine, once again feeling the sting of guilt that she is too busy and self-absorbed to call her closest friends. She knows that some quality time with a friend would be the best antidote to her depression, but it would consume too much energy to make the effort. Besides, everyone she knows is in bed long before she even gets home at night. Exhausted from the day's stress, Jamie says good night to the computer, puts a scoop of coffee beans in the machine's hopper and falls asleep to the familiar hum of electronic appliances.

About thirty miles away, Deborah has just said good night to her weekly meditation group. She always looks forward to these Thursday night gatherings, and again to Sunday nights, when a different group of friends comes over for a community dinner. She realizes that sharing home-cooked meals and meditation with others has added an essential element of ritual, purpose and belonging to her life. She spends some time playing with her cat and two dogs, watering her many plants, and enjoying the residual scent of incense in the house. She remembers what a relaxing morning she had, drinking coffee on her porch overlooking abundant open space. Two deer had grazed a few feet away, while a flock of geese flew overhead. She had had a leisurely visit with her neighbour, who had stopped by after spontaneously shovelling snow from her sidewalk. Working in her home office for a few hours, she had taken a break, checked in by phone with several friends, and taken her dogs for a walk in the public open space nearby. She then walked two blocks to the neighbourhood grocery, buying enough organic food to last a few days. Deborah remembered an especially moving exchange of e-mail messages she had had with an out-of-state friend before getting back to work on a freelance editing project.

Even though she now had to provide her own medical insurance and retirement plan, she was pleased with the flexibility and freedom that freelance work allowed. She thought of so many of her former colleagues, who still worked in jobs they hated out of fear of losing a regular pay-cheque and benefits. Deborah could sympathize, as many of them had families who depended on them financially. She might still be trapped in the corporate world if she had children to support.

She remembered the unbearable stress level during those 20 years that she had worked in such high-pressure environments. Back then, no amount of yoga or meditation had been sufficient to release the accumulated stress; she had been sick all the time and was chronically depressed and exhausted. Worst of all, the aggressive business climate in her corporation had turned colleagues, who should have been friends, into threats and competition. Deborah shuddered at these memories, feeling a profound sense of gratitude that she had been able to muster the courage to be self-employed.

It was starting to snow and she remembered to put out extra food for the deer and birds in her backyard. Deborah's nose was tickled by the pleasant smell of wood smoke from her neighbour's new, low-emission stove. The laughter of children playing on sleds brought a smile to her face, reminding her to pause and catch a few large snow flakes on her tongue. Enjoying a simple dinner at home, she had cleaned up the kitchen, heating water for tea and lighting candles and incense before the arrival of her meditation group. Several people had stayed for a while after meditation to share support and to swap stories about their spiritual practices. As always, Deborah felt blessed by the emotional nurturing and spiritual intimacy of the group. Belonging to this community had made such a dramatic difference in her sense of well-being. No matter what kind of problem arose, her "beloveds" were always there with material, emotional, or spiritual support. And they knew they could always count on her in return. How wealthy she felt! As she walked outside with her departing friends, Deborah noticed that the sky had cleared, revealing a billion bright stars unobscured by urban street lights. Before bed, she opened a window slightly to admit the crisp winter air. Falling asleep to a coyote serenade, she said a silent prayer for the well-being of the planet.

What contrasts emerge as we compare a day in the life of Jamie and Deborah? Both work, own their homes and are materially comfortable. Yet, Jamie's day is hectic, stressful and long. She is never in touch with the natural world, interacting almost completely through electronic media. Her clothes, her furniture, her hair style, her house and car, all look exactly like those of the cohort she works with. She works, eats, exercises and sleeps in climate-controlled buildings that never allow fresh air or natural light to enter. Although she feels that she has many friends, she has no time to spend with them. Jamie is too busy and stressed even to receive the love and support of her own mother or sister. When she suffers from an all-too-frequent sense of loneliness and emptiness, she soothes herself with the impersonal distractions of binging on junk food, buying several new outfits through her personal shopper, having her house professionally redecorated, or planning a solo trip to a private luxury resort. She has excess money but derives little pleasure from spending it on herself, by herself. Her life is very full, and very empty.

Not only does Jamie lack a sense of spiritual meaning and purpose in her work, she has no time for close relationships that might help to fill this need. Sociologists and psychologists have recognized for many decades that such a lack of social integration can lead to alienation and despair.[39] While enjoying a high level of affluence and personal autonomy, Jamie and others like her are nevertheless statistically much more likely to commit suicide than those who are less autonomous and affluent, but who have stronger social ties. In addition to the need for social integration, biologists have documented in humans an innate, biological need for connection with the world of nature and natural processes.[40] When this need is denied, Jamie and others like her suffer physical and psychological imbalance leading to alienation and despair. The absence of strong social ties, combined with a lack of connection with nature, thus creates an even higher risk of depression and isolation. Such depression and isolation, in turn, can create and exacerbate addictions, eating disorders and other self-destructive syndromes which place sufferers such as Jamie at much higher risk for mental and physical stress-related diseases. And so the vicious cycle of malaise and addictive consumption continues. Accordingly, in the U. S. population, we see over 21 per cent of suicides committed by white men, who are the most economically and politically autonomous, yet the most disconnected from other humans and from nature. White men are over four times as likely to commit suicide as white women, and over ten times more likely than African American women, who have more limited social and economic choices yet much greater social connectedness.[41] We can see, then, that a high level of connection with others and with nature are strong protective factors against the stresses of post-modern life.

In contrast to Jamie's competitive, isolating and stress-filled day, Deborah enjoys a sense of spaciousness and calmness in her day. She spends a significant portion of her day with animals, getting her exercise in fresh air, sunlight and nature. She has many friends and makes a priority of devoting significant time to nurturing those relationships. She enjoys a strong sense of well-being due to the safety, belonging, and support shared by her community of close friends. Even though she has never been close to her biological relatives, Deborah feels that she is a vital member of a family, one formed by choice and mutual commitment rather than by blood ties or obligation. She meditates daily so that any accumulated stress is released from her nervous system. Deborah balances the time she spends on the computer with quality time alone or with friends. She seeks to balance the abundance in her life with service to others by helping the local homeless, teaching at the community college and volunteering her services in her religious congregation. She is not stressed that the stock market has taken a downward turn because her money is invested in local and international projects, with people who share her values and desire to help others. She has plenty of time to notice and appreciate the simple beauty and comfort of her home. Her life is not as busy as Jamie's, but is infinitely more full.

Jamie's strong ambition drives her to be successful economically, while Deborah defines success in spiritual terms. Her life is successful because she has a high degree of relational, as contrasted with material, wealth. Her lifestyle does not lack any material comforts, yet electronic appliances and an older car are at the background rather than the forefront of her life. She minimizes the amount of time and energy spent in acquiring and using such conveniences, keeping it available instead for those activities that increase her sense of connection with life: nurturing relationships within the context of a strong community, meaningful work, service to others, time alone and in nature, exercise, eating well and a spiritual practice that informs and enriches all of her activities. Because she takes care of her own needs in a balanced way, she has energy to focus on the needs of others.

Common sense would tell us that Deborah's lifestyle is healthier and more fulfilling than Jamie's, yet the opposite message is promulgated by our materialistic culture. We are bombarded by advertising telling us that the rewards of material consumption are intrinsically satisfying, an end in themselves. We consume as we are told, yet we find that, like the empty calories of synthetic food, such fleeting pleasures are ultimately devoid of any satisfaction. More hungry and depleted than ever, we become aware on some level that, in its hollowness and addictive self-perpetuation, materialism will never fulfil its promise of providing real nourishment to satisfy our craving. We long for a way to bridge the gap between those external, artificially-created desires and our true, innate need for connection, meaning and wholeness; a way to bring together spiritual principles with their enactment in everyday life. Gandhian economics provides such a way.

Gandhian Economics: A Framework for Spiritual Living

1. Introduction

We have argued that, even though spiritual living is an individual act based on one's values, it is not independent of a social framework. Some social frameworks promote and encourage spiritual living while others are inimical to it. In India, where spiritualism and a spiritual lifestyle have deep roots going back thousands of years, the ideal social framework is defined by an ashram, or residential spiritual community. Gandhi settled four ashrams: Phoenix and Tolstoy Farm in South Africa and Sabarmati and Sevagram ashrams in India. All of these ashrams were settled on wastelands; Sabarmati ashram was near the Sabarmati Central Jail. These ashrams, based on the principle of a joint family, provide an excellent framework for spiritual living because they offer the members both isolation and joint service, thereby providing both safety and inspiration. The ashram's lifestyle is now being replicated in modern centres of yoga and spiritual living.

Some of the basic requirements of ashram living follow from "voluntary simplicity" and joint family. Joint family living is in fact a major institution. It provides training and development of faculties that promote a spiritual lifestyle. Pyarelal describes the nature of joint family and the human qualities it requires: "where so many people with diverse tastes, habits and temperaments are cooped up day and night in a narrow space from week to week, month to month and year to year, it requires no little diplomatic skill, delicacy, tact, especially on the part of the head of the family, to maintain a healthy and sweet atmosphere. The members on their part have to develop the attitude of mutual help and regard, the capacity for give-and-take and adjustments to one another's idiosyncrasies. A single tactless remark, a slip of oversight, an uncouth habit, heedlessness or disregard of another's feelings may set people's nerves on edge and make life hell for the whole family. Competition in this narrow world is keen; even the youngsters feel the edge of it; little things assume big proportions; the slightest suggestion of unfairness or partiality gives rise to petty rivalries, jealousies and intrigues. To smooth them requires infinite patience, resourcefulness and knowledge of human nature. Delicate and conscientious care in the minutiae of everyday life or its lack can make in the narrow confines of the joint family all the difference between peace and discontent, happiness and misery."[42]

Gandhi learned a great deal from living in the joint family in the earlier years of his life and developed some of these principles for ashram living. The important point here is that joint living requires not only negotiating skills but a basic capacity for caring, loving, giving, and forgiving. It is this capacity to love, to give and to serve that is necessary for a spiritual life. It is not only Gandhi who learned these qualities everyone else who has lived in the community setting of a joint family or ashram comes into direct contact with these qualities.

The joint family institution provides a training ground for the capacity to love, to give and to serve. Once one learns to love, love is not confined only to the members of the family or ashram. It expands, naturally, to those beyond the immediate family or ashram. In the case of Gandhi Ashrams, their love took the form of *ahimsa* and non-killing of even poisonous snakes that abounded in all four ashrams. As Gandhi explains, "The ground, which had been a waste, was infested with snakes, and it was no small risk to live with little children under such conditions. The general rule was not to kill the snakes, though I confess none of us had shed the fear of these reptiles, nor have we even now. The rule of not killing venomous reptiles has been practised for the most part at Phoenix, Tolstoy Farm and Sabarmati. At each of these places we had to settle on waste land. We have had, however, no loss of life occasioned by snakebite."[43] In other words, if one learns to love people, one also learns to love nature and all that it entails.

We have talked of the joint family and ashrams as an institution for cultivating capacities to love, to give and to care. However, the joint family and ashram are not merely institutions based on simple relationships with other members and parts of nature, they are also important economic institutions which involve production and consumption of goods, investment and allocation of resources and outputs, strategies for productivity, efficiency, specialization and growth, mechanisms for trade with other similar institutions, formulations of incentives, etc. They therefore contain economic principles.

2. Gandhian Economics: Basic Principles

In addition to implementing the five principles of spiritual living articulated earlier, one can derive basic economic principles from the lifestyle in a joint family or ashram. Since Gandhi developed a number of ashrams in two different countries, his experiments provide a useful starting point. Because of our starting point, we have called the economic principles derived therefrom Gandhian economics. However, these basic principles are much more general and apply to a large variety of similar institutions. These principles are also derived from Gandhi's own life and, hence, have deeper roots in spiritual literature and practice. As he writes, "I must tell you in all humility that Hinduism, as I know it, entirely satisfies my soul, fills my whole being and I find a solace in the Bhagavad Gita and the Upanishads ... when disappointment stares me in the face, and when I see not one ray of light on the horizon, I turn to the Bhagavad Gita and find a verse to comfort me; and I immediately begin to smile in the midst of overwhelming sorrow. My life has been full of external tragedies, and if they have not left any visible and indelible effect on me, I owe it to the teachings of the Bhagavad Gita."[44] As Easwaran argues, spiritual principles are universal and can be found in many other places as well, such as the Sermon on the Mount or the Dhammapada.[45] To develop any economic system, especially a system based on spiritual values, one has to distinguish between three states: (a) the desired or ideal state, (b) a transition or path to this ideal state, and (c) the existing real state from which the transition begins.

The desired or ideal state is conceptual since it does not exist at the moment and one may question if it will ever exist. However, all spiritual thoughts believe in the existence of an ideal state: some after death, others here and now. Gandhian thought persists in the possibility of achieving this ideal state; otherwise, striving toward it is meaningless.[46] For the individual, this ideal state is *moksha, nirvana* in Buddhist language. For the society, it is *swaraj*. *Swaraj* has been misrepresented as independence but, in fact, it is a far more comprehensive concept. "The root meaning of *swaraj* is self-rule. *Swaraj* may, therefore, be rendered as disciplined rule from within ... 'Independence' has no such limitation. Independence may mean license to do as you like. *Swaraj* is positive. Independence is negative."[47]

Many times there is a serious problem in translating words from one language to another, and more so from one paradigm to the other. Since Gandhi was operating from the spiritual paradigm, Gandhian ideas can best be explained by the spiritual paradigm and get twisted when expressed in the scientific-rationalist paradigm.[48] As Gandhi says, "The word *swaraj* is a sacred word, a Vedic word, meaning self-rule and self-restraint, and not freedom from all restraints which 'independence' often means.[49] Self-rule and self-restraint are important elements of *swaraj*; these are important characteristics of spiritual living. Gandhi has developed the concept of *swaraj* in great depth; in fact, he titles his famous 1909 book, *Hind Swaraj*, which was banned by the then British colonial government.[50] *Swaraj* must thus satisfy two conditions: (i) self-realization for the individual, and (ii) political cum economic self-rule with proper restraints for groups of people at various levels: community and nation. The ruling principle in the ideal state is *satya* - Truth.

Gandhi and other spiritualists are particular about the transitional path. Conditions laid for this path are stringent indeed. The ruling principles are *satyagraha* and *ahimsa* – non-violence. The term non-violence does not do justice to *ahimsa* because *ahimsa* is positive, while non-violence is negative. *Ahimsa* is a quality of mind and action. It is directed to not only human beings but to the whole of nature, because the unity of life is the guiding fact. *Ahimsa* is not only the ruling principle for individuals, but also for communities and nations.[51]

Even though the principles of this transition stage are defined, their application depends on the third state of where we are. The existing state formulates all sorts of complications and constraints on the transitional process. The existing state defines the starting point, the context wherein various policies are articulated and formulated.

There is a good deal of material on these issues that is articulated in Gandhian economics.[52] Gandhian economics belongs to spiritualism. The fundamental distinction between Gandhian economics and Classical economics, of both the right and the Marxian variety, lies in the underlying assumptions about human being and human conduct and, therefore, its moral underpinnings. Gandhian economics is situated within a culture and its mores. While Capitalist and Marxian economics spans the left and right quadrants on the horizontal or X-axis, Gandhian economics extends over the vertical or Y-axis.[53]

In view of its embeddedness in culture, Gandhian economics is based on the construct of an idealized community, similar to the constructs of equilibrium and perfect competition. This idealized society is described as *Ram Rajya*: a society in which rulers, or decision makers, are asked to make decisions for the people because the decision makers have won their hearts, rather than their votes or legal authority. These conditions are based on the proposition that ends are contained in the means, so that means are important in themselves. This is contrary to the idea that "ends justify means."

In view of the obvious limitations of space and scope of this chapter, we refer only to the most basic principles in Gandhian economics.[54] Diwan has formulated six basic concepts of Gandhian economics: (i) *swadeshi*; (ii) bread labour; (iii) *aprigraha*; (iv) trusteeship; (v) non-exploitation; and (vi) equality.[55] All these concepts are related, with no hierarchy among them. They all have spiritual underpinnings and are equally important. And, all these concepts are integrally related to the five principles of spiritual living, as described above.

Swadeshi follows from *swadharma*: spiritually-defined duty. *Swadeshi* – loosely translated as self-reliance in a place – is *swadharma* applied to one's community at a particular place and environment. *Swadeshi* is a policy/strategy set that enriches *swadesh*. *Swadesh* is defined by (i) a community or nation; e.g., the U.S., its geography, heritage, history, traditions, etc. and (ii) its people. *Swadeshi* has, therefore, two defining economic conditions: those that enrich (a) the community or nation not only in terms of an increase in its GNP, but also the quality of its ecological environment, and (b) its people, implying an increase in their real wealth in terms of materials, social relations and ecology. The local environment being one of its fundamental parts, *swadeshi* is highly ecological and a necessary condition for ecological sustainability. It implies a downward shift in cost functions.

Bread labour provides the ethical dimension to *swadeshi* at the level of personal action. One cannot be self-reliant or obtain *swaraj* if one is unable to produce necessities of life by one's own labour. This concept generates the distinction between "values-in-use" and "values-in-exchange" and "values-in-threat," as well as between "stranger-defined-work" and "self-defined-work."[56] This contrasts with the concept of employment. It defines the set of commodities that a community will produce.

Aprigraha is "willing surrender" or non-possession, which is also "possession by all." It means that a person must not possess anything that one does not need and that someone else needs.[57] The Gandhian concept of theft is based on *aprigraha*. "I suggest we are thieves in a way. If I take anything that I do not need for my own immediate use and keep it, I thieve it from someone else ... so long as we have got this inequality, so long we are thieves."[58] *Aprigraha* implies a demand function, with an increase in the level of minimum consumption combined with a general lowering of the price level.[59]

Trusteeship is best described as *sauchi* - purity of character. It is a real reflection of *swaraj*. Trusteeship is laced with spirituality and requires personal integrity, honesty and sensitivity. Gandhi's life is an example of such personal character and trusteeship. It follows from and builds on *aprigraha*. It means that everyone who possesses any capability, natural gift, etc. must regard it as a gift from God and use it only for the benefit of all. In other words, these capabilities should not be used for personal profit, privilege and power. "If the trusteeship idea catches, philanthropy as we know it will disappear ... A trustee has no heir but the public."[60] Trusteeship implies a negative relationship between privilege and decision-making power.[61]

Non-exploitation follows from trusteeship and the transitional *ahimsa* principle. It is both a simple and a complex concept. It is simple at the ethical level because it is obvious. No ethical person wishes to exploit anyone. It is also complex because exploitation takes forms in which it is not so obvious. One can argue that the very principle of survival of the fittest, of competition and, therefore, of the market where strangers meet to get the best price, is exploitative. "There can be no living harmony between races and nations unless the main cause is removed, namely, exploitation of the weak by the strong. We must revise the interpretation of the so-called doctrine of the survival of the fittest."[62] This involves a complex system of subsidies that shifts the price vector by lowering the prices of necessities and raising those of luxuries.[63] Equality follows from non-exploitation and yet is a goal in itself. Inequality is, itself, a form of exploitation.[64]

3. Gandhian vs. Mainstream Economics

By now, it will be clear that Gandhian economics, based as it is on different assumptions and ethical principles, is very different from the mainstream economics taught in college text books. For example, these concepts define different types of affluence: material versus relational. This distinction between two different types of wealth explains the divergence between a growing GDP and the declining quality of life in industrialized countries.[65]

The institutions through which policies following from Gandhian economics operate are: (a) ideas that (i) there is a "unity of life" including all matter, living and inert; (ii) human beings are more than physical bodies, and (b) organizations: (i) family, (ii) face-to-face communities in a particular place - a family needs, for its sustainability and even existence, a functioning community - and (iii) larger population units made up of such communities. Because of the importance of these institutions, the economic principles imply "production by masses" instead of "mass production," or "small is beautiful" instead of "economies of scale."

Though the emphasis here is on the local level, it relates to the global economy. Such a global economy is made up of concentric circles, each defined by community economy. Global issues are relevant even for community problems because of the Gandhian propositions that (i) there is an elite-mass contradiction in every society, and (ii) local elite exploit local masses, while international elite exploit people all over the world.

The role of government in Gandhian economics is to develop and maintain these institutions. Since the object is to strengthen communities, the government must promulgate laws that promote decentralized decision making.

The test of every policy is not profit, employment, or growth but, instead, how it strengthens family and community and, through it, character and sensitivity. The world today is suffering from many problems: ecological distress, family breakdown, economic inequality, crime, etc. The basic cause of all these problems is the destruction of communities. The research agenda, for the present and immediate future, is to formulate policies based on Gandhian economics in order to regenerate communities and ensure sustainability.

It is not possible, in this chapter, to go through all the major differences between Gandhian and Mainstream economics. We present below in tabular form, partly for illustrative purposes, differences between these two schools:

Table 2: Differences between Gandhian and Mainstream Economics

Issue	Gandhian	Mainstream
Resources	Abundant	Scarce
Human Image	Body, mind, and soul	Body and mind
Emphasis	Community	Individualism
Objective	Service and sharing	Self-Interest
Philosophy	Small is beautiful[66]	More/Bigger is better

Issue	Gandhian	Mainstream
Mechanism	Enough Trustees	Maximization Entrepreneur
Effect	Non-Exploitative Equality	Exploitative Inequality
Wealth	Relational	Material
Production	Values in use and exchange	Values in exchange and threat
Problems[67]	Divergent	Convergent
Measures	Quality of Life	Standard of Living
Institutions	Decentralized communities	Market
Human Character	Self-reliant	Dependent/alienated
Ecological Impact	Enhancement	Destructive[68]

It may be useful to debunk some myths. The most important myth is TINA: There Is No Alternative to the existing system. All imperial societies have promoted such a myth. In simple language, it is a myth about the legitimacy of power and is formalized by the logic that, if it exists, it must be right.

Since the present system has both strengths and weaknesses, advantages and disadvantages, successes and failures, there is a need for an alternative. TINA needs to be replaced by BINA: Bring In New Alternatives. There is a genuine place here for Gandhian economics on both the intellectual and policy planes.

The other myth is that the present system based on mainstream economics is rational. There is nothing further from the truth. The current system is anything but rational. In fact, it is highly irrational. One need only observe any particular phenomenon to recognize the fact of irrationality.

A few examples will elucidate this irrationality:

(i) Look at the decline in urban areas all over the U.S. Here are economic principles virtually making housing investments worth trillions of dollars obsolete; a whole lifestyle based on urban America archaic to the point of causing major harm to many industries, houses, communities, local governments, etc. By comparison, look at the suburban sprawl; a lifestyle being defined as unsatisfying even by those who admire it[69]

(ii) Look at the ecological wasteland that industrial progress has created. Scholars are now redefining progress.[70] The Worldwatch Institute brings out the facts about ecological degradation on a regular basis through its books, occasional papers and bi-monthly magazine. The evidence is overwhelming. Gore states emphatically, "The hard truth is that our economic system is *partially blind.* It 'sees' some things and not others. It carefully measures and keeps track of the values of those things most important to buyers and sellers, such as food, clothing, manufactured goods, work, and, indeed, money itself. But its intricate calculations often completely ignore the value of other things that are harder to buy and sell: fresh water, clean air, the beauty of the mountains, the rich diversity of life in the forest, just to name a few. In fact, the partial blindness of our current economic system is the single most powerful force behind what seems to be irrational decisions about the global environment."[71]

(iii) Or look at even the narrow issue of air travel. The fares have no relevance to any travel characteristic: distance, time, space, congestion, etc. To justify what goes on in the airline industry as rational decision, one has to develop a confusing, complicated, convoluted argument.[72]

The other side of such myths is that a Gandhian economy is impractical and simplistic, so that it will result in a return to the non-technological lifestyles of the past. However, when one looks at the facts, one immediately recognizes the falsity of this proposition. Let us look at the impracticality argument. Gandhi responds, "This world is held together by bonds of love. History does not record the day-to-day incidents of love and service. It only records incidents of conflict and war. Actually, however, acts of love and service are much more common in this world than conflicts and quarrels. We find innumerable villages and towns flourishing in the world. If the world was always full of quarrel and discord, they could not possibly exist."[73] He continues, "I claim that, even now, though the social structure is not based on the conscious acceptance of non-violence, all over the world mankind lives and men retain their possessions on the sufferance of each other. If they had not done so, only the fewest and most ferocious would have survived."[74] Gandhian economic rules thus are far more practical than those of mainstream economics.

Gandhian economic policies to create, sustain and strengthen families and communities will require a major investment of resources, easily to the tune of thousands of trillions of dollars. Such policies will also need highly sophisticated technologies that can deal with multiple objectives, and will require redesigning houses, transport systems, agricultural systems, etc.

Conclusion

We began this chapter by documenting the debilitating post-modern malaise which increasingly defines life in the world's wealthy, post-industrial countries. Since this malaise is most characterized by its emphasis on materialism, we looked to a viable antidote, spirituality, for direction and potential solutions. We noted that spiritual solutions could ultimately be meaningful only if they were able to be enacted in daily life.

In exploring the theory and practice of creating a spiritually-oriented life, we identified five essential elements of spiritual living: abiding by the Golden Rule, or "doing unto others as you would have others do unto you;" an appreciation and respect for all life forms; a commitment to non-violence; the inseparability of means and ends; and the creation and sustenance of a strong community. We contrasted a day in the life of two actual women to illustrate the differences between a spiritually-oriented lifestyle and the more typical post-modern materialist lifestyle.

Next, we explored the theory and practice of a spiritual life through the principles of Gandhian economics. We endorsed the Gandhian assertion that individuals are best able to engage in spiritual living within a supportive social context, such as the ashram or joint family. We noted that a community such as the joint family is not only a relational institution but also an important economic institution, which therefore contains economic principles.

Six basic principles of Gandhian economics were articulated: *swadeshi*, or self-reliance of a community in a particular place; bread labour; *aprigraha*, or willing surrender by the individual and shared possession by the community; trusteeship; non-exploitation; and equality. We noted that, in implementing these Gandhian principles, it is necessary to define the desired or ideal state to which we aspire a transition or path to this ideal state, and the existing real state from which we are starting.

We contrasted the assumptions of Gandhian economics with those of mainstream economics, debunking the commonly accepted myths that: 1) TINA - There Is No Alternative to the existing system, and 2) that the present system is rational. As examples of this irrationality, we cited the economic nonsense of urban decline accompanied by suburban sprawl, the ecological degradation created by industrial consumerism, and the blatant contradictions of the air travel industry. We offered evidence refuting the other side of such myths, which charge that Gandhian economics is impractical and overly simplistic, threatening to negate the material advances of the high-tech lifestyle. We ended on a hopeful yet cautionary note, stating that, although imminently practical, the theory and practice of spiritual living through Gandhian economics will require major changes in terms of policy development, funding priorities and the applications of technology.

Acknowledgements

An earlier version of this chapter was presented as a paper at the Eastern Economic Association Annual Meeting in Crystal City, Virginia on March 25, 2000. A condensed version has also been prepared for presentation at the IAREP/SABE 2000 Conference in Vienna, Austria, July 12-16, 2000.

The authors wish to thank those who have given feedback and helpful suggestions, particularly Professor John F. Tomer of Manhattan College, New York, for his many insights on social capital and well-being.

Notes and References

1. The concept of social capital is explored extensively in Robert Putnam, *Making Democracy Work: Civic Traditions in Modern Italy*, Princeton: Princeton University Press, 1993, and in his article, "Bowling Alone: America's Declining Social Capital," in *Journal of Democracy* Vol. 6, No.1, January 1995, pp. 65-78. Simply stated, social capital is the communal trust enjoyed by a society that facilitates coordination and cooperation for mutual benefit, p. 67.

2. Romesh Diwan, "Gandhian Economics: Enoughness as Real Wealth," in Trent Schroyer (Ed.), *A World that Works: Building Blocks for a Just and Sustainable Future*, New York: Bootstrap Press, 1997, pp. 86-91

3. *Ibid.*, p. 86.

4. Elizabeth Bethea, *A Critical Mass: The Psychology of Social Change*, Ann Arbor: UMI, 1999, especially Chapter IV, "Old Wisdom, New Paradigm;" pp. 49-63.

5. This assertion of the fundamental unity of life has been explicated by scholars from all prominent spiritual traditions. For examples of classic statements from diverse perspectives, please see Eknath Easwaran, *The Compassionate Universe: The Power of the Individual to Heal the Environment*, Petaluma, CA: Nilgiri Press, 1989; M. K. Gandhi, *An Autobiography. The Story of My Experiments with Truth*, Boston: Beacon Press, 1957; Aldous Huxley, *The Perennial Philosophy*, New York: Harper and Row, 1990; and William James, *The Varieties of Religious Experience*, New York: Signet, 1958.

6. Romesh Diwan and Kerstin Gollner, "Rational vs. Relational Paradigms," Paper presented at the annual meeting of the Eastern Economic Association, New York: Feb-March 1998, p. 22.

7. John F. Tomer, "An Inquiry into the Nature of Well-being: The Importance of Personal and Social Capital," paper presented at the Eastern Economic Association Conference in Crystal City, VA on March 25, 2000, p. 21.

8. For extensive documentation of the economic manifestations of this post-industrial malaise, please see Diwan, 1997 *op.cit.*, Romesh Diwan, "Gandhi, the US and the World: A Bridge to the Twenty- First Century", *Gandhi Marg,* Vol. 20, No.3, October December I998, pp. 291-312; Peter F. Drucker, *The Post-Capitalist Society,* New York: Harper Collins, 1993; Hazel Henderson, *Paradigms in Progress: Life Beyond Economics*, Indianapolis: Knowledge Systems 1991; Hazel Henderson, *Building a Win-Win World: Life Beyond Global Economic Warfare*, San Francisco: Berrett-Koehler, I996; Trent Schroyer (ed.), *A World that Works: Building Blocks for a Just and Sustainable Future,* New York: The Bootstrap Press, 1997; and Marilyn Waring, *If Women Counted: A New Feminist Economics,* San Francisco: Harper Collins, 1988.

9. The great existential philosopher and psychiatrist, Viktor Frankl, *Man's Search for Meaning: An Introduction to Logotherapy,* Boston: Beacon Press, 1959, documents the manifestations of this malaise at a personal level, noting that its ultimate resolution is found only through the discovery of transcendent, spiritual meaning or purpose, rather than through any material solution.

10. For instance, the Justice Policy Institute, in a report titled "The Punishing Decade: Prison and Jail Estimates at the Millennium," notes that, by the end of the year 2000, the U. S. will have spent $41 billion in public monies to operate prisons and jails. The growth in the imprisoned population skyrocketed during the 1990s, exceeding that of the 1980s by 61 per cent and showing an increase of nearly 30 times the average prison population growth of any decade prior to the 1970s.

11. Figures for this section derived from U.S. National Center for Health Statistics, *Monthly Vital Statistics Report*, September, 1997; John J. Macionis, *Sociology* (7th edn.), Upper Saddle River, NJ: Simon and Schuster/Prentice Hall, 1999, pp. 529-551; and *U.S. News and World Report,* December 11, 1995.

12. Michael D. Kelleher, *Profiling the Lethal Employee: Case Studies of Violence in the Work Place*, Westport, CT: Praeger 1997, Joseph A. Kinney, *Violence at Work: How to Make Your Company Safe for Employees and Customers*, Englewood Cliffs, NJ: Prentice Hall, 1995, and Debra Niehoff, *The Biology of Violence: How*

Understanding the Brain, Behaviour and Environment Can Break the Vicious Circle of Aggression, New York: The Free Press 1999, document the pervasive manifestations of violence in the workplace in the U. S.

13. Analyses of the costs of workplace violence are found in Kelleher, 1997, and Kinney, 1995.

14. Richard J. Gelles, 1984, quoted in Macionis, 1999, *op.cit.*, p. 472.

15. Statistics on divorce, domestic violence, child abuse and child poverty from Macionis, 1999, pp. 453-477.

16. The conservative/liberal debate around whether voter apathy stems from indifference (because people are generally content with their lives) or from alienation (because people doubt that participating in elections will make any difference in the *status quo*) is covered in Macionis, 1999, pp. 438-9

17. Crime statistics from U. S. Federal Bureau of Investigation, 1997, cited in Macionis, 1999, pp. 219-224.

18. For alternatives to the explanations traditionally offered by classical economics, please see Diwan, 1998, *op.cit.*; Henderson, 1991, 1996 *op.cit.* Schroyer, 1997 *op.cit.*

19. Emile Durkheim, 1858-1917, is considered by many social scientists to be the founder of modern sociology. His ground-breaking research into the phenomenon of suicide continues to maintain its validity 100 years later.

20. Suicide statistics from U. S. National Center for Health Statistics, cited in Macionis, 1999, *op.cit.*, pp. 4-5.

21. Secular leaders such as Al Gore and religious leaders such as H.H. the Dalai Lama and Thich Nhat Hanh have explored the spiritual dimensions and implications of post-modern malaise and have offered potential solutions involving the spiritual realm. For details see Al Gore, *Earth in Balance : Ecology and the Human Spirit*, New York: Plume Edition, 1992 and Thich Nhat Hanh, *For a Future to be Possible: Commentaries on the Five Wonderful Precepts*, Berkley: Parallax Press, 1993.

22. A tremendous literature on spirituality exists in the popular realm, for example, the work of physicists Fritjof Capra, Paul Davies, and Gary Zukav, physicians Deepak Chopra, Don Miguel Ruiz, and Andrew Weil, and spiritual teachers Swami Chidvilasananda,

Eknath Easwaran, Matthew Fox, and Ram Dass, to name but a few.

23. Bethea, 1999 *op.cit.*, explores the tenets of traditionally spiritually-oriented societies from an historical and cross-cultural perspective, pp. 49-63.

24. Please refer to Endnote 5.

25. The concept of *praxis*, or theory into action, is defined and explicated in Bethea, 1999, *op cit.*

26. Diwan, at The Other Economic Summit, 1997, noted that consumption is a part of life, not the point of life. Also see Diwan and Gollner, 1998 *op.cit.*

27. Diwan "Gandhian Economics: Enoughness as Real Wealth," pp. 86-91. in Schroyer, 1997, *op.cit.*

28. Eisler explores the ancient transition from social systems organized around cooperation and partnership to those based on competition and domination. She proposes that a return to the partnership model of society is currently necessary for the creation of global integrity and sustainability. This point is developed further in Bethea, 1999, *op.cit.*, in terms of representing a *metaparadigm* shift which theoretically overlays the current *linear* paradigm shift from post-industrialism to the information economy.

29. Economists such as Henderson, 1991, 1996 *op.cit.*, and Schroyer, 1997 *op.cit*, have proposed alternatives to popular scarcity-based models of economics. Diwan, 1997, *op.cit*, p. 86, quotes Gandhi in noting that the Earth provides enough to satisfy every person's need, but not one person's greed.

30. Tenets of Hinduism articulated by Romesh Diwan at Eastern Economic Association Conference, Crystal City, VA, March 25, 2000.

31. Hinman explores the moral implications of choosing violent actions. Bethea, 1999, *op.cit.*, pp. 54-55, notes that the element of choice is a critical factor in both secular and religious conceptualisations of ethics.

32. *Webster's Collegiate Dictionary*, Tenth Edition, 1999, p. 1319.

33. The problematic tendency of humans to *overkill* is woven throughout much of the scientific coverage of ecological problems, including Fritijof Capra, *The Web of Life: A New Scientific Understanding of Living Systems,* New York: Anchor Books,

Doubleday, 1996; S.R Kellert and Edward O Wilson (eds.), *The Biophilia Hypothesis*, Washington, DC: Island Press/ Shearwater Books, 1993.

34. See note 22. Also see Pam McAllister, *Reweaving the Web of Life: Feminism and Nonviolence*, Philadelphia: New Society Publishers, 1982 and Thomas Merton, *Gandhi on Nonviolence*, New York: New Directions, 1964.

35. See Diwan in Schroyer, "Gandhian Economics: Enoughness as Real Wealth", 1997, *op.cit*., pp. 86-91, for extensive coverage of this concept.

36. For discussion of this point from a feminist perspective, please see Bethea, 1999, *op. cit*., p., and Stanley, 1990, *op. cit.*

37. Holly Near, 1985.

38. See note 27. Also see Easwaran, 1978, *op.cit*., McAllister, 1982, *op.cit*., and Merton, 1964 *op.cit*.

39. From Emile Durkheim's classic work, *Suicide,* New York: Free Press, 1966..

40. Biophilia, the innate human need for deep connection with nature and natural processes, is explored in depth in, S.R. Kellert and E.O. Wilson (eds), *op.cit.*

41. US National Centre for Health Statistics, 1996 in Macionis, 1999, *op.cit*., p.5.

42. Pyarelal, *Mahatma Gandhi , The Early Phase*, Vol. 1, Ahmedabad: Navajivan, 1965, p.193.

43. Gandhi, 1957, *op.cit*., pp. 429-430. Gandhi, and anyone who is able to extend the capacity to love even poisonous creatures, believed that these creatures will , in their turn, not harm one because this is the spiritual law and the meaning of God. In an instructive way, Gandhi continues, "Even if be a superstition to believe that complete immunity from harm for twenty five years in spite of a fairly regular practice of non-killing is not fortuitous accident but a grace of God, I should still hug that superstition". p.430

44. C.F . Andrews, *Mahatma Gandhi's Ideas*, London: George Allen & Unwin, 1949, pp.72-73.

45. Eknath Easwaran, *Bhagavad Gita for Daily Living, To Love is to Know Me*, Vol.. 3, Petaluma, CA: Nilgiri Press, 1984.

46. In fact, all saints believe in the existence of such an ideal state. It is because of this belief that Gandhi is called a Mahatma, or saint. Huxley, 1944 *op.cit.*, not only assumes its existence, but finds sufficient evidence in its favour.

47. *Collected Works of Mahatma Gandhi (CWMG)*, Vol. 45, New Delhi: Publications Division, Government of India, p.263.

48. This problem of interpretation through a different paradigm is quite serious. Scholars from the spiritual paradigm find very different meanings in the same words and ideas than those from the scientific-rational tradition. An important recent example is from Frawley's study of *Rig Veda*. "Most of the translations and interpretations of the *Rig Veda* used today were produced by nineteenth century European scholars. Their work often reflects the bias of their times; the imperialism, materialism and Christian missionary spirit, the tendency to look upon Asia and its cultures as inferior, to even blame the spiritual traditions of Hinduism and Buddhism for the political decline of these cultures... If the *Rig Veda* is a spiritual document, we cannot expect that it can be understood by an interpreter who has no sense of the spiritual. To examine an object, we must have the sensitivity for what it is. We do not look to a chemist to judge a great painting. Hence we should not look to intellectual scholars to understand the mystery religions of the ancient world. Nor should we be surprised if they fail to appreciate them or *even degrade them*" David Frawley, *Wisdom of the Ancient Seers- Mantras of the Rig Veda*, Salt Lake City: Passage Press, 1922, p.25.

49. *CWMG*, Vol. 45, p.264. Emphasis added.

50. Gandhi felt so sure of his views that he added, "After the stormy thirty years through which I have since passed I have seen nothing to make me alter the view expounded in it" . See M.K.Gandhi,. *Hind Swaraj or Indian Home Rule*, Ahmedabad: Navajivan, 1939, p.18.

51. There is a serious misunderstanding among certain intellectual circles about the meaning of *ahimsa* for nations and communities. It is not as simple as offering the other cheek and never defending the community. Discussion on this issue, however, deserves a large paper.

52. A brief description of Gandhian Political Economy appears in Romesh Diwan "Gandhian Political Economy" in Philip O' Hara

(ed.) *Encyclopedia of Political Economy*, Routledge, 1999, pp.937-39.

53. Huxley, 1944 *op.cit*; E.F. Schumacher, *Small is Beautiful: Economics as if People Mattered*, New York: Harper and Row, 1973 articulate its reasoning in philosophical terms.

54. For further details one may refer to Romesh Diwan and Mark Lutz,(eds.) *Essays in Gandhian Economics*, New Delhi: Gandhi Peace Foundation, 1985, Diwan and Gollner, 1998 *op.cit.*; Romesh Diwan, "Gandhian Economics and Contemporary Society" in Ramjee Singh and S. Sundaram (eds.), *Gandhi and the World Order*, New Delhi: APH, 1996; Diwan 1998, *op.cit.* and Romesh Diwan "Mahatma Gandhi, Amartya Sen and Poverty" *Gandhi Marg*, Vol. 20, No.4, January-March 1999, pp.421-444; These contain references to more literature.

55. Romesh Diwan, "The Economics of Love: Or an Attempt at Gandhian Economics, *Journal of Economic Issues*, Vol. 16, No.2, June 1982 conceptualizes these concepts mathematically and formulates them in the current economic idiom.

56. It is discussed at length in `Economics of Bread Labour," chapter 7, in Diwan and Lutz, 1985, *op.cit.*

57. It may be useful to recognize that there is a fine distinction between ownership and possession; ownership being mostly notational or legal, while possession is the actual fact that ensures use. Ownership may also imply possession.

58. M.K. Gandhi, *Socialism of My Conception*, Edited and Published by Anand T. Hingorani, Bombay: Bharatiya Vidya Bhavan, 1966, p. 45.

59. The argument is developed in Diwan, 1982, *op.cit.*

60. Gandhi, 1966, *op.cit.* , p. 271. From *Harijan*, April 12, 1942 in an answer to a question.

61. The argument is developed in Diwan, 1982, *op.cit.*

62. Sabarmati Sangrahalaya, Ahmedabad #13117. March 20, 1928.

63. The argument is developed in Diwan, 1982, *op.cit.*

64. Diwan 1999 *op.cit.,* analyzes the concept of poverty based on the concept of inequality, domination, and exploitation.

65. Diwan and Gollner, 1998, *op.cit.* discuss these differences at greater length.

66. Schumacher, 1973, *op.cit*, is titled such and explains the idea in great detail.

67. E.F. Schumacher, *A Guide for the Perplexed*, New York: Harper and Row,1977 makes a fine distinction between convergent problems in which the solution eventually is the same, and divergent problems in which two persons can, and do, reach completely opposite conclusions.

68. There is now ample evidence on this fact. Gore, 1992, *op.cit.* and Edward O. Wilson, *In Search of Nature*, Washington.DC:, Island Press, 1996.

69. As Karl Weisser, "Suburban Sprawl Issue Reaches Halls of Congress" , *Times Union,* Albany, NY: July 5, 1998, p. B1 argues, the sprawl is now becoming a major issue, being talked about by Presidential candidates.

70. Clifford Cobb et al, "If the GDP is Up, Why is America Down?" *Atlantic Monthly*, October, 1995, pp.59-78..

71. Gore, 1992, *op.cit.*, pp. 182-3. Emphasis added.

72. This paper does not permit further exploration of this argument. Suffice it to add that one can find an equally credible case to explain it on the basis of monopoly power and the nature of technology.

73. Gandhi, 1966, *op.cit.*, p. 12, *To Ashram Sisters*, p. 113

74. *Ibid.*, p. 15, *Harijan*, Feb. 22, 1942.

6

Gandhi on Modernity : A Revisionist Paradigm

K. Raghavendra Rao

(A biographical note seems called for. Human beings are kept happy and hopeful through coincidences and contingencies that characterise even the most planned life. When I was a student of English Language and Literature during 1945-48 at Madras Christian College, Tambaram, years of nationalist turbulence, I recall listening to a stirring speech on the campus by Shri Ravindra Varma – I am not sure whether he was still a student but had left college or was visiting the campus as a young Congress student leader. I have a vivid memory of him, clad in khadi , bursting with youthful energy, delivering a highly charged patriotic speech. I do not remember the content of the speech but only its fury and force and the short figure from whose mouth the speech was rushing out. Even now I have a fairly clear picture of the event. I consider it an honour and pleasure to write something in his honour, and also regard it as commemorating that exciting history.)

I

As a professional academic I have been moving around, into and above Gandhiji for the last four decades, finding him perpetually fresh and challenging. At the end of a long journey into the Gandhi territory, I have come to the conclusion that one of the gravest mistakes committed by me and several others was to banish Gandhiji from the modernist camp without qualification by branding him as an arch enemy of modernity. Now it seems clear to me that it was a mistake both in intellectual strategy and in the theoretical interpretation of Gandhiji. This sharp exiling of Gandhiji from the world of modernity was no doubt due to the 1960s reification of modernity in American sponsored discourse as antithetical to tradition. Subsequent attempts to establish logical and historical connection between modernity and tradition went to the other extreme of obliterating all distinction between the two. For instance, the Rudolphs, attempted to argue that Gandhiji was, in fact, an agent of modernity.[1] But this was obviously untenable since the idea of modernity they used was really incompatible with the Gandhian position. More recently, the emergence of the so-called post-modernity discourse has opened up the possibility of alternative paradigms of modernity to the dominant American one, which had identified modernity virtually with the American reality. Today , it is possible to suggest alternative paradigms of modernity. If this is carried out, Gandhiji can be shown to be an exemplar of one or some of these paradigms. In the first part, I propose to look at these alternative paradigms or models, relying on the historically and conceptually innovative work of the philosopher of science, Stephen Toulmin, which came out as recently as in 1990.[2] I shall also complement his alternative paradigms within the Western history with some indigenous paradigms of modernity recoverable from our own history and tradition, In the second part, I shall try to relate these alternative paradigms of modernity to Gandhiji. In the brief and final third part, I shall try to focus on the essential claim and argument of this paper. Before going into the discussion properly, I want to make a minor but relevant point usually missed in discussions of Gandhiji. This is the simple point that, even if Gandhiji was opposed to modernity ideologically, as defined in the dominant paradigm, he had to make peace with modernity as an empirical-existential conditionality. He was constantly compelled, if not always consciously, to concede small victories for it. Being a very practical man of action, he had to reckon with the reality on the ground and calculate pragmatically the chances of executing his moral-ideological programme in an environment hostile to it.

Without going into the technical details with which Toulmin packs his text, it is enough for our purpose here to see the essence of his thesis. It should also be mentioned here that Toulmin is too modest a scholar to claim any finality for his position. While making a strong presentation of his case, he also leaves the matter open for further research and development. In the first place, he states that his intention is to rescue the project of modernity from the current destructive attack on it by the post-modernists, not by upholding the modernity paradigm they attack, but by returning to an alternative paradigm that was historically available as an option in the West but was not taken up in favour of the now attacked paradigm. Secondly, he argues that the West had generated historically two paradigms of modernity, one during the period of Renaissance humanism in the sixteenth century, and a second paradigm generated during the period of scientific revolution in the seventeenth century. However, it was the second paradigm that dominated history and thus led us to the present crisis of modernity, together with its negation, post-modernity. Thirdly, he argues that the solution is not to abandon the project of modernity as such but only the second paradigm. In other words, he advocates a return to the first paradigm and a reconstruction of our institutions on the basis of the first paradigm.

What then are these paradigms? Toulmin identifies the following central features of the Renaissance humanist paradigm of modernity : 1. Equal emphasis on rhetoric or the art of persuasion and logic, that is, persuasive presentation of truth and the logical construction of truth, orality and print textuality; 2. The emphasis on the particular as against the universal; 3. Emphasis on the local as against the general; and 4. Emphasis on the timely as against the timeless. All these four features of the epistemology implied in the first paradigm are interconnected. Orality and the need to take account of the addressee and the specificity of his circumstances leads logically to an emphasis on the particular and the detailed. This, of course, means that we need to take serious account of the local and the concrete. Finally, all the three culminate in an emphasis on historical contingency and specificity, on the time-bound as against the timeless. In a way, what this amounts to is to abandon the Platonic epistemology in favour of an Aristotelian realism. The seventeenth century rationalist and scientific revolution rejected this paradigm and established a new paradigm, a paradigm that emphasised textuality against orality, abstract and formal logic as against communicative effectivity, the universal against the local, and the ahistorical as against the historical determinate. Toulmin argues that the savage attack on modernity mounted by post-modernists and their nihilism and pessimism, are all directed against the second paradigm. Hence , the way out of the crisis is not to abandon modernity as such but only its second paradigm.

If we delink modernity from its allegedly universalistic second paradigm, as Toulmin would have us do, we need not go to the first paradigm of modernity spawned by the West. We have the other option of returning to our own indigenous paradigms. These were suppressed by the global conquest and dominance by the West. Today, we should attempt to rescue the indigenous paradigms so that we may avoid the historical fate of the dominant Western paradigm. We may also develop links with the first Western paradigm on the basis of intellectual equality. If this is done systematically, we will be in a position to insert Gandhi into the modernity discourse. What I propose to do now is a very tentative and hesitant theoretical and historical reconstruction, which may be further elaborated by more specialist expertise in the related fields of scholarship. I suggest that we can recognise three versions of modernity as embedded in our history and tradition, and on the basis of their collation we can construct an indigenous Indian paradigm of modernity. These three versions are : 1. The Buddhist which emphasised the crucial significance of individual experience and practice as against abstract theory but also rationality without absolutising it; 2. The medieval religious reformist Bhakti movement which emphasised equality, individual experience and also the need for the transcendental category of God; and 3. The more explicitly revolutionary Lingayat movement under the leadership of Basava in 12th century Karnataka that upheld a humanistic vision of life based on equality, individual rationality and community without abandoning the need for the transcendental categories of Godhood and grace. What is common to all the three versions is the assumption that human life is a value in itself but not an absolute value as it needs the supplement of the transcendental categories and therefore human beings need to engage in a continual activity of balancing the demands of reason and faith. This involves an emphasis on the moral nature of human experience which is subject to the rule of the good and the evil, and also the need for a choice between the two based on individual rational deliberation. But this is not sufficient since men need the benefit of divine grace. At the same time, mere divine grace is also not sufficient in the normal course of things, though exceptional situations cannot be ruled out. It is a paradigm which is not absolutely homo-centric and it is also not absolutely theo-centric. That is, why it constantly emphasises the balance between the faculties of reason and faith, and both are conceptualised as eminently human faculties. In an important sense, these versions can be accommodated within the larger framework of the classical Indian goals or *purusharthas* of *dharma, artha, kama* and *moksha* (morality, material gain, sensuality and spiritual liberation.)

We can now derive an indigenous Indian paradigm of modernity as follows. It may be conceptualised as having the following structural features

1. The value of human life here and now, as lived in space and time, but not as an absolute value,
2. Hence a recognition of human rationality as a basis for ordering a good human life,
3. The need for the transcendental values of God and grace, and hence the need for the human faculty of faith, and
4. The complementarity of man and God, reason and faith, time and the timeless and the particular and the universal , and history and the transhistorical.

It is obvious from this formulation that the Indian paradigm of modernity as conceptualised here is incompatible with all absolutisms whether religious or humanistic. One can see that this paradigm is pretty close to the Renaissance humanistic paradigm of modernity which is discussed by Toulmin in his path-breaking work.

II

In light of the alternative paradigms of modernity suggested above, we may proceed to examine Gandhiji's central positions and theoretical assumptions underlying them. The writings of Gandhiji are massive but their essence lies encoded in his most fundamental theoretical text, HIND SWARAJ , which was produced quite early in his life in 1909. We may legitimately assume that his subsequent writings should be read as securely anchored in this short text and that the later writings should be seen as minor modifications in detail or elaboration in response to practical application.

Two cardinal concepts underpinning this seminal text need to be noticed first. The first is the concept of reasoning as a basic individual faculty and its role as a tool for arriving at truth and for deriving practical wisdom from the perception of truth. Of course, this presupposes the larger notion of man as a rational being and his history as a record of the play of this rationality at both individual and collective levels. The second concept is the concept of God which is both the cause and effect of all that there was, is and can be. It is well known that Gandhiji later detranscendentalises the category of God by reversing the relationship between God and truth. Earlier he had held that God is truth but later he held that truth is God. This radicalised the category of God. It is my contention that both these concepts are compatible with the paradigms of modernity implied in Renaissance humanism and Indian religious humanism.

In the Preface to the first English version of the original Gujarati text of 1909, Gandhiji emphasises the role of reasoning as a subjective process in the formation of his text. But he does not equate this subjective process with originality, and explains that what had been dormant in him had become activated as a result of his reading of other texts. He puts this paradox in these words: "These views are mine, and yet not mine. They are mine because I hope to act according to them. They are almost a part of my being. But, yet they are not mine, because I lay no claim to originality. They have been formed after reading several books. That which I dimly felt received support from these books..."[3] While the notion of absolute subjective originality belongs to the homo-centric paradigm generated in the West in the 17th century, it is no part of either Renaissance humanism, or Indian religious humanism.

The two traditions conceptualise man as a conscious and rational agent without absolutising him by banishing the transcendental from human life. Therefore, Gandhiji's epistemology accords well with the paradigm of modernity presupposed in these two traditions.

Not only does Gandhiji emphasise subjective reasoning without absolutising it, he also regard it as a major source of human historical praxis, that is, as an important propeller of historical momentum. That is why, he can declare, "... As long as man is contented with his present lot, so long as it is difficult to persuade him to come out of it..." [4] In other words, man can make his history by his rational and critical ability. Gandhiji implies but does not explicitly state the position that modernisation cannot be equated with Westernisation, by imitating the English version of it. He puts it graphically and metaphorically thus, "....You want the tiger's nature, but not the tiger.: but that is to say, you would make India English..."[5] His rejection of the dominant Western paradigm of modernity is on the ground that it "takes note neither of morality nor of religion."[6] At this juncture, it needs to be noted that Gandhiji equates religion with morality, and also civilization with morality. And the modernity thus transformed is not a temporal concept but one based on fundamental value assumptions. The English version of modernity or modern civilization operates on the basis of a passion for money. It is a money-crazy and commercial civilization and is based on modernity rooted in that civilization.[7]

Gandhiji emphasises religion as central to his vision of civilisation and, by implication, his concept of modernity. But this is a position that is liable to be misunderstood by those committed to secular values, and hence needs some elaboration. By religion he does not mean any particular religion, but "that religion which underlies all religions.[8]" In other words, he refers to some essential and ideal category. Not only this, he also links religion with morality. In other words, he held that all religions were a composite of two parts – an essential and ideal part and an accidental and adventitious part. His version of modernity would regard as central only the first part. One of the most important concepts of the dominant paradigm of modernity, though not that of the two alternative paradigms suggested earlier, is the concept of the nation. Gandhiji does not reject it but radicalises it in his own direction by trimming it to suit his political ideals of a decentralized, small-scale polity and society. First he rejects the English and imperialist argument that India was not a nation before their arrival and then provides an alternative conception of the Indian nation. He writes, " ... The English have taught us that we were not one nation before and that it will require centuries before we become one..." [9] Gandhiji rebuts the imperial critique that India was not one nation because it was multi-religious.[10] He rejects the overintegrated model of the nation-state envisaged in the dominant Western paradigm of modernity, which tended to reduce diversities to uniformity and homogeneity in terms of culture, including religion. He further advances the global argument that no nation in the world was unireligious. He says, "...In no part of the world are one nationality and one religion synonymous terms: nor has it even been so in India.."[11]This loosely integrated concept of the nation follows logically from his emphasis on small-scale, relatively self-sufficient communities, enjoying substantial local political autonomy.

Of course, ultimately, the notion of modernity is a secondary and derivative construction based on larger categories like the nature of man, God and the cosmos. While the paradigm of modernity rejected by Renaissance humanism, Indian religious humanism and Gandhiji is based on the notion of man as an absolutely self-adequate creature and the cosmos as an instrument for man's self-aggrandizement characterised by an absence of God, the Gandhian modernity is founded on a creative but not absolute man and a cosmos which transcends man and regulates him through transcendental categories of God, grace and morality. For Gandhiji, man is limited physically by the nature and capacities of his body especially his hands and feet.[12] Man is also intellectually limited and hence he must be self-disciplined in terms of his claims to knowledge of both himself and the other.

This would naturally lead to a Gandhian emphasis on duties rather than rights and a need for self-mastery or *Swaraj*.[13] Indian civilization was based on these civilizational values and these values needed to be preserved in their essence. But this did not mean a critical indifference to the defects in the way Indian values had been historically distorted.[14] What Gandhiji is doing here is to separate out what he considered the ideal essences of Indian values from their existential contamination, and thus provide a critical perspective on these values. His discussion of the relationship between means and ends also reinforces this position.[15] One of the causes for the corruption at the level of values is the corruption of means. Indian values which are to serve as a foundation for an Indian paradigm of modernity should, therefore, be so practised that ends and means match within a unified moral framework.

The point he makes is that Indian critical operations must work within an Indian historical framework, and any external critique emanating from a framework outside this should at least take this framework into serious account. In Gandhiji's words, "In our own civilization there will naturally be progress, retrogression, reforms and reactions..."[16] In short, we need to be self-critical and this cannot be done without the exercise of critical rationality by individuals. If this is not modernity, what else can it be? If we miss this point, we are likely to misunderstand his advocacy of the virtues of rural simplicity or his defence of *Varnashrama* as attempts to justify them in their current corrupt form. In the last fifty years of our independent existence as a nation, we have practised the paradigm of modernity now critically rejected in the West itself and foolishly counterpoised Gandhiji to modernity in general. It is time now that we go back to our Gandhian foundations in search of a paradigm of modernity suited to our local needs.

III

In conclusion I may claim that I have shown that the Gandhi-modernity debate needs to be reopened, and located on a new theoretical plane. Most fundamentally and urgently, our paradigm of modernity has to answer the profound Gandhian question. Modernity for whose benefit? For the benefit of a handful of urban Westernised or for the benefit of the vast masses whether urban or rural? It will not do to starve and impoverish millions in the name of modernity by resorting to the trick of separating the question of modernity from the question of the welfare of our toiling masses. Any modernity, theirs or ours or anybody else's must wrestle with the great Gandhian challenge.

Notes and References

1. Susanne and Lloyd Rudolph, *The Modernity of Tradition*, Chicago : The University of Chicago Press, 1967.
2. Stephen Toulmin, *Cosmopolis*, Chicago: The University of Chicago Press, 1990.
3. All references to HIND SWARAJ are from Rudrangshu Mukerji, (ed.)*The Penguin Gandhi Reader,* New Delhi: Penguin Books India, , 1993, p.3
4. *Ibid*, p.11.
5. *Ibid*, p.12.
6. *Ibid*, p.20
7. *Ibid*, p.20.
8. *Ibid*, p.21.
9. *Ibid*, p.26.

10. *Ibid*, p.26.
11. *Ibid,* p.26.
12. *Ibid*, p.35.
13. *Ibid*, p.26.
14. *Ibid*, p.36.
15. *Ibid*, p.42.
16. *Ibid*, p.57.

7

Is a Gandhian World Social Order Desirable and Possible?

T.K.N. Unnithan

The popular image of Gandhi depicts him as an ardent nationalist who was engaged in selfless and dedicated service for the liberation of India from British colonial domination, through non-violent techniques of political action. This, indeed, is true. Gandhi was deeply involved in the struggle for political emancipation and social and economic reconstruction of India. And to that he devoted his whole attention. However, what is often not understood is that Gandhi did so in a world context. His contributions to Indian political independence should not be viewed as concerning only one or two nations in an isolated manner. Gandhi himself had said: "My mission is not merely the freedom of India, though today it undoubtedly engrosses practically the whole of my life and the whole of my time. But through the realisation of the freedom of India, I hope to realise and carry on the mission of brotherhood of man. My patriotism is not an exclusive thing. It is all-embracing and I should reject that patriotism which sought to mount upon the distress or exploitation of other nationalities."[1]

Gandhi's concept of patriotism embraced the entire human society. His fundamental ideas have a universality and they transcend national barriers. These broader, universalistic aspects of the Gandhian thought system and contributions are relatively less known. What are the specific universal and transcendental aspects of the Gandhian movement in a world context? Is it possible to visualise a Gandhian world social order based on the fundamental Gandhian principles of truth, non-violence and *sarvodaya*? What are the possibilities of establishing such a peaceful world social order in the context of nationalism and national sovereignties? An examination of these questions will constitute the core of the discussions that follow.

Gandhi's movement for national independence was, in a way, aimed at the reordering of world power-structure which was based on the imperialistic-colonialistic pattern of international relations. He wanted freedom for India, not to isolate her from the rest of the world, but to promote international cooperation. Because true international cooperation was possible only when the interacting nations were sovereign and equal before international law. In Gandhi's own words, "My notion of *Purna Swaraj*[2] is not isolated independence but healthy and dignified interdependence. My nationalism, fierce though it is, is not exclusive, not designed to harm any nation or individual. Legal maxims are not so legal as they are moral. I believe in the eternal truth of 'sic utere tuo ut alienum non laedas' - use thy own property so as not to injure thy neighbour's."[3] By ending colonialism he hoped to remove one of the root causes of exploitation and domination of weaker countries by stronger ones[4]. As Erik Erikson in his book, 'Gandhi's Truth' points out, Gandhi and the Indian nationalists maintained that British colonialism had resulted in the exploitation and draining of the Indian sub-continent in four areas of national life, the economic and political, cultural and spiritual.[5] Therefore, it is that Gandhi had declared, "We hold it to be a sin before man and God to submit any longer to a rule that has caused this four-fold disaster to our country."[6] As Erikson puts it, "While the British Empire may have promised to Indians and others a wider identity supervised by an elite of British choosing and training, it neglected to cultivate (as America neglected to do for the American Negro) those components of identity which neither a defined group nor an individual can do without and this is a "criminal" neglect indeed. It is the task of anti-colonial revolutions to transvaluate such a condition so that identity elements which nevertheless developed, and which at the time seemed more or less accidental, ornamental or expendable by-products of history, are turned into insignia of such pervasive dominance that to neglect them would be a sin in the face of existence. The case of India, then – or better, the case of England and India –is only the most extreme illustration of the historical trend known as colonialism: extreme in the magnitude of the population involved, in the distance between professed ideal and historical actuality, in the divergence of success achieved and disaster wrought, and in the perverse discrepancy of public glamour and degrading poverty."[7] Gandhi attacked the evil at its very root; he wanted to destroy the institution of colonialism, to begin with in India, and thereby put a stop to the 'fourfold exploitation' with a view to restore India's identity. Gandhi wanted to achieve this in a novel way through a non-violent revolution, through the *satyagraha* movement. Unlike the Marxist-Leninist line which undermines the individual role in history and maintains that an unjust social and economic system can be attacked by bringing the state under the dictatorship of the proletariat through a revolution, Gandhi held that "the root of the problem does not lie in the authority of the state, but in the character of the individual which has made the existence of that state possible."[8] Therefore, Gandhi set to bring about a radical transformation of the unjust social system not through coercion or through transference of power to a centralised state, but through individual reformation and non-violent social and political action. This he called the *satyagraha* movement, a movement led by a moral force which is generated by a sincere desire to follow the path of truth in individual behaviour and social action.[9] The significance of the concept of *satyagraha* lies in the integration of the philosophy of non-violence with a theory of social action.[10] Gandhi aimed at the implementation of moral ideals in social life and his doctrine of non-violence that guided the *satyagraha* movement was explained by him as "vindication of truth not by infliction of suffering on the opponent but one's own self."[11] *Satyagraha* was not merely an instrument for realisation of political, economic and other material ends but also a state of spiritual and moral self-transformation in man.[12] Through such a movement he strived to secure an India of his dreams, an independent India free from colonial domination, where individual behaviour and social action would be based on 'satyagraha', where the individual would have the integrity to contribute to a high moral order which would create and maintain social justice and harmony."[13]

After obtaining political independence Gandhi wanted India to become an ideal democracy. A democracy established on the principle of non-violence was to be of a unique kind. Gandhi's ideal non-violent democracy was a federation of decentralised, self-sufficient, self-administered, interdependent and cooperative village republics.[14] In such a democracy power was decentralised. In an ideal non-violent democracy of Gandhi's conception there was no need of a state. Gandhi had said, "Political power means capacity to regulate national life through representations. If national life becomes so perfect as to become self-regulated no representation become necessary. There is then a state of enlightened anarchy. In such a state everyone is his own ruler. He rules himself in such a manner that he is never a hindrance to his neighbour. In the ideal state, therefore, there is no political power, because there is no state."[15] But Gandhi knew the limitations in realising such an ideal. So he added, "But the ideal is never fully realised in life. Hence, the classical statement of Thoreau that that Government is best which governs the least."[16] Here Gandhi's 'anarchy' is not the one that leads to disorder but that which relates to a condition of statelessness as a result of the existence of an enlightened harmony that dispenses with the necessity of a state to enforce behaviour patterns. The power structure of a non-violent society would be distributed in such a way that each individual or each cooperative unit of individuals would constitute a power unit, and society would equilibrate itself on the basis of the existence of this power structure. In his ideal stateless democracy or enlightened anarchy there was no use of force in any form, whereas society acquired an equilibrium by individual perfection. Such a non-violent society would consist of groups of settled villages and life would be regulated through cooperation, bread-labour and mutual love.[17] Individuals in a non-violent society were to work for the establishment of a social order which ensured the greatest good of all.[18]

A non-violent India was expected to strive for removal of injustice anywhere and crusade for the cause of suffering humanity in any part of the world. Gandhi's patriotism "was not exclusive; it was calculated not only not to hurt another nation but to benefit all in the true sense of the word."[19] Gandhi had said that "we want freedom for our country, but not at the expense or exploitation of others, not so as to degrade other countries. I do not want the freedom of India if it means the extinction of England or the disappearance of Englishmen. I want the freedom of my country, so that other countries may learn something from my free country, so that the resources of my country might be utilised for the benefit of mankind. My idea of nationalism is that my country may become free, that if need be, the whole country may die so that the human race may live. There is no room for race hatred there. Let that be our nationalism."[20] His movements for self-government (*swaraj*) and for the use of home-made goods (*swadeshi*) might have come into conflict with the interests of other countries, especially those of England. But then Gandhi's movements were directed primarily against the injustices done by England in keeping another nation in subjugation by force, thereby denying it opportunities for free development. He believed that by enabling India to be free he was not only helping India but also Britain in an indirect way, i.e. by removing the possibility for England to be unjust to another nation. Besides, the moral strength which an independent India could give to other subject nations was another factor which convinced Gandhi that true nationalism was a contribution to internationalism."[21] Thus, Gandhi wanted national independence before international cooperation. "You want cooperation between nations for the salvation of civilization, I want it too, but cooperation presupposes free nations worthy of cooperation. If I am to help in creating or restoring peace and goodwill and resist disturbances thereof, I must have the ability to do so and I cannot do so unless my country has come to its own. At the present moment, the very movement for freedom in India is India's contribution to peace. For so long as India is a subject nation, not only is she a danger to peace, but also to England which exploits India. Other nations may tolerate today England's imperialist policy and her exploitation of other nations, but they certainly do not appreciate it; and they would gladly help in the prevention of England becoming a greater and greater menace every day. Of course, you will say that free India can become a menace herself. But let us assume that she will behave herself with her doctrine of non-violence, if she achieves her freedom through it and for all her bitter experiences of being a victim of exploitation."[22] Gandhi's prediction, indeed, came true. India's achievement of freedom generated a wave of nationalistic movements in many subjected nations. The Afro-Asian resurgence and realisation by colonial powers of the necessity to end colonial rule and the subsequent gaining of freedom by several countries could be linked with Gandhi's freedom movement.

Thus a colonialistically oriented world social structure has given way to a more democratically oriented one. The world power structure underwent a transformation in a non-exploitative direction. Yet the world is not devoid of exploitation, the old imperialistic colonialistic pattern of power structure has been replaced by new types of alignments and power blocs. The world society of today retains its feudal characteristics in spite of the fact that colonies have received their freedom. The economic domination of a few countries still indirectly influences the less affluent developing countries. The time lag in economic development and technical progress is fully utilised to compensate for the loss of colonial power or realise neo-imperialistic ambitions. Though every national independent state is sovereign and such sovereignty is respected and all states are treated as equals before international law, in actuality the world scene today is a big power gamble in spite of the existence of the United Nations. "It (the United Nations) has already revealed its impotence to settle any serious conflict among the great powers. The great and small powers ignore it in connection with most important problems – the United Nations has degenerated into a mere screen for the power politics of the artificial and incidental majority of world state. Having neither the moral authority nor adequate physical power, it cannot perform the miracle of eliminating war and erecting a temple of eternal peace."[23]

In this context a number of alternatives are thought of. Because wars and conflicts destroy human values and happiness, they continue to be of serious concern to human society. A world government by abolishing national sovereignties is talked of as an alternative. But as Sorokin maintains, "a large part of the movement for one world is a camouflaged imperialism of nations and groups bent on promoting their special economic, political and cultural interests and unwilling to make any genuine sacrifices on behalf of the cause of world government – the totality of the foregoing evidence is sufficient to prove why taken alone the establishment of a world government or the abolition of state sovereignty could in no way either eliminate or decrease war or lead to a just and lasting peace".[24]

It is in this connection that the Gandhian view of world social order merits consideration. Gandhi did not believe in the efficacy of a United Nations.[25] Because, " the United Nations, for all its virtues, is no help to creating, maintaining or enlarging the number of Gandhian states. The United Nations was established with few Gandhian principles which argue against its stateness."[26] A modern state with its military strength always possesses potentialities for suppression of freedom internally and creation of wars or international conflicts externally, establishment of a world state by merely extending the characteristics of a modern state, with or without surrendering national sovereignties would suffer from the deficiencies of the latter, viewed from a Gandhian angle. A world sovereign state above all national states may after all not be able to establish or maintain a peaceful world society in spite of the military strength or power it may possess. Gandhi's opposition to the U.N. is to be understood in this perspective. he was opposed to the U.N. in so far as it possessed the attributes of a nation-state in regard to military potential and in regard to its opposition to decentralization of power and freedom of human development. However, it may not be construed from this that Gandhi was totally opposed to any type of international organization. If the U.N.O. functioned on the basis of the Gandhian principles, Gandhi would not have difficulty in accepting the same. Gandhi, for example, had said, "The better minds of the world desire today not absolutely independent states warring one against another, but a federation of friendly interdependent states".[27]

"I would like to see India free and strong so that she may offer herself as a willing and pure sacrifice for the betterment of the world. The individual being pure sacrifices himself for the family, the latter for the village, the village for the district, the district for the province, the province for the nation, the nation for all."[28] "My religion has no geographical limits. There is no limit to extending our services to our neighbours across state-made frontiers."[29] "I believe that true democracy can only be an outcome of non-violence. The structure of a world federation can be raised only on a foundation of non-violence, and violence will have to be totally given up in world affairs".[30] In the words of Nehru, "Gandhi was an intense nationalist, he was also at the same time a man who felt he had a message not only for India but for the world, and he ardently desired world peace. His nationalism, therefore, had a certain world outlook and was entirely free from any aggressive intent. Desiring the independence of India he had come to believe that a world federation of interdependent states was the only right goal, however distant that might be".[31] Gandhi had said, "I do want to think in terms of the whole world. My patriotism includes the good of mankind in general. Therefore, my service to India includes the service of humanity. Isolated independence is not the goal of the world state. It is voluntary independence. I want to make no grand claim for our country. But I see nothing grand or impossible about our expressing our readiness for universal interdependence rather than independence. I desire the ability to be totally independent without asserting the independence".[32] Such a federation of independent sovereign states will not circumscribe the national state but would permit it full freedom, will remove the causes of friction and conflict that may arise from time to time and promote harmony and social justice. The Gandhian model of power distribution in a national or world context is enunciated in the following statement which Gandhi made in elucidating his concept of decentralized state power. "There will be ever-widening never ascending circles – at last the whole becomes one life composed of individuals never aggressive in their arrogance but ever humble, sharing the majesty of the oceanic circle of which they are integral units. Therefore, the outermost circumference will not wield power to crush the inner circle, but will give strength to all within and derives its own strength from the centre."[33]

Will national sovereignties come to clashes in such a Gandhian world federation? The answer is given by Paul Power in his 'Gandhian Model for World Politics', "If the clash of interests said to follow class membership is not part of a Gandhian model for world affairs, what of the collision of sovereignties? Considered as power or force that must rest on violence sovereignty does not seem to be compatible with Gandhi's ethical thought. Yet, the "India of His Dreams", non-violent as it would be, is not stateless; there is sovereignty in the meaning of authority which directs the national community through consent to legitimate power. Gandhian states possess this kind of sovereignty which emerges from within national societies to give them identity, substance and purpose. In their dealings these states would tend to avoid creation of an inter-sovereign system, including military alliances and international organizations. Rather, they would emphasize right conduct with fellow Gandhian states and also with those political entities, sovereign in the traditional way, that hopefully will reorganize their internal life to become Gandhian. The absence among the Gandhian states, of conventional international organization will facilitate the growth of the number of units in the fellowship."[34] Further, a Gandhian state, established on the basis of decentralized power, cottage industries and village government, will not have the military capacity to threaten others.[35] Thus, the Gandhian model has certain institutionalised built-in mechanisms to prevent conflicts of a national and international type.

What are the practical possibilities of establishing such non-violent, self regulating, free, interdependent, cooperative world social order? The practical possibilities or desirability of such a world society may not be denied. However, it is extremely doubtful whether the current world forces tend to aid the creation

of such a world social order. Paul Power[36] mentions that Gandhi's ideas aid a theory of cultural regionalism, dedicated to peaceful adjustment, but not surrender of underdeveloped nations to the modern forces of science, materialism and secularism. Such a regional theory is in contrast to the one dealing with economic functionalism, political union or military security." "Gandhi's regionalism is a step towards establishing inter-cultural equilibrium as the optimum relation between the East and the West, and in the interim represents a moderately timed acculturation which is about the best hope for the traditional non-West in today's world. In either case his regional ideas help to remedy cultural domination and conflict."[37] But Gandhi's ideas do not contribute to regionalism ; they really transcend regional or national barriers. They are directly concerned with injustice wherever it occurred. The impression that his contributions aided a theory of cultural regionalism has arisen from the fact that his attention was focused on colonial countries as he considered colonialism a form of injustice practised at the international level. This should not lead us to conclude that he advocated unity of certain cultural aggregates to the exclusion of others. While a cultural equilibrium will be a compatible concomitant of Gandhian teachings the concept of cultural regionalism will not be consistent with a non-violent world social order. For, any cultural regionalism will result in some kind of conflict of ethics. As Bart Landheer[38] says, the problem of the establishment of a peaceful and non-violent world society may result in phenomenon of conflict of various levels of ethics, e.g., small group, national and international. According to Landheer, the basic difficulty in the establishment of a peaceful society lies firstly in the lack of symbolism of a world humanity which still remains partial and vague in the consciousness of the average man, secondly in the confusions regarding the nature of a world society itself which is mentally constructed as an extended replica of national society! "Mankind as a whole does not have a clear existence in our minds, except in case of national catastrophes, when the oneness of human nature suddenly makes us aware of the fate of others. We think about international affairs as analogous to national ones while in reality they are basically different and require social forms that are not like those of the national state. International society is organized as if it were a large state while in reality it is not, as the essential attributes of the states are missing. As a result, we have no clear image of ethical values upon the global level."[39] It is here that the Gandhian model offers us a solution. Gandhi's image of a world society is based on a system of ethical values relevant to the world as a whole. The non-violent world federation of states based on Gandhian principles would not be a world state created by surrendering national sovereignties, but a cooperative organization that would allow each state to keep its own identity and sovereignty which is compatible with the values of non-violent social order. A non-violent social order at the national or global level would not connote a social organisation where there was merely no violence. A truly non-violent social order should embody a set of norms and sanctions regarding avoidance and control of violence as well as the practice of good-will in day to day behaviour of individuals. The quality of social relationships would be a richer and higher type in such a society. By the same logic, an economically advanced country, where there is no manifestation of violence of any form, need not be truly non-violent if there also does not exist a positive good-will among the people. Gandhi's non-violence was action-oriented love, which according to him represented truth and hence God. For him God was truth and love, ethics and morality, fearlessness and selfless service. Hence his stress on moral values and he refused to subordinate means to ends. As he believed "in the inviolable connection between the means and the ends as there is between the seed and the tree" he insisted on the acceptance of non-violent means for securing social goals: if the means were non-violent there was no need to be concerned about the ends, they would inevitably be desirable. Gandhi believed that non-violence was " a power which can be wielded equally by all, young men and women or grown-up people, provided they have a living faith in the God of Love and have, therefore, equal love for all mankind. When non-violence is accepted as the law of life it must pervade the whole being and not be applied to isolated acts". He also believed that the 'law of non-violence was good enough for individuals and the masses of mankind'.

According to Pitrim Sorokin, "creative altruism in man can strengthen the moral basis for the establishment of a non-violent society; altruistic love as ideally formulated in the 'Sermon on the Mount' which Gandhi considered identical with his non-violence can lead to increase in unselfish and creative love in inter-individual and inter-group relationships in social institutions and culture."[40] Such motivations will result in alternations of the personality, cultural and social systems and thus give rise to a system of ethical values that will have relevance in the context of a peaceful non-violent social order at the national and global levels.

The Gandhian view of a world social order thus rests on the following prerequisites :

1. Individual personality development and character reformation on the basis of strict self-discipline in regulating one's behaviour in accordance with the norms of a non-violent social order.

2. Capacity on the part of the individual to suffer and sacrifice and to fearlessly pursue the path of truth and non-violence in all individual and social actions.

3. Faith in God along with the capacity to treat all religions as equal.

4. Acceptance of *Sarvodaya* (welfare of all) as the ultimate social goal and the pursuit of this goal by identifying one's own well-being with the well-being of the entire society through non-violent actions for the removal of all systems of exploitation and injustice and for the impartation of justice and promotion of egalitarian values even if against contrary religio-cultural sanctions.

5. Establishment of self-governing, decentralized social units, that interact cooperatively for mutual benefit and follow non-violent policies and promote non-violent social

relationships in contrast to those that promote alienation, exploitation and conflict, at the local, national and international levels.

Gandhi's doctrine of non-violence or *stayagraha* techniques of social action was intended not only to solve national problems of injustice but also international conflicts and wars. He considered war as a morally degrading and brutalising phenomenon and hence emphasised disarmament and creation of a non-violent civilization.[41] Pacifism, according to him, must be total and not partial, must find its expression in a broad movement that seeks not merely abolition of war but of the entire non-pacifist civilization.[42] And Gandhi maintained that the dread of atom bomb or nuclear weapons would not abolish wars or usher in a peaceful social order.[43] The abolition of wars and establishment of a peaceful world social order, however, was possible, according to Gandhi, through the positive philosophy of non-violence.

Thus, the Gandhian view of a world social order is essentially one of a moral order. *Satyagraha* (soul force) symbolised for Gandhi the attainment of moral ends through moral means. *Satyagraha* as a philosophy of social action was not merely an instrument to attain political, economic and other material ends, but for the spiritual and moral transformation of man.[44] Gandhi's *satyagraha* or soul force was generated out of a motivation to follow the path of truth and non-violence and was based on self-help, self-sacrifice and faith in God.[45] Gandhi's theory of non-violence is a positive philosophy and not a passive ethics. It is based on the assumption that men who wish to practise it must have certain moral and spiritual pre-requisites, a positive love for all beings and the pursuit of truth. The tradition of non-violence perhaps existed in all cultures but Gandhi converted it into a practical ethics which could be applied in day to day life. This offered tremendous possibilities for contemporary India as well as the whole world. Here was an alternative to physical force which had so far been acknowledged as the *sine qua non* of the social order in the soul force (*satyagraha*) or the spiritual and moral power.[46]

Enunciating Gandhian thought Acharya Kripalani supplements this point in the following passage: "The moral principles which guide the conduct of individuals in the social field must also guide their conduct in the political and the international fields."[47] "If we are to be saved from the cruel contradictions of a moral man living in an immoral (or at best amoral) political and international world order, we must find a unifying principle in life which will save us from this moral dichotomy. This unifying principle, Gandhi holds, is supplied as in social life so in political and international life and conduct by morality."[48] And Gandhian principles of the moral order are not based on self-interest or individual enjoyment, but on the social objective of *sarvodaya*, happiness for all. Emile Durkheim maintains that the logic of altruism cannot be deduced from egotism, the love of society from the love of oneself, the whole from the part.[49] Gandhi's altruism was derived from the concept of mankind, even all creation. Gandhi's was a 'creative altruism', which was characterized by pure, continuous and unbounded love for all. He could easily be placed in Sorokin's category of top altruists, "persons the scope of whose love is widest, being co-terminus with the whole universe, and God; the intensity of whose love is highest; whose love is wisest and most creative and whose acts are motivated only by love itself, continuous and durable."[50] Assessing the contributions of Gandhi, Albert Schweitzer wrote, "Gandhi continues what Buddha began. In the Buddha, the spirit of love set itself the task of creating different spiritual conditions in the world; in Gandhi, it undertakes to transform all worldly conditions."[51] Would the world tend to order itself in the directions indicated by Buddha and Gandhi or dismiss them as other worldly, Utopian, and set to destroy itself by the creation of artificial power blocs, perpetuation of exploitation and promotion of international conflicts? Sanity would undoubtedly advocate for choosing the twin path of spirituality and morality in international relations and establishment of a self-sustaining harmonious world social order. But are we sane?

Notes and References

1. D.G.Tendulkar, *Mahatma*, Vol.2 , Bombay: Vithalbhai K.Jhaveri and D.G. Tendulkar, 1951, p.464.

2. *Purna Swaraj* means full self government or independence
3. M.K. Gandhi, *Young India,* 26-3-31, see N.K. Bose, *Selections from Gandhi* , Ahmedabad: Navajivan Publishing House, p. 118.
4. M.K. Gandhi, *Young India,,* 12-11-31, see N.K. Bose, *ibid.*
5. Erik H. Erikson, *Gandhi's Truth,* New York : W.W. Norton & Co., 1969, p. 265.
6. *Ibid.*, as cited from Pyarelal; *Gandhi, Early Phase,* p. 62.
7. Erikson, *op. cit.*, p. 267.
8. N.K. Bose, *Studies in Gandhism,* Ahmedabad: Navajivan Publishing House, 3 rd edition, 1962, p. 311.
9. T.K.N. Unnithan, *Gandhi and Free India,* Groningen: J.B. Wolters, 1956, pp. 40-41.
10. T.K.N. Unnithan and Yogendra Singh, *Report of UNESCO Project on Tradition of Non-Violence inEast and West* (mimeographed)
11. *Ibid.*
12. *Ibid.*
13. M.K. Gandhi, *India of My Dreams,* compiled by R.K. Prabhu, Bombay :Hindu Kitab Ltd., 1947.
14. M.K. Gandhi, *Picture of Village Swaraj,* Harijan, 26-7-42. See also Gandhi's last will and testament.
15. M.K. Gandhi, *Young India,* 2-7-31, see N.K. Bose, *Selections From Gandhi.*
16. *Ibid.*
17. T.K.N. Unnithan, *Gandhi and Free India, op.cit.*, p. 48.
18. M.K. Gandhi, *Sarvodaya,* Ahmedabad: Navajivan Publishing House, 1951.
19. M.K. Gandhi, *Young India,* 3-4-24, see N.K. Bose, *Selections From Gandhi.*
20. N.K. Bose, *Selections from Gandhi*, p. 42.
21. T.K.N. Unnithan, *Gandhi and Free India,* p. 109.
22. M.K. Gandhi, *Young India,* 12-11-31, see N.K. Bose, *Selections from Gandhi.*

23. Pitirim A. Sorokin, *Reconstruction of Humanity* , Bombay: Bharatiya Vidya Bhavan, , 1962, p.25.

24. *Ibid.,* pp.28-31.

25. D.G. Tendulkar, *op. cit.,* Vol.VII, p.390.

26. G. Ramachandran and T.K. Mahadevan (Ed.), *Gandhi: His Relevance for Our Times,* New Delhi: Gandhi Peace Foundation, , 1967 (article on a Gandhian Model for World Politics by Paul.F.Power).

27. M.K. Gandhi, *Young India,* 26-12-24, See N.K. Bose, *op.cit.*

28. *Ibid., p.119.*

29. M.K. Gandhi, *Young India,* 11-8-20, See N.K. Bose, *op.cit.*p.42.

30. M.K. Gandhi, *Correspondence with Government,* See N. K. Bose,. *op. cit., p.41.*

31. J. Nehru, *Mahatma Gandhi* , Bombay : Asia Publishing House, 1966, pp.36-37.

32. *Ibid.,*

33. M.K. Gandhi, *India of My Dreams, op. cit.,* pp.26-27. Also see Unnithan, *op.cit., p.48.*

34. Paul.F.Power, *op. cit.*, p.284.

35. *Ibid., p.283.*

36. Paul. F. Power, *Gandhi on World Affairs* , Washington, D.C: Public Affairs Press, pp.98-99.

37. *Ibid.,*

38. Bart Landheer, *Ethical Values in International Decision Making* , The Hague : Martinus Nijhoff., 1960.

39. *Ibid.,* p.8.

40. P.A. Sorokin, *Studies of the Harvard Research Centre in Creative Altruism* 1959. Also see Sorokin: *Explorations in Altruistic Love and Behaviour.*

41. T.K.N. Unnithan and Yogendra Singh, *op.cit.*

42. M.K. Gandhi, *Harijan,* Nov. 12 (1938) see N.K. Bose, *op.cit.*

43. D.G. Tendulkar, *op.cit.,* p. 143.

44. Unnithan and Singh, *op.cit.*
45. M.K. Gandhi, *My Experiments With Truth* , London, 1949, pp. xi-xii.
46. Unnithan and Singh, *op.cit.*
47. J.B. Kriplani, *Gandhian Thought*, Chandigarh: Punjab University Press, 1964, p.7.
48. *Ibid.*
49. E. Durkheim, *Division of Labour in Society,* Free Press, Paperback edition, 1964, p. 414
50. Sorokin, *op.cit.*
51. Albert Schweitzer, *Indian Thought and its Development* , Bombay: Wilco, 1960, p.224.

8

Breaking the Shackles: Gandhi's Views on Women

Usha Thakkar

Gandhi worked not only for the political emancipation of the nation, but for liberation of all the suppressed and oppressed sections of society. One of the noteworthy results of his life-work has been the awakening of women, which made them shed their deep-rooted sense of inferiority and rise to dignity and self-esteem. For Gandhi, "When woman, whom we all call *abala* becomes *sabala*, all those who are helpless will become powerful".[1] The welfare of the weaker sections of society was dear to his heart. He had no qualms about the priority of social over political ends. In his opinion, to postpone social reform till after the attainment of *Swaraj* was not to know the meaning of *Swaraj*.[2]

Women, urban and rural, educated and uneducated, Indian and foreign, were attracted to his ideas and deeds. While some like Sarojini Naidu, Lakshmi Menon, Sushila Nayyar and Rajkumari Amrit Kaur rose to prominence, there were thousands of unsung and unnoticed heroines of India who learnt the meaning of liberation from him and contributed with all their energy to the struggle for independence. Life sketches and reminiscences of women freedom-fighters give us glimpses of their crusade against injustice and inequality.

An attempt is made in the present paper to understand Gandhi's views on women in the context of social, economic and political issues.

Social Regeneration

Gandhi respected traditions of the society, but not at the cost of loss of individual dignity. His practical and dynamic advice was "It is good to swim in the waters of tradition, but to sink in them is suicide".[3] He never hesitated to criticise the evils which had gripped the Indian society, and tried to mobilise public opinion against such evils. He realised that there were deep-rooted customs hampering the development of women, and women's freedom from such shackles was necessary for the emancipation of the nation.

According to Gandhi, the custom of child-marriage is both a moral as well as a physical evil, for it undermines our morals and induces physical degeneration. The *purdah* system, according to him, was "vicious, brutal and barbarous". He questioned the basis of the practice of pushing women in seclusion: "Why is there all this morbid anxiety about female purity? Have women any say in the matter of male purity? We hear nothing of women's anxiety about men's chastity. Why should men arrogate to themselves the right to regulate female purity? It cannot be superimposed from without. It is a matter of evolution from within and, therefore, of individual self-effort.[4] He called prostitution "moral leprosy" and despised the fact that " the beast in man has made the detestable crime a lucrative profession".[5] He appealed to prostitutes to give up their "unworthy profession" and become "*sanyasinis*" of India.[6]

Gandhi viewed marriage as a sacrament imposing discipline on both the partners, not a licence for physical union and emphasised spiritual union in marriage. He insisted on monogamous marriages and put forward a plea for inter communal marriages between caste Hindus and Harijans. In his opinion, "Woman is the companion of man, gifted with equal mental capacities. She has the right to participate in the very minutest details in the activities of man and she has an equal right of freedom and liberty with him. She is entitled to a supreme place in her own sphere of activity as man is in his".[7] Gandhi was clear that "Woman must cease to consider herself the object of man's lust. The remedy is more in her hands than man's. She must refuse to adorn herself for men including her husband, if she will be an equal partner with man".[8] When Gandhi was asked whether a wife could go against the will of her husband to take up national service, he supported the claim of a wife to devote herself to a noble purpose. He cited the example of Mirabai in support of his argument. In his opinion, every wife " has a perfect right to take her own course and meekly brave the consequences when she knows herself to be in the right and when her resistance is for a nobler purpose".[9] According to him, the only honourable terms in marriage are mutual love and mutual consent.[10]

For him, sexuality ought to be kept at the minimum inside marriage and totally eliminated outside it. The method of birth-control, he favoured, was by exercising self-restraint in life and restricting physical union only for getting children. Referring to his own life, he observed that he began to enjoy his married life only after he abandoned sex. For him, " the conquest of lust is the highest endeavour of a man's or a woman's existence whereas physical union for the sake of carnal satisfaction is reversion to animality which has to be avoided by both.".[11]

Gandhi realised the miseries of widowhood for a woman as "men have ordained perpetual widowhood for women and conferred on themselves the right to fix marriage with another partner on cremation-ground itself".[12] For him, "Voluntary widowhood consciously adopted by a woman who has felt the affection of the partner, adds grace and dignity to life, sanctifies the home and uplifts religion itself. Widowhood imposed by religion or custom is an unbearable yoke and defiles the home by secret vice and degrades religion."[13]. He believed that it is better for a widow to remarry openly rather than commit sin secretly.[14]

Gandhi sees these widows as a strong reservoir of energy, which could be put to use to bring light to the dark corners of the nation. In his opinion, "It is worth considering carefully in what way the country can avail itself of the services of hundreds of widows, young and old".[15] As Gandhi respected widows who dedicated themselves to the service of humanity, he had great regard for women who chose the path of staying single to serve society and the nation. In his opinion, not every Indian girl is born to marry. There are many girls willing to dedicate themselves to service instead of servicing one man.

Gandhi had visualised a great role for women in eradicating the evil of communalism. His appeal to women was to refuse to cook, and to starve themselves in protest so long as their men "do not wash their hand of these dirty communal squabbles". Gandhi's appeal reached women everywhere in India. He expected great things from them in the areas of work concerning purity of life, removal of untouchability, propagation of *khadi,* communal harmony and *Swadeshi.* His logic was simple: "If Kaikeyi could obtain all that she wanted from Dashrath by dint of *Duragraha*, what could they not achieve with the help of *Satyagraha?"*.[16]

Gandhi's own experience of Kasturba's resistance to acceptance of untouchables as members of the family perhaps made him aware of the role that women can play in the removal of untouchability. "If the Hindu heart is to be cured of the taint of untouchability, women must do the lion's share of the work". [17] His appeal to women was "If you consider *Harijans* untouchables because they perform sanitary service, what mother has not performed such service for her children."

When Gandhi told women that the economic and the moral salvation of India rested mainly with them, [18] he was not paying mere lip-service to them. He was evoking a creative and constructive spirit that was suppressed in them. A simple factor like their choice of clothes and jewellery was transformed by Gandhi into a force for *Swadeshi. Khadi* came to be identified with opposition against foreign rule and love for the nation, and giving away her jewellery means that a woman is shedding her own shackles.

Political Emancipation

Gandhi revolutionised not only Indian politics, but also the whole perception of life for women. In his words, "My contribution to the great problem (of women's role in society) lies in my presenting for acceptance of truth and *ahimsa* in every walk of life, whether for individuals or nations. I have hugged the hope that in this, woman will be the unquestioned leader and, having thus found her place in human evolution, will shed her inferiority complex."[19] Women's entry into national politics through non-violent methods brought miraculous results. On the one hand, women became aware of their inner strength, and on the other, the process brought human and moral elements into politics.

Gandhi had tremendous faith in women's inherent capacity for non-violence. And his experience of participation by women in politics from his days in South Africa till the end of his life bears testimony to the fact that they never failed his expectations. With Gandhi's inspiration, they took the struggle right into their homes and raised it to a moral level. Women organized public meetings, sold *khadi* and prescribed literature, started picketing shops of liquor and foreign goods, prepared contraband salt, and came forward to face all sorts of atrocities, including inhuman treatment by police officers and imprisonment. They came forward to give all that they had – their wealth and strength, their jewellery and belongings, their skills and labour – all with sacrifices for this unusual and unprecedented struggle.

Gandhi's call to women to involve themselves in the freedom struggle had far-reaching results in changing their outlook. "The cause of *Swaraj* swept all taboos and old customs before it".[20] Many women in their individual lives shed their age-old prejudices against the caste system. They had no hesitation in leaving the boundaries of their protected homes and going to the jail. They even broke their glass bangles (a sign of ill omen for married women) when they were told that they were made of Czechoslovakian glass. Women's participation in the freedom struggle feminised nationalism and the nationalist struggle helped them to liberate from age-old traditions.

Though Gandhi never challenged the traditional set up, he inspired women to carve out their own destinies within it, and thereby changing its very essence. Women learnt from Gandhi that one can be strong, even if seemingly weak, to protest against injustice. They realised that they do not have to accept the norms of male-dominated politics. They evolved their own perspectives and formulated their own methods. In a way they presented a critique of the colonial unethical state.

Gandhi could see woman as connected with service and not with power. When a woman wrote to him in 1946 about the political scene and the paucity of women in it, he wrote: "So long as considerations of caste and community continue to weigh with us and rule our choice, women will be well-advised to remain aloof and thereby build up their prestige.... Women workers should enrol women as voters, impart or have imparted to them practical education, teach them to think independently, release them from the chains of caste that bind them so as to bring about a change in them which will compel men to realise women's strength and capacity for sacrifice and give her places of honour. If they will do this, they will purify the present unclear atmosphere." [21] His advice to women was to teach people in villages simple lessons of hygiene and sanitation. Seeking power would be, for them, "reversion of barbarity". [22] And still Gandhi believed that, "Women must have votes and an equal status. But the problem does not end there. It only commences at the point where women begin to affect the political deliberations of the nation." [23]

Economic Self-reliance

Gandhi visualised a humane society, free from exploitation and in justice, built by responsible men and women. Gandhi, however, maintained that the spheres of work for woman and man were different. "She is passive, he is active. She is essentially mistress of the house. He is the breadwinner. She is the keeper and distributor of the bread. She is the caretaker in every sense of the term." [24] Gandhi was of the firm opinion that if women have to work outside the home, they should do so without disturbing it. They can take up some work, which would supplement the income of the family, and spinning, according to him, was perhaps the best work they could undertake. Spinning and weaving for women were "the first lesson in the school of industry". The spinning wheel can be the "widow's loving companion", of livelihood for the poor family and a means to supplement the income of the family of the middle class, and for the well-to-do women, it would be a means to relate their lives to those country's poor women.[25]

Though women had no direct control over economic matters, they were the managers of homes. Gandhi was quick to grasp this fact. So, to popularise the message of *Swadeshi*, a cardinal economic principle for him, he demanded the support of women. In his opinion, the *Swadeshi* vow cannot be kept without the help of women. "Men alone will be able to do nothing in the matter. They have no control over the children, that is the woman's sphere. To look after children, to dress them, is the mother's duty and, therefore, it is necessary that women should be fired with the spirit of *Swadeshi*."[26]

Ideal Models

Gandhi often presented ideals before women, drawn from Indian traditions, mythology and history. He often talked about Sita, Draupadi, Damayanti and Mirabai as great women. There is nothing new for a social reformer drawing inspiration from the tradition. What is new here is the fact that this innovate interpretation of these characters gives a glimpse of the dynamic element in his thinking. He did not accept the negative elements of the Hindu tradition. He visualised the Indian women as new Sitas, Draupadis and Damayantis, "pure, firm and self-controlled".

For Gandhi, Sita was not a weak and dependent creature, but a strong woman conveying the message of *Swadeshi*, who only wore "cloth made in India" and thus kept her heart and body pure. [27] Moreover, she should defy the might of Ravana by sheer moral courage and she would not waste "a single moment on pleasing Rama by physical charms".[28] Implying thereby that a woman could assert herself in doing what she considered right even if the husband thought otherwise. Another ideal model presented by Gandhi was Draupadi who was not dependent on men and saved herself by an appeal to Krishna when the Pandavas failed to protect her. [29] Here the appeal to Krishna is to be understood as following one's own conscience. He saw Mirabai, as a symbol of courage, who followed her chosen path by defying the social norms of the time.

It is interesting to note that Gandhi does not advise a woman to be an ideal wife or ideal mother. Deviating from the traditional framework, he advises women to be sisters. Pointing out the greatness of a sister over a wife, he maintained that a sister is to all the world, while a wife hands herself over to one man. Moreover, it is possible to become the world's sister only by making *Brahmacharya* "a natural condition" and being 'fired by the spirit of service". Women have the potential to do immense service to the unfortunate, by doing this they can be "Sisters of Mercy".

Though Gandhi gave the traditional role a new vigour, he had undaunted faith in the chastity and purity of woman. He was sure that the "dazzling purity" of a woman could disarm even the most beastly of men.[30] In his opinion, an ideal woman would rather give up her life than her purity. Construction of the woman in such terms seems to be at times too idealistic in contemporary times. According to Madhu Kishwar, "Gandhi's very vocabulary, in its exaggerated idealisation of women as 'sisters of mercy' and 'mothers of entire humanity' reveals the bias of a benevolent patriarch." [31]

And yet, there is something in his ideas that is essentially radical. He did not see women as helpless objects of reform. Neither did he think of bringing change only in some spheres of life, such as marriage or education. His vision of change was comprehensive. He connected the moral with the political, the social and the economic, presenting an eclectic view of life. For him the means had to be identified with the ends; similarly, he did not differentiate between the private and the public worlds of women. He also enhanced the dignity of woman's housework, advising his men followers to take to spinning and to do ordinary works in everyday life. He himself imbibed so many of a woman's qualities, that he became 'mother' to many.

Gandhi saw that the low status of women was the result of prejudices and adverse traditions, which were centuries old. It was difficult to get women interested in the larger problems of life and society because they knew nothing of them, having never been allowed to breathe the fresh air of freedom.[32] The only factor that would enable women to come out of this situation was the determination and strength of the women themselves. Though men should help in the cause of women, ultimately women will have to determine their destinies. Gandhi sympathises with women, but he does not want to pity them all the time. Neither does he want them to be irresponsible, pleasure-loving beings.

In Gandhi's philosophy, the women of India found a new identity. His words and deeds have inspired thousands of women, and will continue to do so, in their struggle against injustice and inequality.

Notes and References

1. *Message to All India Women's Conference*, sent before December 23, 1936.
2. *Young India*, June 28, 1928.
3. *Navajivan*, June 28, 1925.
4. *Young India*, November 25, 1926.
5. *Young India*, August 18, 1927.
6. *Navajivan*, September 11, 1921.
7. Speech at Bhagini Samaj, Bombay, February 20, 1918.
8. *Young India*, July 21, 1921.
9. *Young India*, October 21, 1926.
10. *Young India*, December 27, 1928.

11. *Harijan*, November 21, 1936.

12. *Navajivan*, June 28, 1925.

13. *Young India*, August 5, 1926.

14. *Young India*, September 23, 1926.

15. Message to Gujrati Hindu Stree Mandal on or before November 14, 1917.

16. Cited in D.G. Tendulkar, *Mahatma* Vol.II, New Delhi: Publications Division, Govt. of India, 1961, p.347.

17. *Harijan,* March 9, 1934.

18. *Young India*, August 11, 1921.

19. *Harijan*, February 24, 1940.

20. Margaret E. Cousins, *Indian Womanhood Today*, Allahabad: Kitabistan, Series No.5, 1937, p.63.

21. *Harijan*, April 21, 1946.

22. *Harijan*, February 24, 1940.

23. *Young India*, July 21, 1921.

24. *Harijan*, February 24, 1940.

25. *Young India*, August 11, 1921.

26. *Speech at Women's Meeting*, Bombay, May 8, 1919.

27. *Speech at Women's Meeting*, May 19,1925.

28. *Young India*, July 21, 1921.

29. Reply to Women's Address in Noakhali, May 14, 1925.

30. *Harijan*, March 1, 1942.

31. Madhu Kishwar, "Gandhi on Women", *Economic and Political Weekly*, October 5, 1985, p.1701.

32. *Young India*, February 3, 1927.

9

Development Paradigm Transition: From The Second to the Third Millennium

Amalendu Guha

Introduction

Growth is not development and development is not growth. Growth is vertical and creates vertical social, economic, political, cultural and ecological relations, while development is horizontal and intends to create and maintain horizontal relations between and among social beings, in these very mentioned domains and dimensions. Most of the economists and social scientists mistook growth for development. The theories of the Nobel Prize winners in economics and other noted economists centred their theories and equations around the efficiency models and functional behaviour of capital, technology, economic management mechanism as well as alternative methods of capital productivity, credit productivity, technological efficiency, etc. in which the human resources were neglected and considered merely as market for the output produced with the efficient use of the above inputs and natural resources. The growth economists thought, therefore, much of cost-efficiency and economic efficiency instead of human or social proficiency. But the genuine development is to be effected by the masses, for the masses and, in relational process and behaviour, has to be of the masses. The mission and vision of development economists is the establishment of effective correlation between Man and Matter, or, in other words, between Man and Natural plus Created Resources, in the common human interest. Therefore, the development economics, in essence, is human economics. Capitalism and the laissez faire economic system worked for the efficient use of matter, capital and technology and not much for human welfare and workfare. It worked for market and could not produce any effective theory as well as appropriate means and measures for generating sufficient and common absorbable financial capacity at the social and human levels covering the entire human beings. Therefore, it left a vacuum consisting 30 per cent of the human resources of the globe which can be recognised as the below survival level or marginalised class or social strata. They form the social and economic vacuum of the global society, lacking income or purchasing power to possess the goods and services entering into their fundamental human and social needs- satisfaction. They are left as economically and socially unproductive and workfare is denied to them, because the very economic system of competitiveness and combativeness has left this 30 per cent global population as undesired "socially and economically surplus", in the sense that they cannot be used for "efficient economic system and function". This is the essence of mass unemployment, human marginalisation and pauperisation.

Development, in the next century and millennium, is to have newer sense and essence. Development should mean the generation of the necessary and appropriate economic, social, political, cultural and ecological ways, means and measures for producing socially and humanly needed goods and services to meet the fundamental social and human needs of the entire humankind and, in which, the entire masses will be the producers and beneficiaries of the above. This will be a new special and human relation, in which needs, rights and duties will, trialectically, interact each other. Global Common Society is the vision of the next millennium and development behaviour of the above type may pave the way for achieving such type of society.

New and Alternative Development Approach for the Global Poor

There are about one-third of the population of the globe who are living at the below-subsistence or below survival level. They live with either one meal or two half-meals a day. The growth economists and the Nobel Prize winners for the last four decades have failed to give any practically usable model for sustainable and relevant development as well as practical poverty-alleviation solution for the below survival level population of our earth. The philanthropic approach for resource transfer from the centre to the peripheries or localities will never, really, take place. The rich will never part with or share their accumulated wealth and created welfare with the poor. The governments are really weak to adopt and implement measures for the transfer of resources from the urban centres to the rural and human peripheries.

The multinational companies effect mass production for the market and the people having purchasing power at their disposal, not for the entire masses. The now-defunct East European socialist countries effected social production and converted the masses into state clients, with homogenization of their needs and without taking into consideration of their choices and options and by excluding the criteria of equity. So long, there has taken the outflow of the material, financial and economically active human resources from the territorial localities or peripheries to the urban centres and sub-centres. This led to the all round processes of resource-pauperisation of the peripheries. In order to attain poverty-alleviation and enable the economically and resource-emptying peripheries to attain relevant self-reliance and sustenance, there arises the necessity of organizing and effecting a new development system, whose basic premises are the following.

- organization of the mobilisational and participatory development functions at the locality level, on the basis of the local social/ human values, culture, mode of life, traditions, basic needs, etc.,
- organization of production process by the masses on the basis of the use of the local natural and human resources as far and as much as possible, in order to achieve the optimum locally usable goods and services,
- organization of employment in such a way as to accrue income to the employees of the localities,

- organization of distribution in such a way as to meet the needs of the population of the localities,
- organization of the use of local savings and accumulation (on the pattern of the use of only the positive aspects of the Grameen Bank in Bangladesh) in local interest and in the localities, through stoppage of outflow of the same to the urban centres and sub-centres.
- adoption of attractive measures to effect the inflow of financial resources from the urban to the rural localities, etc.

Such type of organisation of production by the masses and distribution of the effects of their labour in the localities will stop the outflow of human capital to the centre and will make the localities autonomous, besides keeping the resources and the effects of development at the localities. This is the mechanism of the poverty-alleviation economy of the global poor.

Developing from and at the below level is, therefore, the exclusive necessity for the development of the peripheries and the socio-economically marginal or peripheral people. For this reason, development by the masses should be the development philosophy at the beginning of the next millennium. This mass development culture is an organic whole, in which all the actors and factors should be interdependent. Such interdependent interaction makes development socially effective and in a socially justifiable way. Such development is predominantly human. Development culture and behaviour of this type assures social stability and may enable the doing away with the unevenness of development mal-behaviour of mass production at the centre, in which the common masses are made the market. The mass-man should not be regarded as an element of the market, but a value-creator.

Globalisation of the economy, particularly and practically of trade, is an accomplished fact now. But we have forgotten the real essence of the globalisation of economy, which means the globality of the local economies whose interaction and interdependent behaviour should be based on horizontal and reciprocal advantages. In order to achieve the same we need the globalisation of peace and a tensionless situation. Such state and stage is attainable when appropriate measures are taken to eradicate the social, economic, political, cultural and ecological causes of tensions and conflicts between and among nations, social groups, ethnic and religious communities, dominating centre and dependant peripheries, etc.

Mass production at the centre of capital and technology cannot be beneficial for the masses, because it does not create income or purchasing power for the common masses, recognised as market by the owner of capital and technology. This is the very essence of difference between mass production at the centre and production by the masses at the localities. Mass production is hurried economic production while production by the masses is slower and less economic, but socially secure process when evaluated from the aspects of income generation and livelihood security perspectives. Monetary income and possession of purchasing power is the source and initiative of propensity to spend and consume. Such propensity cannot be created through borrowings or credit-capital. The rural and peripheral human resources have nothing to sell but their labour. If this rural or peripheral labour is combined with financial and credit capital in the relation of production, it becomes a creative combined force and actor of production, which is completely different from the capitalist mode and relation of production. This can be regarded as co-operative common mode and relation of production. Transfer of credit-capital from the centre and sub-centre to the rural or local periphery means the empowerment of the poor. This will be a new production and socio-human relation.

In the structured capitalist and the now-defunct East European state-capitalised socialist system, there took place the accumulation of both the capital and resources in the centre and sub-centres. It happened through the transfer of both the savings and natural resources from the localities to the centre. It created the concentration of wealth and welfare in one pole and poverty as well as deprivation in the other pole. Common masses, thus, became clients to the patrons of the centre. In order to undo such economic destabilisation and disparities, there arises the necessity for creating civil societies and civil economies, which may generate employment and stop labour-drainage from the peripheries towards the centre. Its ultimate effects are localised socialisation of human resources, natural resources, capital, income generation, distribution of purchasing power, enabling the consumption of the basic needs-satisfying goods and services at the mass satisfaction level, etc., and finally, the establishment of equitable local societies.

In such equitable local and common societies the human resources should be regarded as human capital and there should not take place any disputed division between a man's intellectual property and his physical input property. Both of these are to be considered as socially necessary functional actors, for their creative contributions. The decentralisation of production or production by the masses, though cannot be the production of scale, will place the common people in possession of power of gainful employment and services necessary for themselves. Such system and mechanism will generate both the wealth and welfare at such common local society level. Its very basic theoretical and practical framework is self-propelling WORKFARE, which is superior to the welfare provided by the patron to the clients. Workfare system creates a civilisation and culture of co-working, co-producing, co-sharing, co-living and co-existing with human dignity.

Food Security : Mass Production or Production by the Masses (as Development Security for the Global Poor)

Food security for the common masses in the 21st century is the much desired goal. The below subsistence or the poverty-ridden level population of the globe accounts for around 30 per cent. The mass production of food grains and purchasing power-dependent and based distribution has not solved the problem of the global poor. Both capitalism and former state-capitalised socialism have failed to produce any effective solution to eradicate poverty and depauperise the economically marginalised society. For assuring and enabling food and other basic needs security, we need production by the masses, which creates employment and, hence, income or purchasing power at the mass or locality level. Mass production with mass control of distribution was experimented in the former East European state-capitalised socialist system, but has failed. Mass production presumes the homogenised quantified target for production, but does not take into consideration the real and realistic heterogeneous needs of the consumers.

Again, there is consumption behaviour differentiation. Therefore, mass production carries within itself own limitations. If at both the multinational and national levels mass production happens to occur, then there will be crisis in market, and this has been noted on a global basis during the last decade, in spite of economic prosperity.

As and when both production and consumption become localised, particularly the basic needs-satisfying goods and services and the products and services matching own values, habits and necessities, the temptation for effecting or importing massive production, indefinitely and at any cost disappears. Mass production demands concentrated mass accumulation of monetary and technological capital and power-cum-capacity of using natural resources in the hands of the few. Such concentrated economic power of the MNCs, monopolies and conglomerates can effect mass production, but cannot do away with unemployment and poverty. When the production is effected by the masses at the localities level, the distribution can be equalised. Distribution can never be equal when markets are spread beyond the localities and national territories.

Production by the masses cannot be mass production of economic scale, but the production by the masses generates mass employment and satisfies mass needs. This is what we need for eradication of local unemployment and poverty. Production by the masses is a production of sharing. In modern economic thinking one is to put accent on the following conceptual framework, namely that, capital + technology is the processing mechanism of the natural resources, by the human resources for adding human and social utility values to the needed natural resources.

Mass production at the centre creates economic and social alienation at the periphery which is not a participant in the mass production that takes place at the centre but only a market at the bottom. But in the process and course of production by the masses at the human and territorial level an effective and lasting social and economic relation is created which is diametrically opposed to centre's alienation policy and effects. Again, production by and for the masses at the mass level enables the creation of social values and these values are more important than the centre's mass production-generated economic values. If economic values are preferred to social values then there will arise the tragedy of the deterioration of the quality and values of social life. Development and promotion of the destructured local social economy will not produce much economic wealth and welfare as well as accumulation, but will generate social wealth and social welfare comprising of social and family happiness and satisfaction, which cannot be measured and quantified economically. Non-monetary wealth helps the generation and prevalence of social security and social health. The non-governmental and non-structured socio-economic system and functional mechanism, at the local level, in the forthcoming century and the millennium may enable the achievement of balanced social health, social security, social values and social economy.

Centralised production is the prime feature of both private capitalism and state capitalism, in which profit motivation is privatised and monopolised for the owner of capital and technology in case of the former and state capitalised in case of the now-defunct East European socialism. Now, at the end of this century, we are to invent and introduce a new socio-economic system where an individual is to be freed from economic slavery and bindings of capital and will be a participant and beneficiary of a decentralised production and distribution system. The strongest economic arguments in favour of localisation of production and consumption are the following :

a) in a decentralised or localised production system there cannot take place concentration and centralisation of profits, and
b) the question of capturing and controlling market disappears when the concentration by large or mass scale production does not exist.

Profit-motivation leads to competition and group violence and, sometimes, to economic anarchism. Localised production and distribution avoids these evils and crises.

The centre or the cities have developed and overdeveloped while the periphery or the villages remained underdeveloped so long. Now, the core functions of development have to be moved from the centre to the periphery. The periphery or the grass-root localities are to be the production units of the masses instead of remaining as market of the mass-scale producing capitalist monopolies or state capitalism. Why is this necessary ? In mass scale production system the capital-input ratio is higher than the labour-input ratio and the replacement ratio of labour by capital also becomes higher, on the ground that capital productivity is higher than the labour productivity. But in the rural or grass-root localities of our globe, particularly in the economically underdeveloped territories, labour or human resources are abundant while capital is scarce. Because of labour-abundance their development is to be more labour-input or use-oriented. Where the ratio of labour- input or cost of an article or product is higher than the capital-input ratio, it means more employment or the use of present capital; less use of capital and technology or the result of past labour and; distribution of the income type of wealth to the human resource factor, the important factor and actor in the produced article or product.

If the income is generated and used at the mass or grass-root, it means that monetary wealth is distributed at the mass level and accumulation, though at small scale, will remain in the peripheries instead of moving towards the centre, the core of capital and technology. Such savings, again, can be used at this very human-resource abundant and usable periphery. Market-dependency on the centre, particularly for the products and services related to basic needs satisfaction, will also be reduced considerably. Export of raw materials to the overdeveloped and developed centre, which the periphery and sub periphery actually need, generate unemployment in the peripheries, and cones-quently, poverty. Modern economists of today should think that the production of food crops and other crops and other basic value-oriented goods and services generate more welfare type of wealth in the local societies because their use-values are more important to them.

Coming back to the food security needs, which are the most basic of all human needs, the gene revolution has opened new avenues for increased agrarian production through tremendous achievements in bio-technological research. Built-in protection against malicious crop viruses will enable increased production and if access to such advanced gene technology is destructured and made available to the local and small scale farmers all over the world, it will enable us to feed the very 30 per cent global poor and depressed population. The subsistence farmers will benefit much from this gene revolution. The gene technology has generated the following benefits :

a) the crops are insects-protected;
b) these are herbicide tolerant;
c) these involve low input-cost; and
d) these enable less use of chemical insecticides and herbicides, etc.

Some of the achievements and ongoing successful projects are:

i) development of new Chinese rice hybrids that can provide higher yields to the tune of 20 per cent to 40 per cent;
ii) redesigning of the rice plants by the IRRI in Philippines to achieve 30 per cent higher yields; and

iii) enabling the cultivation of the newer gene-added-crop-varieties in acidic soil, etc.

The bio-technological research has been proceeding towards such a stage as to produce crops with high Vitamin-E content which may result in the decline of the aging process of the body-organ.

Concluding Remarks

Unless development economics can eradicate poverty and effect economic destructuralisation, it cannot be regarded as development economics. To assure food, housing, clothing, health, basic education and employment should be the prime goal of development in the forthcoming century and millennium.

10

Religion and Nation-State: The Untenable Linkage

T.K Oommen

I

Both state and nation are products of historical evolution and they existed more or less independently in the long span of human history. They came to be linked only some 350 years ago when the Treaty of Westphalia was signed in 1648. Before that there were empire-states, city-states, theocratic states and the like. The Treaty initiated the notion of nation-state which idealized the co-terminality between nation and state. A nation-state was also assumed to be a democratic state in that it is the end-product of self-determination by the people that eventuates in the emergence of the state. And yet, neither the fact nor the assumption regarding nation-state is empirically sustainable.

When one examines the state-nation linkage, one gets several permutations and combinations. These are: (1) nation-state wherein a nation has its own exclusive state. Such examples are only a few such as Japan and Portugal; (2) several nations co-existing in one state (e.g., former Soviet Union, India); (3) one nation divided into several states: Poland before World War II, Arabia and Kurdistan; (4) onation divided between two states; Germany before unification, the Punjabs, Indian and Pakistani; (5) one nation divided into two, one part of which is a sovereign state and the other part is in another state: Ireland, Bengal; (6) a nation of which one part lives in its homeland and the other part is dispersed into the territory of another state: the Sindhis.

Although nation-state has been an ideal for the past 350 years, there is an inherent tension in the union between nation and state; they pull in opposite directions. The state wants to count, to label and homogenize; nation wants to preserve identity, celebrate diversity and nurture pluralism. 'National integration' often connotes assimilation and homogenisation leading to the eclipse of identity. This is the source of tension in linking state and nation, particularly in multi-national states such as India. The democratic multinational state, through its constitution, assures equality to all citizens irrespective of their nationality. But the 'minorities' are persuaded and/or coerced to abjure their identity, particularly that based on religion and language. That is, the tension between state and nation at its root is a tension between equality and identity. Integration is sought to be achieved by offering equality to citizens but denying identity to nations. If we want to have both equality and identity we must keep the conceptual distinction between state and nation; citizenship and nationality.

The co-terminality between state and nation is not a fact but a figment of imagination and hence the notion of terminal loyalty to the state is not sustainable. Further, the idea of terminal loyalty smacks of a hierarchy of loyalties, the loyalty to the state being the supreme one and all other loyalties subordinated to it. This is an untenable proposition in a culturally plural democratic society. What we ought to establish is a set of horizontal loyalties each of which is functional in a specific context. Thus, an Indian Catholic should have his ultimate loyalty to the Indian state in the political context but in the religious context his ultimate loyalty may have to be to the Pope. And there is no contradiction in this as all human beings are simultaneously involved in a web of identity-set. Instead of a hierarchy of loyalty, we should think of contexts of differentiated loyalties.

If the tension between state and nation is anchored to equality and identity, the tension between nation and religion is based on the struggle for supremacy between two identities. The identity of nation emerges in the unity between territory and language; the identity of religious community is based on the similarity in beliefs and rituals. The contestation for supremacy between these identities has a long history and remains unresolved. A third contender for supremacy in the identity struggle is race. There was co-terminality between identities based on religion, language and race earlier, but after the geographical explorations of sixteenth century and colonialism which followed it, this co-terminality was disturbed. Today the same racial group may belong to different religious faiths and speak a variety of languages.

Three prominent attributes of collectivities were sought to be homogenized through project modernization in different parts of the world. These are race, religion and language. Several points need to be noted here. First, race and religion are delinked from territory as hinted above. Language also is de-territorialized to some extent but most linguistic communities have their specific homelands and hence remains the only plausible basis of democratic nation formation. Second, homogenisation of racial groups can be brought about only through interracial unions. Brazil tried it through its policy of 'racial democracy', but the attempt has only elaborated the racial stratification system; no homogenisation came about. At any rate voluntary unions between races are likely to remain limited; unions through coercion are not democratic and hence not admissible. Third, homogenisation of religious groups within a nation is possible only through coercive conversion of one group to another (one cannot be a Hindu and a Muslim or a Muslim and a Christian at the same time) or through the physical liquidation of all the minority religious communities by the dominant community with the connivance of the state, that is fascism. Neither of these solutions is democratic and hence acceptable. Fourth, homogenisation of linguistic communities is not necessary because one can learn more than one language; one's own mother tongue plus the official and/or the dominant language.

II

With these preliminaries in mind, let us look at the linkage between religion and nation. Religion and nation are not and cannot be linked; nationalism based on religion is not tenable. Why? Whichever way one defines a nation, contiguous territory – a common homeland – is an absolute necessity for it to emerge and exist. You cannot have part of your nation in Asia and the other part in Africa or America. Separated parts become entities like Sindhis in India or they establish new nations in new homelands as French Canadians did. On the other hand, religious communities are invariably territorially dispersed. A faith community does not have a common homeland. That is, de-territorialisation of religion is a fact.

One could argue that this fact applies only to those religions which convert – Christianity, Islam, Buddhism or Sikhism. But geographical dispersion can also occur through migration or colonization. Thus, Judaism is one of the most geographically dispersed religions in the world.

Hinduism does not convert, but only gradually assimilate. But Hindus do migrate. Thus, countries such as Surinam, Fiji or Mauritius have substantial Hindu population. That is, the co-terminality between religion and territory is disturbed due to conquest, colonialism and immigration. Therefore, any effort to establish a nation based on religion is doomed to fail.

If religion and territory were co-terminus and if religion was an accepted basis of nation formation, there would have been only a few nations in the world as world religions are only a few. The three Semitic religions – Judaism, Christianity and Islam; the four Indic religions – Hinduism, Buddhism, Jainism and Sikhism; and the couple of religions of Chinese origin – Confucianism and Shintoism – together make less than a dozen (I don't know whether you have noticed that all world-religions are of Asian origin). But today there are more than 80 'nation-states' which profess Christianity, over 50 which are predominantly populated by Muslims, over a dozen Buddhist majority countries, and even Hinduism is a majority religion in two countries – India and Nepal. Thus, if Hindu Rashtra is to be built, the first item on the agenda of the Indian state should be annexation of Nepal! If religion alone could be the basis of nation, Muslim Pakistan would not have split into Bangladesh and Pakistan; and there is no rationale in Pakistan and Afghanistan with contiguous territories remaining separate states. Latin America is predominantly Catholic and yet there are over a dozen 'nation-states' in that continent.

This brings me to my third point. Religions are utterly diverse and heterogeneous from within. Intra-religious intolerance is as much pronounced as inter-religious animosity. The tension between the numerous denominations in Christianity is well-known, although the Catholic- Protestant conflict is the one which is mostly pronounced. The conflicts between Sunnis and Shias are well-known and the Ahmedias are not even counted as Muslims by the two major Muslim sects. The tension between Sikhs and Nirankaris is too familiar to us. Hinayana and Mahayana Buddhists are not always at peace. Common religion, namely Mahayana Buddhism, which it shares with China does not 'integrate' Tibet with China. The Hutus and Tutsis, the fierce enemies in Africa, are both Catholics. That is, from all accounts even the people of the same religious community or even the same sectarian/denominational groups within them cannot constitute peaceful 'nations'. In the case of Hinduism, the deep wedge based on castes and languages make it highly fractionated. And as I noted earlier, Hindus are not only in India. Nepal's official religion is Hinduism and some 25 million Hindus live outside South Asia. Therefore, one-nation one-religion is an untenable proposition.

Is the postulate 'one culture, many religions', an idea floated often in India these days, plausible? The postulate is a summation of confusion because religion is an important dimension of culture; many religions necessarily imply difficult layers of culture. Religious pluralism should mean the dignified co-existence of these cultural layers. To bring them all under one cultural rubric, whether one calls it Indianisation or Hindutva or something else, is an agenda to homogenise them, to annihilate their specificities is the exact opposite of cultural pluralism.

What are the implications of establishing a nation, based on one religion? First, since no part of the world is exclusively populated by one religious community, to establish nations based on religions would mean one of the following: (a) annihilation of minority and/or weak religious groups, (b) their assimilation – either voluntary or forced or (c) their marginalisation within the polity. That is, there are two inevitable consequences in establishing a religion-based nation: genocide and/or culturocide -- systematic liquidation of cultures. Both are utterly anti-democratic and admittedly fascist. If culturocide is attempted, this should inevitably lead to homogenisation of cultures and hegemonisation by the dominant community. When demands are made in India to stop beef-eating or pork-eating, this is precisely what is implied. Last years's newspaper reports about objections to meat-eating on the day Mahavir Jayanti and Idul Zuha coincided was a pointer towards hegemonisation. For the Muslims, it is customary and sacral to eat the meat of sacrificial goat on the day of Idul Zuha, for Jains, who are congenital vegetarians to eat meat is an abhorrent act, particularly on Mahavir Jayanti. Now the question is whose belief or ritual should prevail? In a multi-religious democratic nation the customs of all religious communities ought to be respected; this is the essence of religious pluralism.

Second, if a religion-based nation is established, those who do not belong to the 'national religion' are not simply minoritized but also marginalized in the 'nation' as a whole. The Buddhists, Christians and Hindus are marginalized in Bangladesh as well as in Pakistan. In Sri Lanka Hindus, Christians and Muslims are marginalized. In India, although Hinduism is not the official religion, for all practical purposes Muslims, Christians, Sikhs and Buddhists, particularly the former two, are marginalized. Not only that. The majority religious community of the country may also get marginalized in some parts of the country as exemplified by the case of Hindus in the Kashmir Valley or to some extent in Nagaland and Mizoram or even in the Punjab.

Not only that the religious minorities are marginalized, some of them are viewed as outsiders. This is the case with Muslims, Christians, Zoroastrians, Bahais and Jews in India. There are several manifestations of this. The most recent is the willing celebration of the *Jayantis* of founders of Buddhism, Sikhism and Jainism but the refusal to acknowledge and celebrate 2000 as the Year of Christ. This culturally orphans the 25 million Christians of India. And the curious fact is that there is hardly any alien elements among the Christians of India. In fact, the overwhelming majority of Christians are converts from Adivasis and Dalits, admittedly the earliest natives of India. The act of conversion pursued by Christians and Muslims is invoked to de-nationalize them, to label and stigmatise them as 'outsiders'. Not only that. Even states with official religions will treat co-religionists as outsiders when they are outside their homelands. Thus, those Muslims who migrated to Pakistan from Uttar Pradesh with great enthusiasm are now treated as outsiders. The same is the case of Bihari Muslims in Bangladesh. That is, a state based on religion provides no guarantee to treat the dislocated co-religionists as co-nationals.

Third, in a polity wherein an exclusionary religious orientation prevails the secularists, agnostics and atheists will have no freedom of expression. The responses to the contents of Satanic Verses or to the drawings of Saraswati and Sita by M.F. Husain or to the film Fire vividly illustrate this. When actual or contrived mass protests against such documents or events occur, the states tend to ban them in the name of maintaining law and order. This, in turn, would mean that both the state and oppositional forces get intimidated and silenced by violent protests.

Even states which are constitutionally 'secular' do not adhere to secularism in practice. For example, although Indian secularism is defined as equal respect to all religions and/or equal distance from all religions, consider the following facts. First, the proclivity to ignore the specificity of religious practices of Adivasis and Dalits and their being labelled as Hindus, if they are not converts to one of the so-called world-religions. This undermines the religious identity of these communities. Second, the expansionism that Indian Constitution and Hindu Code Bill indulge in by defining Indian Protestant religions such as Buddhism, Jainism and Sikhism as Hindu for certain purposes. This is done to achieve 'integration' of the followers of Indic religions but denies autonomy to these religions. Third, the exclusivist practice in the cases of non-Indic religions with regard to the policy of protective discrimination. Two reasons are advanced in defence of this. One is, these religions do not recognize the caste system. But this is equally applicable to Indian Protestant religions as they all emerged out of revolts against caste system. The second is an assumption that those who convert experience upward social mobility. But there is no clinching evidence to demonstrate this. Fourth, reluctance on the part of the caste to act as a reformer in the case of non-Indic religions while acting as a reformer in case of Indic religions thereby violating the principle of keeping equal distance from all religions.

The argument that minority religious collectivities resist change is equally applicable to the majority religious community too; recall the fierce resistance to Hindu Code Bill from conservative Hindu elements.

I must also note here the trivialisation that nationalism has undergone recently. During the colonial era, wresting self-rule (*swaraj*) was the goal. Not only self-rule, but economic development, social reform, uplift of all (*sarvodaya*) and particularly the uplift of the poor (*antyodaya*) were the guiding principles. And Indians have not hated even the oppressive coloniser who exploited them for two centuries. But today what passes for nationalism are a curious mix of things – exploding nuclear devices, defeating the 'enemy' in games of cricket, football or hockey, and torturing cross border migrants. That is, nationalism survives through demonisation of the other. Greater the capacity for destruction and revenge of the 'nation', the higher is the intensity of nationalism; greater the ability to overkill the enemy, larger is the glory of the nation. This is a negative and oppressive concept of nation and nationalism. And what is more, religion is the anchorage of this rendition of nation and nationalism. What we need is an emancipatory and inclusive notion of nation and nationalism. And this is possible only if the dominant religion is accommodative.

In his address to the World Parliament of Religions in 1893, Swami Vivekananda said with great gusto: 'I am proud to belong to a religion which has taught the world both tolerance and universal acceptance. We believe not only in universal toleration but we accept all religions as true. I am proud to belong to a nation which has sheltered the persecuted and the refugees of all religions and all nations of the earth'. How strange and alien these words sound today in year 2000 after a little over 100 years!

It is important to recall here that the exponents of religious nationalism are utterly irreligious; they have only utilized religion to build religious majoritarian states. V.D. Savarkar, perhaps the most important ideologue of Hindu Rashtra, was an agnostic, even an atheist; he never visited temples or sacred places. His notion of Hindutva is an enunciation of how to govern a Hindu majority state. That is, Hindutva is a political agenda while Hinduism is a religion. Similarly, M.A. Jinnah, the founder of Pakistan, was not a believer in Islam but a staunch politician who wanted to provide social justice to the Muslim population in a Hindu majority polity although he overshot the target and ended up with a Muslim state. In both cases the confluence of state and nation is evident and the injustice towards minority religious group is loud and clear.

I have often heard many, including well-meaning liberals, arguing that Hinduism cannot be fundamentalist because it does not have an identifiable founder, an ultimate text and a regulating Church. And yet it is true that both M.K. Gandhi and his assassin Nathuram Godse are widely perceived as 'good Hindus' although by different Hindu groups. I suggest that there is a fundamental difference between them which is fundamental. While M.K. Gandhi conceived of a 'nation' which is inclusive of all religions, his assassin championed the cause of a 'nation' which excluded non-Hindus. Godse championed the cause of a Hindu state,

Gandhiji rejected it lock, stock and barrel. It is this exclusionary orientation which tends to make Hinduism fundamentalist. It is not the Hinduism of Vedanta, of Vivekananda, of M.K. Gandhi which advocates religious pluralism.

Let me conclude by stipulating the conditionalities for the emergence and existence of religious pluralism. First, delink state and nation and pursuantly citizenship and nationality. Citizenship is an instrument of equality and nationality, is an anchorage of identity. Second, abandon the notion of terminal loyalty to the state and endorse the idea of contextual loyalties. The notion of hierarchy of loyalty should be replaced by the idea of horizontal loyalties. Third, delegitimise the idea of an official or state religion which necessarily marginalizes those who belong to minority religions. Further, even in uni-religious polities such a policy will marginalize atheists, rationalists, agnostics and secularists. Fourth, dissociate nation and religion and delegitimise the idea of nation formation based on religion, not only because of empirical untenability of their union but also the inherent undemocratic tendency their linkage entails. Fifth, facilitate the self-definition and identity assertion of all religions irrespective of their sources of origin and presence in a polity. This is in tune with the contemporary democratic ethos. Sixth, accept the notions of multiple identities and identity-set; advocate the selective invocation of contextually appropriate identity. Seventh, do not visualize secularism or rationality as alternatives to religiosity or spirituality; recognize the possibility of their co-existence in different contexts. Eighth, refuse to endorse the advocacy that equality is a substitute for identity. Human beings aggressively seek both. Ninth, recognize cultural diversity as a fact of life and cultural pluralism, that is the dignified co-existence of cultural collectivities and practices, as value orientation. However, insist that cultural pluralism is utterly different from cultural relativism, which encloses all kinds of inhuman practices in the name of cultural purity. Tenth, recognize that all religions have their assets and liabilities and the ingenuity of a religion depends upon its ability to abandon its liability and enlarge its assets. In this process selective borrowing of the assets of other religious traditions becomes an imperative.

11

Education and Living : The Sustainability Connection

K. John Mammen

Donella H. Meadows and associates in their trail-blazing treatise *Beyond the Limits,* published in 1992, contended that the ideas of limits, sustainability, sufficiency, equity and efficiency are not barriers, obstructions or threats, and that sustainability is the ultimate challenge to the energy and creativity of the human race. They put forth the rationale that transition to a sustainable society requires a careful balance between long-term and short-term goals and an emphasis on sufficiency, equity and quality of life, rather than on quantity of output and that it required more than productivity and technology. It necessitated maturity, compassion and wisdom. The success of the Agricultural Revolution and the Industrial Revolution has created the necessity for another revolution, namely, the Sustainability Revolution. The transition to a sustainable society called for visioning, networking, truth telling, learning and loving. The learning-process will have to supplant the education process which means exploring a new path with vigour and courage, being open to other people's explorations of other paths and being willing to switch paths if new evidence suggests that another one leads more efficiently or directly to perceived goals and aspirations.

The foregoing thoughts from *Beyond the Limits* were cited since when concepts like education and sustainable living are deliberated, a pronounced tendency for what Max Black termed "Loose Concepts" can attend. Although Aristotle considered the object of education as the disinterested endeavour to learn and propagate that which is best known and thought, with the passage of centuries the rationale of education has undergone a sea-change. Today it is particularly so in the context of certain imposed societal goals which are linked to economic reforms which stipulate that production and income must rise, distribution of income must improve, unemployment must fall and economic growth is optimised with enhanced volume of exports aided by structural adjustments. Higher education is most extensively and expensively accommodated today to serve the needs of a culture home-grown in the highly industrialized Western countries, which does not have an intrinsic air of societal urgency. When John Kenneth Galbraith gave expression to these thoughts in his book, *The New Industrial State,* in 1967 and very emphatically suggested that in future there will prevail a dispute over the definition of success and that there will be a controversy over both the legitimacy of alternative goals of life and living, and the means of achieving them, many an eyebrow was raised. Galbraith has proved prophetic. Voices are heard both in the West and East that the process of education has to be emancipated from a self-inflicted bondage as a hand-maid of an inhuman and cancerous industrial system. Interestingly, John Maynard Keynes was a forerunner to Galbraith when he expressed a similar train of thought way back in 1932 in his *Essays on Persuasion.*

The inalienable relation of education to human life and living was highlighted at very many U.N. Conferences. The UN Conference on Environment and Development at Rio de Janeiro in 1992 adopted, among other things, a strategy that public information, education and understanding was important in promoting more effective participation of citizens in attempting solutions to environment crisis. The Vienna Conference on Human Rights in 1993 affirmed education as a basic human right. The Cairo Conference on Population in 1994 stressed the link between population-growth and education and the implications of women's access to education. The Beijing Conference on Women in 1995 emphasised the imperative need to guarantee learning opportunities at all levels to women and girl-children. The Social Development Summit at Copenhagen in 1995 identified education as an indispensable means of combating poverty. The Istambul Conference on Human Settlement in 1996 highlighted education as a necessary means of improving quality of life in cities and rural communities. The Food Summit at Rome in 1996 recognised the need for the education of food producers and consumers in meeting the growing shortage of food in various parts of the world.

The World Declaration on "Education For All" (EFA) was adopted at Jomtien (Thailand) in 1990 stressing the need for more effort, resources and imagination in universal education for children and in adult education and literacy. In a mid-term review of EFA in 1996 at Amman in Jordan the Jomtien Declaration of EFA was reaffirmed. And very recently the E 9 countries – India, Pakistan, Bangladesh, Brazil, Egypt, Indonesia, Mexico and Nigeria (with China not participating) met at Islamabad in Pakistan to review the progress made in universalising school education under the EFA resolution.

The Dolars Commission on Education in the 21st Century reported in 1996 that the concept of learning throughout life is the key that gives access to the 21st century. It went beyond the traditional distinctions between initial and continuing education. It also linked the concept of the learning society in which everything affords an opportunity of learning and fulfilling one's potential. The report suggested that in the 21st century education needed to build on the four pillars of learning – 'to know', 'to do', 'to live together' and 'to be'.

At the International Conference on Adult Education at Hamburg, Germany, India's Minister for Human Resources Development put across that education enabled a person to find a solution to his or her problems, and a nation to effectively tackle its societal issues, and that for this the goal of education should be to create 'moral individuals' with a universal outlook and having concern for society. In the learning society of the future, literacy can provide a variety of educational opportunities thereby reducing the mass-elite gap. What is more, adult education is an activity that plays its role throughout a person's life and acts as a supplement to formal schooling.

As part of the 'Special Events' at the World Summit for Social Development at Copenhagen in 1995, the Association of Danish Folk High Schools organised a Workshop on 'Education and Social Progress'. The statement issued on the conclusions arrived at the workshop is an interesting document. It puts forth a contention that "Formal education needs to be maintained and improved while recognising that it has failed crucially in some important respects where popular (folk) education can make a significant contribution". One wonders whether correctives can at all be grafted to or made in the formal education system, 'wherever it has crucially failed', adopting a soft option of improving it. What is warranted is a revisionist and reformative approach since what one witnesses even in Denmark today is the formal education and folk education streams running parallel without providing avenues for the interactive learning processes. Another contention in the statement is thought-provoking: "A strong civil society produces a strong sustainable economy, but it does not work in the reverse. The conditions of sustainability can be destroyed if people do not influence their own development". In poor countries one wonders whether it should be attempted to summon infinite patience to establish first civil society so that a strong sustainable economy can be established. A paper titled "To be a Citizen in the 21st Century", presented at the Rajiv Gandhi Institute for Contemporary Studies in 1996 by Dr. Alough Hareven of Israel, pointedly mentioned that, "For people who are hungry and homeless, being a citizen and sharing in citizenship are empty phrases. So a nation which wishes to evolve a civil society must effectively facilitate people out of their misery". Posing the question "Is it then futile to speak of shared citizenship in countries where such miseries prevail on a large scale"? Dr Hareven reflects that "Closing social and economic gaps cannot be conceived only in terms of government responsibility" and that such a view smacks of "patronistic approach". He generalises to state that the preferred view is that closing social and economic gaps must be the shared effort of the government and of the deprived communities. He interprets

Mahatma Gandhi to advantage to fashion the view that the implicit message is that citizens at large should not play a passive role about their own future. But the question arises whether in fashioning such a role for citizens, a credible charismatic leadership is an imperative necessity. Does it warrant a crisis situation for such leadership to emerge? The question as to how the growth of civic identity as empowerment of the individual and as an identity equally shared by all citizens is to be facilitated, remains inadequately addressed, let alone answered. As Dr. Hareven observes "There are no facile answers and they vary from country to country; they vary also in the immensity of the obstacles which the growth of shared citizenship must overcome". The debate has just commenced.

The Basic Education precept propounded by Mahatma Gandhi did not really catch up in India. Poet Rabindranath Tagore's *Gurukula* pattern of education foray stands stunted as 'Bonsai' at Santiniketan with the passage of years. And in Denmark the Grundtwingian educational reformationist foray seems to be losing ground if one were to look at the crumbling family and societal solidarity blinded by the cataract of affluence and permissiveness. Arthur Morgan's communitarian ideas are not reflected in the American mainstream and remain academic curiosities, with practitioners in isolated isles of experimentation. Was lack of support of critical mass of political will, the reason behind the eclipse of the unexceptionable precepts? This calls for discussion and debate.

Marco Antonio Dias, Director of UNESCO's Division of Higher Education, contended at a UNESCO Conference on Higher Education in Latin America that "Before we decide what kind of university we want, we must decide what kind of society to build". The Sarvodaya Society of Mahatma Gandhi's dream, of which basic education was an inalienable part, stands far removed from the sovereign democratic socialist republic vouchsafed in the preamble to the Indian Constitution and which has undergone a process of metamorphosis over a period of nearly 50 years into a permissive liberalised society with the forces of unbridled competition and marketisation in full play.

Poet Rabindranath Tagore thought that if he could bring light and life into a few villages in India, that will be the India of his dreams and that the inheritors of his legacy would carry on the torch handed over to them – an intent which was sadly belied. Grundtwing's folkschool idea may perhaps be looked at as a protest and an attempted answer to the aberrations of a fundamentalist religious society, German fanaticism and the grammar school and not as a nation-building developmental instrument, although it is a thought-churner and action-conditioner in various parts of the world not excluding India. Arthur Morgan's communitarian foray in education (based on his vision of the community of the future) has remained and continues to remain stagnant in practice pitted as it was and is against a sick society which was taken over by satanic technology, mindless competition and unbridled and affluent consumerism.

Popular enthusiasm for societal typology preferences seems to be on the wane. And yet conceptually one has to reflect on societal paradigms to shape one's mind-set for purposive social action. Delivering the second Lakshmi N. Menon Memorial International Lecture at Thiruvananthapuram in Kerala on 30th November 1996 Dr. A.T. Ariyaratne made a passionate plea that we should rethink about the validity or feasibility of blindly following Western economic theory and practice and wondered that 'perhaps a theory of a "Full Engagement Society" will be a more feasible and realisable concept in our (poor countries) rural situation". He summoned the thoughts of Mahatma Gandhi, J.C. Kumarappa, E.F. Schumacher and Lord Buddha and pleaded that every home and every neighbourhood should become a social laboratory and also suggested that the best point to start is the home and educational institutions. He then stated that world today has an abundance of knowledge and harmless technologies at its disposal which can be used to build a peaceful and contented society without continuing in the path of greed, ill-will and ignorance. Dr. Ariyaratne's view that poverty will be on the increase as competition has taken over co-operation and that a people-based, need-based, alternative economy in which everybody can gainfully participate has to be worked out, is indeed unexceptionable. However, what makes one reason in askance is on the sustainability of a Full Engagement Society which may be an attempted answer to the limitations and constraints of the Keynesian Full Employment Society. Be that as it may.

Now and in the foreseeable future, concern of people in poor countries will surround the twin-concepts of 'preventive' and 'curative' development stemming from the Vienna Conference on Human Rights and the Copenhagen Summit. Preventive development will support people's participation in the growth of civil society and good governance and human rights, whereas curative development will address fighting privation, hunger, poverty, famine, disease and other ills that deprive the poor from meeting their basic needs. Any effective development foray worth the name ought to enhance the quality of life and living of poor people. India has the largest segment of the world's poor and it is with this backdrop that quite a few educational forays in India are to be seen. Closely looked at, these forays appear ill-suited and superficial attempts to tinker with the existing system. A vision of education for societal transformation is conspicuous by its very absence in these forays. The Education For All (EFA) movement in India is at best confined to universalisation of elementary education and adult literacy components. The District Primary Education Programme, financed by the World Bank and other International agencies, look at the first five years of primary education with prime focus on delivery mechanisms. Bulk of these programmes are geared towards mainstreaming students into the formal schools system guided by the same ideological compulsions as those of schools in the West, and enhancing structural facilities. World Bank's approach to education is based on an "Economics-only vision" or rather fraudulent economics as the world's poor might perceive it. There appears to prevail considerable disenchantment at the beneficiary-level and a climate of 'mutual mistrust' between donors and beneficiaries.

If education is to promote sustainable living, it needs to become a liberating and emancipative force. This would warrant a major conceptual change from current demagogic practices. All efforts so far towards reorienting the educational idiom in India have proved only cosmetic touches at best. It is here that Paulo Freire becomes relevant. The school and university level education system still retains the traditions of the colonial heritage. The Western orientation in India's education precepts and practices bear the imprint of a cultural invasion and of Western socio-cultural tastes. Poor countries which achieved political freedom need to seriously rethink on their current educational practices and introduce a change of track in their educational endeavours adopting Freire's method of teaching literacy based on day-to-day experience of students, creating social consciousness that would take learners out of poverty and privation. Freire's liberation education philosophy recognises and honours local culture and community culture, providing many a forum for individuals to empower themselves and creating awareness of the political nature of education to the teaching process. It is conceded that the tie of Freire's teaching ideal to those of people's education i.e. folk education, is close.

Delivering the August Foral Oration in Copenhagen on 9th July 1990, Dr. Ariyaratne outlined his perceptions of a liberated personality and a liberated society. There is a remarkable and reassuring parallel between Freire's thoughts on liberation in regard to education and that of Dr. Ariyaratne. Dr. Ariyaratne stressed "our future as a global community depends on the extent to which we succeed in creating world- wide processes of total personality, family and local community awakening". Dr. Ariyaratne's optimism that before the year 2000 AD the critical mass of consciousness needed to create the basis of a new world order in which sobriety, values of temperance, brotherhood and peace can be achieved by our common efforts, stagnated as a pious wish.

When the linkage between education and sustainable living is deliberated higher education scenario also merits specific consideration. The World Conference on Higher Education took place at the UNESCO headquarters at Paris in the latter part of 1998. It approved a world-wide action-plan aiming to reinforce the contribution of tertiary education to economic and social development and democracy. It is hoped that this plan will open ways for the much-needed reform of national systems of higher education of UNESCO's member-countries. It needs mention that some industrially advanced countries (e.g. U.S.A., Australia) are utilising their higher education facilities for foreign exchange earning from poor country beneficiaries. Dependence on higher education facilities with the industrially advanced countries is mostly from poor countries resulting in foreign exchange drain that will retard the efforts for improving quality of life and living in poor countries. The relationship of higher education on the one side, and social development, higher production and economic growth, the reinforcement of cultural identity and the maintenance of social cohesion, the struggle against poverty and promotion of a culture of peace, on the other side, merits detailed and in-depth consideration. The typology of higher education – its capacity to respond to society's needs calls for carefully focused attention in poor countries which experience braindrain, foreign exchange drain, subversion of indigenous lifestyles, and imposition of wasteful, ostentatious and unaffordable lifestyles. Poor countries need to ponder in-depth when USAID claims that "United States has become the University of the World" and that it is "shaping millions of future leaders of the developing world"!

Norwegian social scientist Johan Galtung has done pioneering studies on lifestyles. His study on "Alternative Lifestyles in Rich Countries" was published in *Development Dialogue* and was discussed at an annual meeting of the World Future Studies Federation. In this study, Galtung enunciated the characteristics of "high-consumption, high-energy societies" and "low-consumption low-energy societies" and argued that a major problem in Third World countries is to guarantee for all a 'Social Minimum" where resources needed for basic-needs satisfaction are concerned. Galtung also cited the corresponding problem of industrialised countries: to define and live according to the idea of a "Social Maximum", a ceiling which should not be trespassed. Although UNDP's Human Development Indices (HDI) are published annually, Sustainable Living Indices have not been computed so far, although enquiries of a desparate, nature have been attempted on nature's limited capacity, man's limited capacity, limit to inequality, limit to exploitation, etc.

The virtues of simple living and high thinking have been aired from time to time. Mahatma Gandhi suggested that "One should eat to live and not live to eat' and that mother earth has enough resources to meet everyone's need and not anyone's greed. Galtung looked at the dialectic between "regular life" and "vacation life" in rich countries. Contextually, one is reminded of Abraham Maslow's hierarchy of needs which ranges between fulfilment of basic needs and self-actualisation. Maslow did not take into consideration the renunciation philosophy of the "Rishis" and "Pillar-saints" of ages past.

Man or woman does not live by bread alone. When one considers sustainable living, one has to pay attention to material and non-material needs like virtues of togetherness, new experiences, innovation, self-actualisation and happiness. Then there is the question of "meaningful life" in general, and individual life in particular and a process of inner human enrichment where such things as insight, joy and happiness are meaningless unless one also contributes to the insight, joy and happiness of others.

What will be the nature of an appropriate education paradigm of the future? Galtung advocated a de-emphasis on schooling and re-emphasis on education and learning processes as also a learning society and even suggested innovative "Education Cafeterias" with various menu-choices! It is in fashion these days to promote "Development Education" in the West as also the East. In a dynamic world, concepts of education and sustainable living need not and ought not remain static. In poor countries where Liberation Education is a felt-need, it should precede Development Education forays to realize enhanced economic growth and quality of life. Edifices of education need be built on firm foundations of appropriate and relevant society – configurations which are culturally compatible lest there should be dismay and disaster later.

THE CONTRIBUTORS

Shakti Bethea holds a bachelor's degree in Psychology and Spanish, a master's degree in Social Work, and a Ph.D. in Integrative Sciences, an interdisciplinary doctorate from the Union Institute which includes the social, political, economic and physical sciences. She practiced social work for twenty years in mental health, public school, medical and community settings and has taught at the University of Denver Graduate School of Social work. Shakti currently teaches at Front Range Community College and also directs the Bethea Institute for Research on the Transformation of Humanity.

Romesh Diwan obtained his Ph.D. from the University of Birmingham and taught in Universities of Glaslow, Punjab and Hawaii before joining the faculty of Rensselaer Polytechnic Institute where he now serves as Professor of Economics. He was Chairman of the Department during 1982-1987. He has published four books and more than 150 articles in a variety of journals. The books are *Alternative Development Strategies and Appropriate Technology: Science Policy for an Equitable World Order, Essays in Gandhian Economics*, *Productivity and Technical Change in Food Grains*, and *High Technology and International Competitiveness* – all co-authored. He has been the founding Chairperson of the Association of Indian Economic Studies and has edited theme – based issues of journals like *Seminar* and *Asian Thought and Society*. He is or has been on the editorial board of *Asian Thought and Society, Eastern Economic Journal, Gandhi Marg, Indian Journal of Quantitative Economics*, and *International Business*. He is listed in Marqis *Who's Who in the World 1995*, 12th Edition and Who's Who in

America, 1984-85, 43rd Edition and later editions. He lives at 15 Northstar Drive, Troy, NY 12180-6512.

Peter Van Den Dungen is lecturer in Peace Studies attached to the School of Peace Studies, University of Bradford, West Yorkshire, BD7 1DP, U.K. His areas of interest are History of Peace, pacifism, and internationalism; United Nations and other international organizations; and Peace education, Peace culture and Peace museums. He has also been monitoring attempts for establishing peace museums world wide and engages in advocacy and activism in this line.

Amalendu Guha has held positions like Professor of International Economics at University of Bucharest, Romania, Research Fellow at International Peace Research Institute Oslo, Research Professor and Project Leader of World Indicators Programme, Chair in Conflict and Peace Research of University of Oslo, Researcher at the Norwegian Institute of International Affairs and visiting Professorships/Research Fellowships in as many as sixty-four universities and research institutes located in different countries. He is a former editor of the Scandinavian Journal of Development Alternatives. Currently he is Professor and Director of the Institute for Alternative Development Research. He has authored/co-authored 28 books and published more than 350 research articles in different Journals. Notable among his books are *Development Alternative, Conflict and Peace: Theory and Practice, Maldevelopment: Process and Mechanism, Development and Human Ecology.*

His address for communication is P.O.Box 870 Sentrum 0104 Oslo, Norway. Phone and Fax: (47)22-410949 Residence (47)22-295417.

K. John Mammen is a Thiruvananthapuram – based Development Economist. He has held research positions at Gandhi Vichar Parishad, Wardha; Viswabharati University; Gandhigram Rural Institute; Centre for Research on New International Economic Order, Chennai and Centre for Research in Education, Innovation and Development, Mitraniketan. He has authored two books, one on the *Economics of Water Resources Development* and the other on *Challenges of Rural Development.*

He contributes regularly articles to leading journals and national dailies. He is recipient of the United Writers' Association Award for Development Economics in 1992.

T.K. Oommen is Professor of Sociology at the Centre for the Study of Social Systems, School of Social Sciences, Jawaharlal Nehru University. He is a former President of the International Sociological Association and has authored several books. Notable among his recent books are *Citizenship, Nationality and Ethnicity: Reconciling Competing Identities, Alien Concepts and South Asian Reality, The Christian Clergy in India and Citizenship, National Identity: from Colonialism to Globalism* and *Agrarian Movements in Kerala.*

Authony J Parel is Professor Emeritus in Political Science at University of Calgary. He has also taught at the University of British Columbia and Concordia University, Montreal and is a member of Clare Hall, Cambridge. He is the author of *Machiavellian Cosmos* and edited works like *Studies under the Upas Tree, Gandhi : Hind Swaraj and Other Writings*, and *Gandhi: Freedom and Self-Rule*.

K. Raghavendra Rao is a Professor of Political Science specialized in political theory, particularly Marxism and Gandhian thought. He had taught in Gauhati, Karnatak and Mangalore Universities and has contributed several illuminating articles in *Gandhi Marg.*

Gene Sharp is Senior Scholar in Residence at the Albert Einstein Institution and is an Associate of the Programme on Nonviolent Sanctions at Harvard University's Center for International Affairs. Professor emeritus of Political Science at the University of Massachusetts at Dartmouth, he has also taught in the University of Oslo, University of Massachusetts at Boston and various other institutions. His books include *The Politics of Nonviolence Action (3 Volumes), Gandhi as a Political Strategist, Making Europe Unconquerable, and Civilian-Based Defence: A post Military Weapons System.*

Sulak Sivaraksa began his career as a Teaching Assistant at the School of Oriental and African Studies and was a lecturer at Thammasat University. He served as the founder editor of Social

Science Review during 1963-69. He was a Visiting Professor at the University of California (Berkley), Cornell University, University of Toronto and University of Hawaii. He was a founder and Director of Shanti Pracha Dhamma Institute, established in April, 1998. He was also the founder and Director of the Thai Inter-Religious Commission for Development. His name has been twice recommended for the Nobel Peace Prize. He received the Right Livelihood Award, often described as the alternative Nobel Prize. He has published several books.

Usha Thakkar, formerly Professor and Head of the Department of Political Science, S.N.D.T Women's University, Bombay, is currently Hon. Director, Manibhavan, Gandhi Sangrahalaya, Bombay. She has researched on Gandhi, Vinobha Bhave, Political Participation of Women, Empowerment of Women Presidents of Village Panchayats. She is a Visiting Professor at the Institute of Gandhian Studies, Wardha, Maharashtra.

T.K.N. Unnithan is Professor of Sociology and a Former Vice-Chancellor of the University of Rajasthan. He has researched on Gandhi's Views on Social Change and Sociology of Non-Violence and Peace. He is currently associated with the Khejri Sarvodaya Trust, Jaipur.

INDEX

Abala, 179
Acculturation, 171
Acharya Kripalani, 34, 174
Adivasis, xix, 206
Adolf de Obieta, 89
Adult education, 33, 212
Afghanistan, 204
Aga Khan Palace, 25
Agricultural revolution, 210
Ahimsa (non-killing), 52, 66, 69, 70, 71, 134, 183
Alipuram Jail, 3, 25
All India Congress Committee (AICC), x, 27
All India Spinner's Association, xi, 34, 39, 42
All India Students' Congress, ix, 11, 12, 14, 17
All India Village Industries Association, xi
Alternative Nobel Prizes, 90
Alternative paradigms, 152
Anti-Asiatic legislation, 68
Anti-imperialistic approach, 116
Antyodaya, 207
Aprigraha, 135
Archbishop, 80
Aristotle, 154, 210
Ariyaratne, A. T., 215, 217
Arnold, Edwin,23
Ashrams, 12, 130-31
August Comte, 99
Aung San Suu Kyi, 76
Aurobindo Ghose, 96

Baba Amte, 81
Bandopadhaya, S. K., 34
Bangladesh, 192, 204
Basic education, 214
Beijing Conference, 211
Bengal terrorist organisation, 102
Bethea, Shakti, xv, 113
Bhagvad Gita, 133
Bhavana (mindfulness), 51, 53, 54, 56
Birth-control, method of, 181
Black, Max, 210
Bose, Subhash Chandra, 10
Brahma Vihara, 48
Brahmacharya, 186
Bread labour, 135, 136
Brij Mohan, 17
Brundtland, Gro Harlem, 85
Brussels, 7
Buddhadasa Bhikku, 60
Buddhism, xii, 47, 48, 49, 50, 51, 58, 203, 205, 206, 215

Cairo Conference, 211
Capitalism, 47, 48, 49, 50, 54
Catholic-Protestant Conflict, 204
Challenges, 13, 61, 66, 17, 72, 74, 151
Child abuse, 116
Child marriage, 80
Choudhury, H.R., 84
Christianity, 203, 206
Common homeland, 203
Communalism, xviii, 182
Computer technology, 16
Conceptual definitions, 114-15
Constructive Action, 50
Consumerism, 52, 54, 55, 56, 59, 61
Coomaraswamy, Ananda, 106
Copenhagen Summit, 216
Corruption, 159
Creative altruism, 175
Cultural pluralism, 209
Current Malaise, 115-18
Czechoslovakia, 68

Daisaku Ikede, 85
Dalai Lama, 8, 76, 79, 80
Damayanti, 185
Damodaran, A.K., 20
Dana (Sharing), 51
Das, Taraknath, xv, 102, 103, 104, 105
Dazzling purity, 186
Decentralized production, 196
Deborah, lifestyle, 126-30
Delusion (*mudra*), 53, 61
Democratic participation, 60, 61
Demonstration, 25
Desmond Tutu, 80
Development Paradigm Transition, 189-195
Dhammas, 50, 51
Dhammapada, 133
Dharma, 155
Dias, Marco Autonio, 214
Dijkstra, Piet, 32
Diploma programme, 40, 41

Discrimination, 76
Disobedience, 68
Disparities, 193
District Primary Education programme, 216
Diwan, Romesh,xv, 113
Dixit, J.N., 30
Dolars Commission, 212
Domestic Violence, 116-17
Draupadi, 185
Drugs addiction, 60
Duugen, Peter Van den, xiv, 76
Duragraha, 182
Durkheim, Emile, 175
Dutch National Youth Council, 32
Dutta, Manoranjan, 10

Ecological distress, 138, 140
Economic destabilisation, 192, 193
dimension, 48
inequality, 138
management mechanism, 189
prosperity, 195
self-reliance, 184-85
Edith Ballantyne, 83
Education cafeterias, 219
Education for All, 211, 212, 216
Einstein, Albert, xiv
Eirwin, Harbottle, 82
Emergency, 23, 26
election, 35
Empire Theatre, 68
Employment, 16, 199
Environmental violence, 45-60
Equality (*samanattata*), 50-51, 56, 135
Exploitation, 47, 51, 52, 137, 163, 167, 219
Export, 198

Family breakdown, 138
First World War, 82
Folk education, 217
Food security, 197-99
Food Summit, 212
Foster, E. M., 109
French Revolution, 59
Freire, Paulo, 217
Full Engagement Society, 215, 216

Galbraith, John Kenneth, 211
Galtung, John, 83, 218, 219
Gambling, 60
Gandhi, Mahatma, 30
accomplishments, 64
constructive programme, xiv, 28, 67
doctrine of non-violence, 174
epistemology, 157
ethical thought, 170
freedom movement 20, 167
ideal non-violent democracy, 165
interpretation of, 34
lesson in new century, 71
message of, 11
movement for national independence, 163
non-violent struggle, 64, 67, 68, 70-72
opposition to UN, 168
patriotism, 162, 166
personality and social philosophy, 79
political character, 70
political emancipation, 182-84
spiritual views, 65
thinking and action, xvi
thought isomorphism, xvii
views on women, xvii, 179-85
Gandhi Media Award, 86
Gandhi Peace Foundation, xvi, 8, 19, 23, 28, 35
Gandhi Smarak Nidhi, 35, 36
Gandhi Vichar Parishad (Institute of Gandhian Studies, Wardha), xi, 8, 28, 29, 34
Gandhi-Tolstoy relationship, 96-98
Gandhian Cricket, 30
Gandhian economics, xvi, 15, 113-29, 130-40
basic principles of, 132-37, 141-43
Gandhian Crown, 17-19
Gandhian proposition, 138
Gandhian World Federation, 170
Gandhian World Social Order, 173-74
Gene revolution, 198
Gillett, Nicholas, 86
Global poor, new and alternative development approach for, 190-91
Golden Common Society, 190
Golden Rule, 141
Gramin Bank, 192
Greed, 61
Guha, Amalendu, xviii, 189
Gurukula, 214

Hareven, Alough, 213

Harijans, 180, 182
Hatred, 61
Hind Swaraj, 96, 97, 103, 105, 109, 134, 136
Hindu Code Bill, 207
Hindu Rashtra, 203, 208
Hindutva, xix, 204
Hiroshima, 76
Hitler, 76
Homogenisation, xix, 202, 205
Human Development Index (HDI), 218
Husain, M. F., 206

Ibul Zuha, 205
Ideal models, 185-86
India's student movement, 10, 11
Indian Youth Congress, 17
Indira Gandhi, 4, 18
Industrial revolution, 210
Industrialisation, 57
Intellectual equality,154
International Council for Adult Education, 33, 212
International Day for Tolerance, 87
International Labour Organization (ILO) Conference, Geneva, 5
International Monetry Fund (IMF), 62
Islambul Conference, 212

Jack, Homer, 89
Jainism, 205, 206
Jaipur Congress, 34
Jallianwalla Bagh, 64
Jamie, lifestyle, 123-30
Jamnalal Bajaj International Award, 87, 88
Janata Government, 23, 26
Japan, 200
Jayantis, 206
Jayaprakash Narain, 11
Jimmy Carter, 85
Jinnah, M. A., 208
Joint Action Committee (JAC), 87
Joint Family living, xv, 131
Judaism, 203
Julius Nyerere, 81

Karuna, 48, 56
Kashmir Valley, 205
Kaur, Rajkumari Amrit, 129
Kausani, 41
Kavi Sammelan, 6
Keynes, John Maynard, 211
Khadi, propagation of, 182
King, Coratta Scott, 89
Kingdom of God, 101, 102
Kishwar, Madhu, 186
Kofi Annan, 81, 82
Krishnaswamy, 21, 22, 25
Kumarappa, J. C., 215

Lakshmi Menon, 179
Letter to a Hindoo, 102-103
Liberation, 52
  education, 219
Lingayat movemeent, 154
Linguistic communities, 202
Lok Sangharsh movememnt, xi
Lucknow session, 18

Madras Christian College, 151
Mahadevan, A. P., 24
Mahatma Gandhi Freedom Award, 84
Mahatma Gandhi Peace Award, 81-84, 89
Mahayana Buddhism, 49, 204
Mainstream economics, 137-40
Malaise, manifestations of, 115-16
  potential solutions to, 118-130
Male-dominated politics, 184
Mammen, John, K., xix, 29, 210
Maslow, Abraham, 219
Mass Production, 193, 194, 195, 196
Metta, 48
Migration, 203
Mikhail Gorbachev, 85
Modern education, 53
Modernity, 151
  alternative paradigms of, 152, 156
  dominant paradigms, 158
  Indian paradigms, 155, 159
  version of, 154
Moral emergency, 49
Moral leprosy, 180
Moksha, 9, 133, 155
Monoculturism, 58
Morarji Desai, 4, 19, 23
Mother Teresa, 76, 79
Mudaliar, A. Ramaswamy, 3
Mudila, 49
Multi-dimensional personality, 41

Nathuram Godse, 208
National integration, 201
National Labour Commission, 8, 23

National Student Movement, 3
Neema Vaishnav, 4
Nehru, Jawaharlal, 3, 13, 17, 18, 23, 169
Nelson, M. G., 98
Nelson Mandela,76, 85, 86
Neo-liberal capitalism, xii, 45
New biographies, 78
New Testament, xv
Nicholas Gillett, 82
Nirvana, 133
Nobel Peace Price, 76, 78, 79, 80, 91
Nobel prize winners, 189
Non-exploitation, 135, 137
Non-violent struggles, 63-64,72-74, 172
Norwegion Nobel Committee, 77

Omar Khayyam, 5
Onam Feast, 31
Oommen, T. K., xviii
Oppression, 76

Pakistan,204, 208
Pandavas, 186
Panikkar, K. M., 7
Parekh, Bhikhu, 106
Parel, Anthony, J., xiv, 96
Parodi, Pierre, 88
Partially blind, 140
Paul Power, 170-171
Peaceful Resolution, 98
Peoples war,10, 24
Pillai, K., Janardhanan, 27
Platonic epistemology, 154
Pleasant Speech (*Piyavaca*), 50
Political dictatorship, 63, 95
Political emanicipation, 182-84
Political revolution, 32
Political transformation, 66
Post-industrial materialism, 117-18
Poverty, 46, 51, 116-17, 164, 191, 195, 198
Prajna, 56
Prostitution, 180
Public glamour, 164
Purdah system, 180
Purna Swaraj, 163
Purusharthas, 155

Quit India Movement, ix, 3

Racial democracy, 202
Rajiv Gandhi, 88
Rajiv Gandhi Institute for Contemporary
Studies, 213
Ramachandran, G., 25, 27, 107
Ramakrishna Bajaj, 111
Ramlal Parikh, 18
Ram Rajya, 135
Rao, Raghavendra K., xvi, 151
Ravindra Verma,
arena of activities, 18
apprenticeship, 26
bureaucratic career, 21
college union, presidentship, 24
commitment to Gandhi's ideals, 18
education, 17
eminent scholar, 6
hand writing, 6
intellectual abilities, 24
joined politics, 22
labour minister, 23
leadership, 10, 16
multi-dimensional services, ix
personality, 14-15
political activities, 22
public life spans, ix
trade union politics, 23
unique humane character of, 37
Religious pluralism, xix, 204, 205
Rembrandt Art Gallery, 6
Renaissance humanism, 153, 156-57
Right Livelihood Award, xiv, 90
Rollan, Romain, 107
Roosevelt, F. D., 78
Ruskin, 96, 105, 106

Sabala, 179
Sabarmati ashram, 130
Sadiq Ali, 38
Sadhaka, 9
Sangha, xiii, 58
Sanjay Matey, 46
Sanyasinis, 180
Sarojini Naidu, 21, 179
Sarvodaya, 28, 163, 173, 175, 207
Satyagraha, 4, 8, 9, 67, 134, 174, 182
movement, 164
Sauchi, 136
Savarkar, V. D., 208
Schumachar, E. F., 215
Schweitzer, Albert, 76, 175
Secularism, 171, 206, 209
Self-actualisation, 219
Self-reliant communities movements, 59
Sen, Amartya, 30

Sevagram Ashrams, 13, 130
Sexual desire, 108
Sexual misconduct, 52
Sexuality, 181
Sharp, Gene, xiii, 63
Sheikh Hasina, 85
Sikhism, 203, 205, 206
Sila (moral precepts), 51
Sivaraksa, Sulak, 45
Smith, Adam, 47, 50
Social capital, 113-15
Social regeneration, 180-82
Social and environmental violence, 45-46
Soka Gokkai International, 85
Sorokin, Pitrim, 168, 173
South Africa, 68, 96, 97, 98, 105-106
Spencer, Herbert, 99, 102
Spiritual approaches, 119-20
Spiritual lifestyles, 123-30, 132
Spiritual living, characteristics of, 134
    essential elements, 120-23
    principles of, 132-35
Spiritual values, 113-14
State Capitalist System, xviii
Strauss, David, 99
Sublime abodes, 48-49
Suicides, 128
Sunnis and Shias, conflict in, 204
Superstition, 60
Sushila Nayyer, 179
Sustainable Revolution, 210
Swadeshi, xviii, 135, 136, 166, 182, 185
Swadharma, 135
Swaraj, 109, 133, 134, 136, 166, 179, 183, 207

Tagore, Ravindranath, 30, 214
Technical revolution, 15
Thakkar, Usha, xvii, 179
Tolstoy, xiv, xv, 96-98, 100, 101, 103-105, 107, 108
Toulmin, Stephen, xvi, 152, 154
Traditional communities, 57
Tranquility, 53
Transnational Tyrannies, 46, 58, 60
Treaty of Westphalia, 200
Trusteeship, 135, 136

Unemployment, 190, 195, 198
Unnithan, T.K.N., xvii, 162
Untouchability, xviii
    removal of, 182
UN Conference on Trade and Development, x, 211
UNESCO, 86, 87, 217-18
Upekkha, 49
USA-UK-Soviet Union, 11
USAID, 218
Uttarakhand, 41

Vadyar, 25
Varnashrama, 159
Vienna Conference, 211, 216
Vijaya Lakshmi Pandit, 21
Vijjian Sangha, 58, 59
Viparsanna, 53
Viscient Montgomery, 8
Vishwa Yuvak Kendra, 8, 23
Vivekananda, 209

Wagha Border, 12
War Resister's International (WRI), 87
Wardha, 40, 41
Washington University, 103
Well-being, 113-14
Western Christian Philosophy, 99
Widow's loving companion, 185
Widowhood, 181
Women freedom fighters, 179
Women's participation in freedom struggle, 183
    low status of, 187
World Assembly of Youth (WAY), x, 18, 32
World Bank, 62, 216
World Order Models Projects, xvii
World Summit, 213
World Trade Organization, 62
World University Service, 22
World Wars, 63
World War II, 8, 10, 14,200

Yoga, 127

Zakir Hussain, 12, 13
Zamora, Mario P., 84